'Thoughtful, insightful, relevant for business and well written; an important contribution to an essential debate.'

David M Armstrong, PhD, MPhil, MA, Partner, PricewaterhouseCoopers

'There are too many out there making it up as they go along. Reading the Green Executive will help you see the opportunity amongst the bullshit.'

Dr Stan Higgins, CEO, North East Process Industry Cluster

'It is most refreshing to read a book in which opinions and advice are supported by facts and figures from authoritative sources. As a practical handbook it deserves to be read and heeded by executives from across the spectrum.'

Professor Dermot Roddy CEng, FIET, FRSA, Science City Professor of Energy, Director, Sir Joseph Swan Centre for Energy Research

'A comprehensive, practical and up-to-date view of art of the possible in sustainable business. Built on the author's insights and those of other practitioners it provides a superb reference for businesses. Doing nothing is no longer an option!'

Ted Shann, Practice Partner, Wipro Technologies

'Timing is everything and this book is needed now. There are huge commercial advantages if your business is green and sustainable. Staff expect it, customers like it and shareholders support it. Opportunity knocks and your door must be open.'

Andrew Bainbridge, Chairman, Major Energy Users' Council & Chairman, Power Efficiency

'Gareth has splendidly shown by providing a comprehensive study of sustainability in all its manifestations that businesses can overcome any problems that are preventing them from becoming a fully green organisation. The book is a must read for all those with an interest in this field.'

Professor Graham Street, Emeritus Professor of Biochemical Engineering, University of Teesside, Chairman Groundwork North East

'This comprehensive, erudite and easily readable work should be compulsory reading for anyone engaged in commerce.'

Jonathan Jowett, Company Secretary and Chairman of CSR Committee, Greggs plc

THE GREEN EXECUTIVE

THE GREEN EXECUTIVE

CORPORATE LEADERSHIP IN A LOW CARBON ECONOMY

GARETH KANE

publishing for a sustainable future
London • New York

First published 2011
by Earthscan
2 Park Square, Milton Park, Abingdon, Oxon OX14 4RN

Simultaneously published in the USA and Canada
by Earthscan
711 Third Avenue, New York, NY 10017

Earthscan is an imprint of the Taylor & Francis Group, an informa business

Earthscan publishes in association with the International Institute for Environment and
Development

Trademark notice: Product or corporate names may be trademarks or registered
trademarks, and are used only for identification and explanation without intent to
infringe.

British Library Cataloguing in Publication Data
A catalogue record for this book is available from the British Library

Library of Congress Cataloging in Publication Data
Kane, Gareth.
  The green executive: corporate leadership in a low carbon economy/Gareth Kane.
    p. cm.
  Includes bibliographical references and index.
  ISBN 978-1-84971-334-4 (hardback)
  1. Business enterprises—Environmental aspects. 2. Management—Environmental
aspects. 3. Sustainable development. 4. Green marketing. I. Title.
  HD30.255.K355 2011
  658.4'083—dc22   2010046143

ISBN: 978-1-84971-334-4 (hbk)

Typeset in Plantin and Gill Sans by OKS Prepress Services
Cover design by Rob Watts

Printed and bound in Great Britain by
TJ International Ltd, Padstow, Cornwall

For Jimmy

Contents

Acknowledgements

First, a great big thank you must go to all those who generously contributed their time and insight to the 'View from the Front Line' interviews: Julie Parr of Muckle LLP, Sally Hancox of Gentoo Housing Group, Richard Gillies of Marks & Spencer, Glen Bennett of EAE Ltd, Surrie Everett-Pascoe from Canon Europe Ltd, Paula Widdowson of Northern Foods, Toon Bossuyt (and Els Heynssens) of BOSS Paints, Stephen Little of The Sage Gateshead, Roy Stanley of the Tanfield Group, Vic Morgan of the Ethical Superstore, Nigel Stansfield of InterfaceFLOR, Nick Coad of National Express, Chris Tuppen of BT, Martin Blake of Royal Mail, Peter White of Procter & Gamble, Roberta Barbieri of Diageo, James Hagan of GlaxoSmithKline and Chris Jofeh of Arup. I'm sure all readers will appreciate their wisdom, experience and honesty. Thanks must also go to the all the intermediaries, personal assistants and contacts who helped arrange the interviews – not least the anonymous employee of BOSS Paints who rescued me when I got stranded in an obscure Flanders suburb.

I am also eternally grateful to Anna-Lisa Kelso and Rita Callender of the Environmental Academy. Their forensic checking of the technical details of Chapters 5 and 18, along with their pertinent comments on the rest of the text, was both essential and much appreciated. Dr Karen Johnson of Durham University also contributed highly useful pointers, technical comments and impressions.

I also need to thank all my clients, colleagues and workshop attendees over the last 13 or so years as many of the models, techniques and key pieces of advice presented in this book have evolved and been battle-hardened through dozens of workshops, sustainability projects and consulting assignments. The team at the Clean Environment Management Centre (CLEMANCE) deserve particular thanks for all our years working together.

Thanks must also go to the staff at Earthscan, in particular Nick Bellorini, Sarah Thorowgood, Claire Lamont, Anna Rice and Dan Harding, for their hard work, expertise and patience. I am honoured that they have had faith in me once again.

Last, but certainly not least, I must thank my ever patient family – my partner Karen and our boys Harry and Jimmy. Jimmy was born halfway through the writing of this book and I am particularly grateful that he started sleeping through the night after just two months – possibly the most significant third party contribution to the completion of the manuscript!

To my family, I love you all.

Introduction

As I write this introduction in the summer of 2010, environmental issues are at the very top of the global news agenda. On 20 April the Deepwater Horizon drilling rig exploded in the Gulf of Mexico, killing 11 workers and starting a huge oil slick. BP, the company who sponsored the drilling, catastrophically failed to deal with the physical leak, the ecological damage it caused and the resulting storm of public anger. BP Chief Executive Officer (CEO) Tony Hayward made a textbook example of how not to handle such a crisis: trying to shift blame onto the contractors operating the rig, downplaying the size of the disaster and complaining about the effect it was having on his own life. In July Hayward stepped down from his position, stating 'life isn't fair'.[1]

Also in the news, seven Indian managers of the Union Carbide plant at Bhopal, India were fined and jailed for two years for the 1984 explosion that released a cloud of toxic gas, killing 15,000–20,000 people. The American chairman of Union Carbide at the time, Warren Anderson, remains 'a fugitive at large' according to the Indian judicial magistrates.[2]

In the meantime, NASA announced that the 12 months to April 2010 were the warmest on record, scotching the myth that climate change had somehow slowed or stopped at the turn of the millennium. It is becoming increasingly certain that the coal that powered the industrial revolution and the oil and gas that ushered in the modern world are exacting their pound of flesh in return.

The Gulf of Mexico oil spill also inspired many commentators to question why BP was drilling for oil in such deep waters in the first place. Is this evidence that we are finding it harder and harder to find oil and gas? Are these fundamental resources, the very basis of modern life, under threat? No one seems to know for sure, but 'peak oil' theory is certainly back on the agenda.

If these two situations, climate change and peak oil, weren't bad enough, there is an emerging factor that would make both problems much, much worse. Currently the consumption that is driving environmental strains is concentrated in a small proportion of the world's population. As the rest of the world develops, as it is doing and has a right to do, consumption will rocket. If we are to avoid catastrophe, we need solutions to these problems urgently.

In response, political rhetoric is starting to coalesce into action. Watching 192 world leaders in Copenhagen in December 2009 trying to come to an international agreement was a demonstration of the importance of this issue internationally, even if the resulting agreement was disappointing. More recently, US President Barack Obama described the BP oil spill as the environmental 9/11 and said it will change the country's environmental policy the way that the terrorist attacks of 2001 changed its foreign policy.[3] Whether it makes his attempts to get his climate bill into law any easier, only time will tell. Across the pond, new UK Prime Minister David Cameron declared that his coalition government 'will be the greenest ever'.[4] Prime Minister Sarkozy of France declared 'Let's face up to our responsibilities, not in speeches but in action, France and Europe are determined to do this',[5] and Chancellor Merkel of Germany said 'Today's generation needs to prove that it is able to meet the challenges of the 21st century'.[6] The Chinese Government is coming to the end of a five-year plan to cut the carbon intensity of its economy. Premier Wen has threatened to use an 'iron hand' and close down factories that don't meet energy efficiency targets in the future.[7] In 2010, China became the biggest investor in renewable energy systems in the world.[8]

One thing is clear – 'The Environment' isn't going away.

Green Business Comes of Age

So where does this leave business? Twenty years ago, the vast majority of industrialists took a very reactive view to environmental and ethical issues. Maximizing shareholder value was the narrow focus, and as long as activities were within the law, all was good. In the last two decades, more and more organizations have ventured 'beyond compliance' to capture the business benefits of reduced costs and brand protection. But the environmental agenda has largely been stuck at a managerial level, treated as a medium-level priority, with only niche companies making it a core business driver.

This is now changing, and fast. The bar has risen to the point where, for cutting-edge companies, sustainability has become a boardroom-level strategic business issue. However, according to business leaders themselves, the skills, awareness and knowledge of executives are inadequate to meet this challenge.[9] The radical transformation required cannot possibly be driven by environmental managers hidden away in their environmental silos.

So this book is for people who want to become green business leaders. If you are going to guide your business towards sustainability, whether it is a cutting-edge start-up, a leading global brand or somewhere in between, you will need new knowledge, new skills and new perspectives. You will need to fully understand the business opportunities and risks posed by the sustainability agenda. You will need to understand the context within which businesses of the future will operate. And of course you will need to understand both the practical and strategic techniques required to transform your business, its supply chain and the market in which it operates. This book provides a roadmap for this journey.

To help guide you I have interviewed 18 senior managers and executives who have already started along this road. They come from a very wide range of businesses from law through to pharmaceuticals. These people, who include some recognized world-class experts, have one thing in common – they are taking a proactive and strategic approach to the sustainability challenge. They tell fantastic and inspiring stories of overcoming difficulties, developing innovative solutions and the personal fulfilment they have achieved in the process. I have been inspired by their stories and I hope you are too.

The Structure of the Book

This book is divided into four parts:

- Part I: Why do it? This section lays out the business case for action, the costs of inaction, the moral case and potential pitfalls of action.
- Part II: The Global Context. This section covers the major environmental issues, the theory behind sustainability and predicts what a sustainable economy might look like.
- Part III: Practical Action. This section describes the various practical options that will make your business greener and help you to position yourself to thrive in a sustainable economy.
- Part IV: Making it Happen. This section covers the skills, techniques and management processes you will need to implement the practical actions and transform your business.

At the end of each chapter is a short vignette entitled 'The View from the Front Line' featuring an exclusive interview with an executive or senior manager with responsibility for environmental, sustainability and/or corporate social responsibility (CSR) performance. The interviewees were chosen to cover a wide spectrum of sectors and a wide range of sizes of businesses. For reference they are listed in table below.

The interviews are a snapshot in time and many things will have changed by the time this book is published – most of the companies concerned will have

List of interviewees

Name	Organization	Sector	Page
Chris Jofeh	ARUP	Design and construction	237–239
Toon Bossuyt	BOSS Paints	Manufacturing	221–222
Chris Tuppen	BT	Telecommunications	123–124
Surrie Everett-Pascoe	Canon Europe Ltd	Electronics	209–210
Roberta Barbieri	Diageo	Food and drink	131–132
Glen Bennett	EAE Ltd	Logistics	193–194
Vic Morgan	Ethical Superstore	Retail/new media	165–166
Sally Hancox	Gentoo Housing Group	Housing and construction	67–68
James Hagan	GlaxoSmithKline	Pharmaceuticals	93–95
Nigel Stansfield	InterfaceFLOR	Manufacturing	49–51
Richard Gillies	Marks & Spencer	Retail	81–82
Julie Parr	Muckle LLP	Professional services	29–30
Nick Coad	National Express	Public transport	179–180
Paula Widdowson	Northern Foods	Food and drink	39–40
Peter White	Procter & Gamble	Consumer goods	17–19
Martin Blake	Royal Mail	Logistics	155–156
Roy Stanley	Tanfield Group	Electric vehicles	109–110
Stephen Little	The Sage Gateshead	Hospitality	141–142

advanced, others may have retreated and some may even have disappeared. But the lessons the interviewees have learnt and shared in the interviews are invaluable.

A Note on Language

The environmental agenda is notorious for its loose use of language. For the sake of variety, I use 'green', 'environment', 'corporate social responsibility (CSR)' and 'sustainability' interchangeably. The terms 'sustainability' and 'CSR' generally have a broader meaning than the others, incorporating social issues as well as purely environmental concerns. 'Sustainability' also tends to be associated with a longer term timescale and implies step changes in performance, whereas 'CSR' implies more modest ambitions.

Although this book is predominantly concerned with the environmental agenda, it is impossible to separate social issues from environmental issues completely. Generally when I use 'sustainability', I am talking in a broader, more long-term sense than when using the other phrases.

Part I
Why Do It?

Understanding the Business Case

The first essential concept for a Green Executive to grasp is the business case for going green *as it applies to their business*. Everything else flows from this business case – your technical strategy, your branding/communications strategy and your management systems, so it is imperative to get a really good understanding of what the unfolding green agenda means to your company.

The following four chapters describe drivers for going green in a generic sense. These generic drivers can be customized and refined with your understanding of your own business environment to develop the case for your business to go green.

Chapter 1 looks at the consequences of taking or maintaining a reactive stance and simply trying to stay compliant with legislation. This has been the traditional approach taken by business but this chapter describes the powerful forces that will pull you backwards when you think you are standing still.

Over the last decade there has been a significant shift away from that reactive attitude to environmental issues. Where once compliance was sufficient, now many businesses want to go beyond compliance to benefit from cost savings and risk management. But as we will see, the really proactive green businesses are now seeing that the big benefits are coming from branding and exploiting opportunities in the new economic landscape. It is this change in perspective we cover in Chapter 2.

In Chapter 3 we look at the moral case for action. Corporate philanthropy has a long history and there are certain lessons we can learn from the past. This chapter also looks at some of the stickier ethical dilemmas and identifies some potential pitfalls.

Chapter 4 raises an extremely important, but often ignored, fact – that going green is not without risk. The chapter looks at some of the banana skins upon which many companies slip up.

Business as Usual Is Not an Option

The Risks of Doing Nothing

We often hear complaints from the business world that going green is too expensive, that environmental legislation is hindering competitiveness or that their sector's environmental impact is insignificant. In this chapter we see that this reactive stance is self-delusional and that doing nothing has a substantial cost and risk associated with it.

Let's face it, the world is going green. The 2009 Copenhagen Climate Change conference may have produced unsatisfactory results in terms of the final agreement, but the sight of all the world's leaders negotiating face to face on cutting carbon emissions was a clear signal that this subject is now at the very top of the global political agenda. If businesses do not shift voluntarily, they will be forcibly shoved in this direction by governments, pressure groups, customers and the general public.

Taking a reactive, compliance-based attitude is a very expensive way of doing business – incremental environmental improvements will only give relief for a short period of time before the bar is raised again. Ever tightening legislation, the threat of prosecution, potential humiliation, rising costs, depreciating assets and losing out to the competition are all risks that must be considered.

The Long Arm of the Law

The number of businesses who are ignorant of the legislation that affects them is staggering. In 2009 the UK's Environment Agency found that only 23 per cent of small businesses could name one piece of environmental legislation that affects them, even though *every* company is affected to some degree by, say, waste management regulations.[1] And it is not just small businesses that are at risk. I have had several robust debates with major household brands who have misunderstood the scope of the European Waste Electronic and Electrical Equipment (WEEE) Directive. They were incredibly reluctant to accept that they were breaking the law, which could have led to prosecution and/or a public relations fall out.

And there is a huge amount of new legislation, much of it requiring significant compliance cost from business, such as the European Union's (EU) Registration, Evaluation, Authorisation and Restriction of Chemicals (REACH) Directive that requires chemicals to be properly tested by manufacturers and importers. The cost of REACH to industry has been estimated by the European Commission to be between €2.8 billion and €5.2 billion over 11 years. Other estimates have put the figure as high as €12.8 billion.[2] In the US, one of President Barack Obama's first acts was to impose new fuel efficiency standards for cars and trucks and a cap and trade bill on carbon emissions is before Congress, albeit progressing with some difficulty. These are just some of the hundreds if not thousands of new or revised pieces of legislation making their way onto statute books around the world.

Being driven by compliance has two main risks: (1) non-compliance – prosecution, clean-up costs, bad publicity; and (2) future standards – vulnerability to tightening requirements.

Non-compliance

Aiming for compliance will not leave you with much of a margin of error, putting your business at risk of non-compliance. If you fall short of requirements, the fines and clean-up costs can be substantial, for example US mining firm Massey was fined $20 million for environmental infractions in 2008.[3] In one of the most infamous environmental disasters, Exxon Mobil Corp is still appealing against the damages awarded against it for the Exxon Valdez oil spill in 1989 – originally set at $5 billion, but since reduced to $500 million.[4] But it is not just 'dirty' industries that can get caught out – a recent breach of UK packaging regulations cost specialist drinks manufacturer Red Bull £270,000.[5]

Breaching legislation can have business impacts above and beyond fines. When Dutch officials impounded Sony Playstations in 2001 due to illegal levels of cadmium in cables, the cost in lost sales and rework was estimated at $150 million.[6] Clean-up costs in the case of an incident can also be huge – BP faces an estimated $40 billion to $100 billion bill for cleaning up the Gulf of Mexico oil spill,[7] dwarfing the $3.5 billion that Exxon Mobil spent cleaning up after the Valdez disaster.[8] And these costs do not include the impact of bad publicity.

Tightening standards

As standards tighten, companies may have to invest over and over again in abatement technology. For example, the EU's Integrated Pollution Prevention and Control (IPPC) regulations and the US Clean Air Act both incorporate the concept of 'best available technology' (BAT). This means that instead of setting absolute targets, regulators require industry to prove that they are using the most effective available pollution control technology every time a permit is renewed. This requirement raises the bar automatically as new technologies become available and implies a constant upgrade of capital equipment – with a constant capital investment required. Designing environmental problems out of the system once and for all is much more cost-effective.

Cap and trade legislation, such as the US Acid Rain Program or the EU's Emission Trading Scheme, is also designed to crank up the pressure on laggard companies. Each business must bid for permits to cover their pollution or trade them with other participants. The total number of permits available to the scheme is gradually reduced, driving up the price of each permit. Those who need the most permits will be hit hardest by the price rises. The UK's new Carbon Reduction Commitment (CRC) Energy Efficiency Scheme will bring cap and trade to businesses not normally thought of as 'polluting', such as large service sector companies.

Public Humiliation

In 2007, Apple Computers had it all – from their stylish iMac and MacBook computers to the must-have iPod, and with rumours of a new phone abounding, their hip, cutting-edge image appeared unassailable. That was until Greenpeace rated them bottom of an environmental league table of electronics companies. Sensing a publicity bonanza, the pressure group set up a clever parody of Apple's website to detail the company's environmental infractions.[9] Apple's legendary CEO Steve Jobs at first dismissed the campaign, but that only instigated a stronger backlash.[10] Jobs then realized the precarious position he was in, with Apple's hip image at serious risk. He did a swift U-turn, launching a radical programme to improve environmental performance and publicized it on the company's home page for a month.

Oil companies have been in the pressure groups' sights for a long time. In 2009 Shell was named as the 'most carbon intensive' company by a coalition of NGOs,[11] however, this pales into insignificance compared to controversy over the disposal of the Brent Spar oil storage buoy and the execution of human rights activist Ken Saro-Wiwa and eight others in Nigeria in 1995. Shell's reputation will remain tainted by these incidents for many years to come and they will find it difficult to build trust with the general public.

It is not just pressure groups who can humiliate companies. Exxon Mobil was attacked by the prestigious scientific body the Royal Society in 2006 for funding organizations set up to deny the existence of man-made climate change.[12] The company changed its tune and now says, 'In recent years, we have discontinued contributions to several public policy research groups whose position on climate change diverted attention from the important discussion on how the world will secure the energy required for economic growth in an environmentally responsible manner.'[13] Arnold Schwarzenegger's State of California famously sued six major motor manufacturers for damage to the environment.[14] The lawsuit failed, but the public point was made.

The message is clear. If you are a high profile business, such as a high street retailer, an energy company, a major construction company, a motor manufacturer, a producer of household goods or in the primary sector (mining, oil, gas, forestry etc.), then you are at direct risk from environmental and human rights pressure groups. These groups need a steady stream of high profile campaigns, such as the Apple example, to keep themselves in the public eye and are always looking for a 'tall poppy' to target. If you are a lower profile business, but you do business with a high profile client, then pressure groups may hold them responsible for your environmental sins. This is a very easy way to lose a major customer and, as we will see, many high profile companies are actively divesting themselves of supply chain liabilities.

Financial Risks

Rising costs

The cost of a barrel of oil doubled between June 2007 and 2008 to a record high of $147.[15] The surge was sudden – the price broke the $100 mark in January 2008 for the first time ever. It then crashed back to about $70 due to falling demand in the 2008/2009 global recession, but has started to rise again since. In October 2009, John B. Hess of oil exploration company Hess Corporation told the Oil and Money conference in London, 'The price of $140 per barrel oil was not an aberration; it was a warning.'[16] Energy security has become a huge international political issue and the volatility of energy prices can present a huge risk to energy intensive industries.

Added to the cost of fossil fuels is the complex raft of energy and carbon taxes that aim to make low carbon options more competitive. Fuel taxes and cap and trade schemes are two tactics used by governments to drive up the cost of high carbon activity.

Waste costs are rising as green taxes escalate and the types of materials that can be landfilled are restricted. The UK Government is increasing landfill tax by £8 per tonne each year up to a level of at least £48 per tonne (from £32 per tonne in 2010).[17] Requirements for pre-treatment of waste and limits to which wastes can be co-disposed also add cost pressures to landfill gate fees. In many areas such as the south east of England, California and China, water resources are becoming increasingly scarce, so costs are also rising.

There are a number of other environmental cost pressures that may not be so obvious. Insurance costs will rise as the cost of environmental fines and remediation from pollution incidents rises. The cost of monitoring and reporting emissions and other environmental data will rise as legislation becomes ever more rigorous.

Depreciating assets

Financial pressures will not just affect revenue costs, but will have an impact on the value of tangible and intangible assets as well. If the economy shifts towards a low carbon future, high carbon capital assets are likely to lose value fast. Who is going to want to purchase an energy inefficient building or a manufacturing plant that will lock the purchaser into a high carbon future? The risk of depreciation of the book value of buildings and other assets is not fully understood by many large corporations. It's not just carbon either – the value of contaminated land will drop as remediation requirements get stricter, and industrial facilities with fugitive emissions and poor pollution prevention measures will be seen as a liability.

Environmental disasters can destroy the reputation of a company and thus much of their intangible asset value. Union Carbide never recovered from the Bhopal disaster in 1984 and was bought at a bargain price by Dow, who are now finding themselves under attack for the sins of the company they purchased.[18] What was purchased as an asset may become a liability.

Competition Is Hotting Up

We explore the business benefits of going green in the next chapter, but the 'do nothing' option puts your business at risk from competitors who choose to exploit those opportunities. For example, the major UK supermarkets have been battling it out for the title of the greenest, with even the budget end of the market improving its sustainability performance rapidly.[19] In the summer of 2009, with the world economy in the depths of recession, Marks & Spencer released an ad campaign with the message 'For us, green is not just a fashion', deriding their competitors for cutting back on environmental projects when the going gets tough.

The bankruptcy of General Motors (GM) in 2009 was partly due to the company being, according to the BBC:

> *slow to move away from producing gas-guzzling SUVs [sports utility vehicles] when consumers were looking for more fuel-efficient vehicles. Toyota, makers of the iconic Prius hybrid, sold more vehicles than GM in 2008, putting an end to the US company's 77-year reign as the world's biggest carmaker.*[20]

When GM returned from bankruptcy, it sold off the highly polluting Hummer brand, promised to invest in the GM Volt electric car and, according to some accounts, even considered changing the colour of its iconic logo from blue to green.[21] This last story could well be apocryphal, or a marketing man's spin, but it still demonstrates how deeply GM felt they needed to change their ways.

As we will see in Chapter 2, if your competitors have a better environmental performance than you, they will:

- have lower operating costs and, as a result, have either a higher profit margin or a more competitive pricing structure;
- be more robust to future change: new legislation, utility prices, green taxation and customer demand;
- have better public relations (PR) and marketing opportunities, and a form of differentiation in tendering;
- have better motivated employees and will attract the best new recruits;
- have a lower risk of prosecution, NGO campaigns and a lighter touch from the regulators.

Well, they'd be mad not to, wouldn't they?

Chapter summary

1   Doing nothing is not an option – you will go backwards rather than stand still;
2   Environmental legislation will only get tighter, in fact some of it is designed to tighten automatically;
3   Public humiliation can be fierce, particularly for 'tall poppies';
4   Utility costs are likely to continue to rise;
5   High carbon or polluting assets may depreciate or even become liabilities in a low carbon world;
6   Enlightened competitors will leave you behind.

The View from the Front Line: Peter White, Procter & Gamble

Procter & Gamble (P&G) was founded in Cincinnati in 1837 by two brothers-in-law making soap and candles. Today P&G is a global consumer goods company with 135,000 employees and a turnover of nearly $80 billion in 2009. The company has a presence on the ground in 80 countries and its 300 different brands are sold in 150 countries. Every day, 4 billion people use a P&G product and the company aims to reach an additional billion consumers in the next five years. P&G also gave the world the 'soap opera', which was an early marketing strategy aimed at housewives.

Peter White is the Director of Global Sustainability at P&G. He has two main responsibilities, first, leading the Global Sustainability Leadership Council that develops the company's strategy and goals and ensures this is implemented across the functions and units. Second, he runs the corporate group that manages sustainability issues for the company.

Why and how did you get involved in this agenda?

I am a zoologist at heart and by training. I did three years voluntary work teaching in a rural school in Nigeria, so I have experience of developing countries. I then did a masters in hydrobiology including a thesis on the fisheries of Lake Naivasha, Kenya, followed by a doctorate in chemical ecology, developing ecological methods of pest control. My claim to fame is that I discovered the sex pheromone for woodworm.

I have done the same job at P&G for 19 years, except they keep calling it something different! I was originally hired to write the book on solid waste management – developing P&G's first lifecycle assessment (LCA) model for packaging in the process. We pioneered the approach of applying LCA to solid waste management, which was the subject of the book and an accompanying computer model. We made this model publicly available and it got taken up and adapted by environmental regulators around the world, including the UK, US, France, Australia and Canada. In 1999 we founded a corporate sustainability group in P&G, which was one of the first globally. In 2006 I got promoted to the global role.

What are the business drivers for Procter & Gamble to engage in this agenda?

P&G has always been engaged in this agenda. The company's environmental management system has been going for over 30 years. Our first scientific publication on environmental science was back in the 1950s.

The first driver is 'doing the right thing'. Since it was founded, ethics and purpose have always been part of the way of life in the company. In 1999 we made a public commitment to sustainability, as part of our ethic of 'doing the right thing'.

On the business protection side, we have long had policies ensuring both social and environmental responsibility – including such areas as human and environmental safety, upholding human rights, workers' rights and sustainable material sourcing, including sustainable forestry.

We had early successes building business on the social side of sustainability: products that produce clean drinking water, save people time in handwashing, products for the elderly and those with osteoporosis. It proved more difficult to build the business through environmentally improved products, since they tend to be about being 'less bad' rather than 'good'. In the 1990s we released a whole range of 'green products' – like our 'pump and spray' refillable propellant-free sprays – but all those products failed in the marketplace. At the time, if you said 'this is green' to the consumer what they heard was 'this isn't going to work, its going to cost more, and I'll have to put twice as much in because you've left the important stuff out'. We still struggle to get that message across today.

Around 2005, with climate change moving up the agenda, we found that our customers such as Walmart and Tesco were saying 'we want much more sustainable product on our shelves'. So now we could build our business by providing the retailers with more sustainable products, whether the consumer was demanding it or not.

So we revitalized our environmental sustainability programme. In 2007 we made our environmental commitment much more explicit by changing the company statement of purpose to include sustainability. The statement of purpose had not been changed before, so this was significant. Today 'we provide products and services that improve the lives of the world's consumers, now and for generations to come' to make it clear we aren't going to go for short-term benefit at long-term cost. We also added a specific principle to our purpose, values, principles – the DNA of the company – to state 'we will incorporate sustainability into our products, packaging and operations'.

What successes have you had?

In 2007 we set some specific goals for environmental improvement in our own operations – to reduce at least another 20 per cent of CO_2, energy, waste and water per unit of production from our plants by 2012. In the first two years we have already achieved around 10 per cent reductions in CO_2, energy and water and 30 per cent in waste, mainly through the industrial symbiosis projects we have undertaken. Since 2002 we had halved the CO_2, energy, water and waste involved in the production of our products.

But we've also introduced sustainable innovation into our products. Take clothes washing as an example: P&G's own operations are almost negligible in energy and carbon terms compared to the energy required to produce the raw materials for the product and to heat the water in washing machines. So we're working on compact and coldwater detergents. The best example is Aerial Excel Gel – it was built from scratch to a sustainability specification, looking at thousands of formulations, to find a compact, low temperature, high performance product. The result cuts the amount of raw material and brings the washing temperature down to 15°C. The gel nature of the product helps the consumer dose correctly. It was also called 'the best detergent we've ever tested' by *Which?* magazine. Performance is key to getting consumers to buy more sustainable products, since most won't trade off performance or value for sustainability.

What are the big challenges for your company?

We currently reach around 4 billion people and would like to reach more. By 2050, there are likely to be 9 billion people and we'd like to reach all of them. If you are trying to do that sustainably, then there are big challenges on sustainable consumption – how do you improve their lives without using fossil fuels? How do you ensure sustainable sourcing of raw materials and recovery of waste?

Moving from fossil fuels and petrochemical ingredients to renewable materials makes sense for long-term sustainability, so long as the renewable materials and energy can be sustainably sourced. Palm oil is a great crop in that the amount of oil per hectare it is one of the highest, but the downside is potential deforestation with loss of biodiversity and an increase in greenhouse gas emissions. So the challenge is to promote and use sustainable palm oil. We have committed to only using palm oil that we can confirm has come from responsible and sustainable sources by 2015. We are currently working with our suppliers to help them get their plantations certified as sustainable so we can meet this commitment.

What's your advice for others in your position?

You need to understand the impacts your company has across the product lifecycle, so you can target your strategies effectively. So for our detergents, we target material sourcing and water temperature in use.

Have a clear sustainability strategy that has synergy with your business model – for example ours is 'no trade-offs'. The mainstream consumer wants performance *and* value *and* sustainability. If you ask them to compromise on the first two for the sake of the last, only 5–10 per cent of consumers will do so.

Employee engagement is essential. We have an empowering, enabling strategy to help employees make it part of their world. We have an awareness programme, a network of sustainability ambassadors to engage people in site specific projects, and we have role-specific training for individual functions such as research and development (R&D), marketing and sales.

Green Business Opportunities

Green Carrots

The world is changing. Governments are trying to transform their economies to address the threats of climate change, resource depletion and threats to biodiversity. Cutting-edge companies have realized that there is a vast array of business opportunities available to those who see 'green' as a source of competitive advantage rather than a bothersome sideshow. This chapter explores those opportunities to give a flavour of the opportunities on offer.

Green performance is certainly associated with strong financial performance. According to Business In The Community, FTSE companies that actively managed and measured corporate responsibility issues outperformed the FTSE 350 on total shareholder return by between 3.3 per cent and 7.7 per cent throughout the period 2002–2007.[1] Green businesses also seem do well in a recession. Management consultancy AT Kearney found that, in 16 of the 18 industries they studied, companies committed to sustainability outperformed industry averages by 15 per cent over the six months of severe recession from May to November 2008.[2] 'Green' is increasingly being seen as an asset and many niche green/ethical companies have attracted investments and/or takeovers from mainstream rivals. L'Oreal purchased The Body Shop in 2006, Coca-Cola invested in Innocent Drinks in 2009 and Cadbury, no slouch in the CSR stakes itself, bought out Green & Blacks in 2005 and was itself bought out by Kraft in 2010.

The Business Opportunities Pyramid

Figure 2.1 shows the pyramid of benefits of going green. Underpinning the pyramid is compliance. While this book is gung-ho about going beyond compliance, breaches of legislation can undo even the best companies, so compliance should never be forgotten in the rush to exploit the positive opportunities.

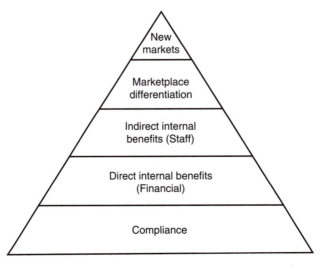

Figure 2.1 *Business benefits pyramid*

In increasing level of benefit (and, ironically, decreasing level of awareness) the stages on the pyramid are:

- Direct internal benefits: cost reduction, improving asset values and risk reduction;
- Indirect internal benefits: staff recruitment, retention and motivation;
- Differentiation in the marketplace: winning business through better branding, reputation and differentiation;
- Exploiting new and emerging markets in the low carbon/green economy.

Direct Internal Benefits

Cutting costs

At its simplest level, going green can save your organization money. For some businesses, this can be a very significant amount of money. Between 2006 and 2008 I carried out simple half-day environmental health checks in 26 businesses ranging from small catering outlets to printing, engineering and construction to major pharmaceutical companies. I identified an average saving in waste, raw material, energy and water costs of £175,000 per annum, per site. Those health checks barely scratched the surface – given longer on site and more time with staff, these savings could have been much higher. In 2008/2009, Northern Foods saved £2 million through their CSR programme, and expect to save £4 million in 2009/2010. Marks & Spencer have earned back the £200 million they budgeted for their Plan A sustainability programme and made a profit on it.

Most people underestimate the full cost of waste, which can be immense – estimates suggest that the true cost can be 10–30 times the disposal cost. I once stood in the goods out area of a bespoke furniture manufacturer looking at damaged 'kits' that had been placed to one side. The environmental manager explained that these orders were held up while someone unpacked each kit, identified which components had been damaged, and ordered replacements to be fast-tracked through the production system, disrupting the planned flow of orders. Someone would then have to reassemble each kit for shipping and only then could the order be fulfilled. I worked through with him the true cost of this waste over and above the cost of throwing a couple of bits of dented chipboard in a skip. The list included raw materials for the replacements, the energy required to make the replacements, the staff costs of sorting out the problem and making the same component twice, disruption to other orders and of course customer (dis)satisfaction. While we talked, forklift trucks hurtled around the warehouse shuffling the kits around – we witnessed two collisions in the ten minutes we were there. My companion looked at me and said, 'I know this is a problem, but no one else seems to think this is a problem.'

Lastly, savings from cutting waste (whether that is wasted materials, energy or water) come straight off your bottom line. If your profit margin is, say, 25 per cent, every £1 from cutting waste is equivalent to £4 worth of new sales. And unlike cutting staff, cutting waste costs improves productivity and morale.

Other direct financial benefits

As we saw in Chapter 1, as the world goes green, assets such as antiquated oil storage tanks, energy inefficient buildings and polluting vehicle fleets will become liabilities. The flip side of this is also true – having low carbon infrastructure and capital assets will add book value to a company in many cases.

We also looked at the financial and non-financial impacts of pollution incidents and compliance breaches. Again, if we flip the argument over, going beyond compliance will substantially reduce the probability of breaching legislation by providing a margin of error. This is an effective form of risk reduction and can also improve the book value of companies.

Staff Recruitment, Retention and Morale

Environmental and CSR initiatives are a determining factor in employee recruitment, motivation and retention according to, among others, the Chartered Institute for Personnel and Development (CIPD).[3] In the US, a survey of over 4000 people carried out by recruitment job site MonsterTRAK found that 80 per cent of young professionals are interested in securing a job that has a positive impact on the environment. Meanwhile, over 90 per cent said they would prefer to work for an environmentally friendly employer.[4] In the UK, a survey of 5000 job hunters showed that 43 per cent would not work for a firm that had no ethical or environmental policies, even if they were offered £10,000 more a year in salary to do so.[5] This desire is manifesting itself in practice – high street retailers WH Smith now include their environmental policy with job application packs as so many potential recruits were asking for it.[6]

It is difficult to quantify the benefits of attracting and retaining the best staff, but anecdotal evidence suggests that this is a key issue in many green companies. Chris Tuppen of BT says the company is being pushed by employees to go green faster than the company feels comfortable with. InterfaceFLOR has a retention rate way above the sector average and, in the words of Nigel Stansfield, the staff have a 'swagger' that he apportions to their enthusiasm for the way the company does business.

Branding and Marketplace Differentiation

Many businesses, including the majority of those interviewed for this book, are finding that the true benefit of being greener is much bigger than the direct financial savings discussed above due to the boost it gives their branding and product differentiation. This is particularly true in the service sector where the cost of raw material, waste, water and energy are a relatively small proportion of the cost of doing business. Greener businesses will become more trusted in the marketplace, attract customers who value environmental performance, and win more public and private sector tenders.

The global market for low carbon and environmental goods and services was estimated to be £3 *trillion* in 2007/2008 and is estimated to grow to £4.3 trillion by 2015.[7] The biggest market internationally is the US with £629 billion, followed by China with £411 billion, with the UK lying 6th with a market of £107 billion. This figure includes traditional environmental industries such as waste and recycling services, pollution control, renewable energy, alternative fuels and green building technologies etc. But it excludes 'green consumer' products such as eco-friendly cosmetics, appliances, vehicles, clothes and food. In the UK alone, these markets were estimated to be worth £32.3 billion in 2006, up 9 per cent on the previous year.[8] The global £3 trillion figure also excludes green business-to-business products or services such as energy efficient appliances, delivery vehicles or teleconferencing, and tenders won due to the environmental performance of the supplier. So the overall global green market is enormous and growing.

The wider business benefits from branding/differentiation are much harder to capture, let alone quantify, than direct economic savings, which can lead to confusion over whether 'green' should show a direct return on investment. We'll be looking at how to address this problem in Chapter 18, but it is important to appreciate that a narrow view on economic opportunities can hold a company back from reaping the true rewards.

Business to consumer

If you sell goods and services to the public, a few markets are already solidly green, but most are still in their infancy – which gives significant scope for growth and competitive advantage to early movers. Booming markets include:

- White goods: the proportion of white goods rated 'A' for energy efficiency sold in the UK rose from 0 per cent to 76 per cent in the ten years to 2006.[9] This represented a market of £1.9 billion in 2007.[10]
- Baby food: 70 per cent of baby food sold in the UK is now organic. This is interesting as organic food only represents just 3.9 per cent of all food production nationally and 0.65 per cent of food production globally.[11] In other words, we are happy to feed 'rubbish' to ourselves, but not to our children.
- Cosmetics: The Body Shop built its reputation on its ethical credentials and has been joined by brands such as Aveda and Natural Collection. £448m was spent on 'ethical' cosmetics in the UK in 2007, up 16 per cent from 2006.[12]

But the key issue here is branding. Marks & Spencer's Plan A was developed partly out of a desire by Chairman Sir Stuart Rose to 'do the right thing' and partly out of a desire to protect the company's position as a trusted brand as the public's values evolve to include sustainability as part of their concept of 'trust'. We saw in Chapter 1 how Apple moved decisively when they realized that poor environmental performance could undermine their brand values. So even in markets outside traditional green niches, consumers are increasingly looking for evidence that their favourite brands are delivering on sustainability.

Business to business/public sector

Much of any organization's carbon footprint lies in its supply chain. As top-level companies and public sector organizations strive to cut their footprints, business-to-business markets for greener products and services are expanding rapidly.

These green markets can be less prosaic than flashy new green products and materials. Most public sector bodies practice some form of green procurement in all their purchasing, even for relatively low impact services. According to Julie Parr of lawyers Muckle LLP, 'The public sector used to simply ask for environmental policies. Now they want to see progress reports and spreadsheets of data. If we don't demonstrate commitment *and* performance, we won't get the contract.'

In a tight competition, the points that accrue from environmental performance can be the deciding factor, as EAE Ltd found out to their benefit. The company won a major government contract for leaflet distribution and the feedback was that their demonstrable commitment to sustainability put them ahead of competitors. They have an onsite wind turbine (among many other green measures) and find that the potent symbolism of that turbine is worth a hundred environmental policies in terms of differentiation. BT claims that their environmental credentials have helped them to £1.9 billion in new business in 2009 (compared with £400 million cost savings over five years). Royal Mail says they have both won and lost eight figure contracts where sustainability was a key factor in the decision.

New and Emerging Green Markets

Government efforts to tackle climate change are creating new markets for low carbon technologies such as efficient vehicles, alternative fuels, renewable energy systems, monitoring systems and building insulation products. This is the fastest growing element of the £3 trillion sector discussed above. In 2008 wind, solar and other clean technologies attracted $140 billion (£85 billion) of investment globally compared with $110 billion for gas and coal for electrical power generation, the first time in the modern era that renewable investment exceeded fossil fuel investment.[13]

The financial stimulus packages announced by governments in 2009 also provided a boost to low carbon markets around the world. According to the *Financial Times*,[14] the UK has committed 7 per cent (or $3.7 billion) of their package to green measures, the US 12 per cent ($117 billion) and South Korea a whopping 81 per cent ($60 billion). China, long blamed by Western politicians and NGOs for its environmental record, has the biggest single green investment of $221 billion (38 per cent of their package).

Legislation is itself creating and boosting markets. The German feed-in tariff (FIT), which guarantees a premium price for small and domestic renewable energy generators, has been credited with boosting renewables to 12 per cent of its electricity supply, compared with 4.6 per cent in the UK (Germany has 200 times as much solar). This has in turn created a quarter of a million jobs in renewables. At the time of writing, 45 countries and 18 states/provinces/territories have similar FITs,[15] with the UK introducing one in April 2010.

These factors will fundamentally alter energy and related markets. Supply chains for many low carbon and 'clean tech' technologies are often immature or even non-existent, providing numerous business opportunities. For example, if there is a large-scale switch to electric vehicles, markets will be created in design, component manufacture, vehicle production, retail, maintenance, breakdown services, battery charging (and associated equipment), customization, fleet hire and disposal. As the sector matures, there is huge scope for innovation and new ways of working will emerge.

To take an example, electric vehicles still have a limited range and relatively slow charging times – some can do a fast recharge in 20 minutes, but that's still a long time to spend in a motorway service station. So entrepreneurs Better Place are bringing battery exchanges to the market where the user drives up and waits while their depleted battery is automatically swapped for a new one in just a couple of minutes.[16] They drive off and the cost is charged electronically to their account. They wouldn't own the batteries, rather they purchase a power service for their vehicle (we'll look at more examples of this kind of business model in Chapter 13).

Again it is not just in advanced technology where markets can be found or created. eBay, the internet auction site, has turned the sale of second-hand goods into a multi-billion dollar business. The Ethical Superstore has created a market for people who want to make purchases on their personal ethical criteria. Carbon offsetting is another relatively new, if controversial, market that has arisen out of the desire to do the right thing.

Annex 1 sets out a matrix of potential business opportunities in the low carbon/green economy, both in the direct supply of technologies, and importantly, some of the supporting products and services required to support those services. While moving into such sectors will not be for every business (as we will see in Chapter 4), it is worth looking at whether there are opportunities that your business is well placed to exploit.

Chapter summary

1 Do not neglect compliance – the bad publicity from non-compliance can undermine other green efforts;
2 Direct cost savings can be significant for energy, water and waste, particularly when the full cost of waste is factored in;
3 Indirect internal benefits, particularly staff motivation, recruitment and retention are harder to quantify but are clearly very significant;
4 Cutting-edge companies see improved competitiveness as the key opportunity, with the returns outweighing cost savings many times over;
5 For many companies, new low carbon and green markets are emerging, ripe for exploitation.

The View from the Front Line: Julie Parr, Muckle LLP

Muckle LLP is a commercial law firm based in Newcastle upon Tyne, UK, specializing in commercial, corporate finance, property, employment, dispute resolution, debt recovery, public sector and private client work. Julie Parr is Director of Service Excellence and has responsibility for CSR and environmental performance.

Why did you personally get involved in this role?

To be honest, it just fits well with me a person. It makes me feel good to know that I'm taking actions to protect the environment, like recycling. It has been great to change things at Muckle for the better and drive out waste in particular.

What are the drivers for Muckle to engage in this agenda?

Initially we wanted to develop a feel good factor among staff. While some of our actions have a cost–benefit, some don't – such as buying recycled paper.

Public sector tendering is one area where a good environmental performance is becoming a key distinguishing factor between tenderers. And, where once an environmental policy was enough, now many organizations are requiring more detailed environmental reports – and even spreadsheets of data – to demonstrate that policy is being put into action.

We now have a slogan for this 'Good Business Sense', which we present in a smile-shaped logo. This is to get across the fun and serious sides of what we are doing.

What are the big challenges for your organization?

Budgeting is always difficult for a medium-sized organization. We would like to measure our carbon footprint, but we will probably have to do this in-house. At present environmental expenditure is regarded as discretionary, although the public sector tender driver is starting to change this.

We need to continue to engage our people so everything we do in the business has an environmental aspect. We're starting to engage the senior partners more and more to get commitment from the top down.

But the biggest challenge is that we don't own our own building. Anything we want to change, like the air conditioning system, lighting systems or even to switch to a green electricity tariff, has to be agreed with six other tenants. This makes it very difficult to reduce our carbon footprint.

What successes have you had?

We started by putting together a 'Let's Think Green Team' of enthusiastic volunteers. The team created a fun quiz for all staff. This asked questions about the company's environmental performance, for example how much does it cost to leave a PC on overnight, or how much paper do we use? From this we've been doing a number of activities to make people think about the impact of what they do.

Legal firms use a huge amount of paper so this is one area the Team focused on. We've managed to cut paper use from 3000 sheets per person per month down to 1000 sheets per person per month. While this is still a lot, we've made a huge saving. We have also cut our IT servers from 13 down to 3 using virtualization.

From this ad hoc start, we have now written an environmental policy and are now formalizing our systems. For example we are engaging our supply chain and looking for ISO 14001 or similar accreditation to demonstrate their commitment. We're also considering whether ISO 14001 is suitable for Muckle itself.

What's your advice for others in your position?

Create a team of people who are interested and engage with the top people to get commitment and buy-in. Make it fun, but communicate business benefits.

The Moral Imperative

The Ethical Dimension

There is almost an unwritten rule of books such as this one that we shouldn't discuss personal ethics, and stick to 'the business case for sustainability' as laid out in Chapters 1 and 2. But it is clear that many of the business leaders who are leading in this space are driven by a clear sense of morality. Most of the interviewees in this book talk about bringing their personal values to their place of work. In the cases of InterfaceFLOR and Marks & Spencer, the drive came from the Chief Executives, Ray Anderson and Sir Stuart Rose, wanting to do the right thing. For companies such as BOSS Paints, EAE Ltd, Procter & Gamble and Arup, an ethical dimension was built in from the very start. Other notable examples of ethical business leaders include Sergey Brin and Larry Page of Google, the late Anita Roddick of The Body Shop and Richard Reed, Adam Balon and Jon Wright of Innocent Drinks.

When we look at some of the environmental impacts of, for example, climate change, there is clearly an ethical case to answer:

- 150,000 people per year are already dying prematurely due to the increased spread of infectious disease as temperatures rise;[1]
- 1 million species could be at risk of extinction due to climate change;[2]
- The climate change we are seeing today is largely due to the emissions from developed nations in the last century, but the effects are being seen in the developing world, for example, 2.3 billion to 3 billion people's water supply is at risk;[3]
- Just 15 per cent of the world's population consumes 80 per cent of economically traded resources, whereas the 33 per cent of the population who live in the poorest countries consume only 3 per cent.[4]

So why are so many commentators reluctant to talk about doing the right thing? In this chapter we look at corporate ethics and how they can affect your business.

Shareholder Value vs. Ethical Values

There are those who believe that the sole purpose of a company is to maximize its profits and any other activity is simply a tax on those profits. The sole social responsibility on business was to keep within the law. This approach was championed in the 1970s and 1980s by economists such as Milton Freidman and politicians such as Ronald Reagan and Margaret Thatcher. In this model, environmental problems would be solved by the market – for example as resources depleted, prices would rise. However, many of the environmental services that the Earth provides are 'free' – for example climate control, and so are outside the conventional economic system.

There is also a financial problem with this value free approach – maximizing short-term profits at the cost of all other considerations can lead to economic disaster in the medium to long term. The 'credit crunch' of 2007 can be blamed in large part on unethical lending (the 'subprime' market) to maximize short-term advantage. The market imploded leading to a failure of many of the companies trading in it. Many private companies, such as the Northern Rock bank in the UK, had to be nationalized by governments. Northern Rock shareholders, who lost everything they had invested, are unlikely to regard the bank's activities as having been in their best interest.

A more progressive view is that business requires a 'licence to operate' from society, whether that society is local communities, consumers of the product or organizations that represent public feeling, such as environmental pressure groups. This is what Northern Foods calls 'enlightened self-interest' – that doing the right thing can deliver for business in the long run. We have seen in the last two chapters how greener businesses will save money, attract new customers, attract and retain staff and avoid the risk of public humiliation or legislative sanction.

But the really radical question is, 'What is business really for?'. Should we accept Friedman's axiom of a single bottom line, or does business have a greater role to play in society and the world? Should we go to work to make the world a better place or just to put bread on the table? Can we solve environmental problems if the globalized economy seeks only profit?

Doing Good

The idea that business can be a force for good in the world has a long history – in fact it could be argued that the idea of corporate social responsibility is as old as the idea of a corporation. Some of the biggest business names in history fall into this category with some clear examples of social values infusing the organization. As we shall see, addressing environmental concerns has been a more recent development.

Cadbury's, the chocolate company, was founded by the eponymous Quaker family in 1824 in order to provide an moral alternative to alcohol, drinking chocolate. The company built 'Bourneville' outside Birmingham in 1833–1900 – a 313 house model village designed to 'alleviate the evils of modern more cramped living conditions'.[5] Although the direct Quaker influence disappeared long ago, the company has prided itself on its CSR performance ever since, including using only FairTrade chocolate in their iconic product, Dairy Milk.

Through the early part of the 20th century this kind of social philanthropy was very popular, although it didn't always extend to product responsibility. Lord Armstrong, the English armaments magnate, established the forerunner of Newcastle University, donated his gardens of Jesmond Dene to the city of Newcastle upon Tyne and was an early promoter of renewable energy in place of coal. But he pointedly took no responsibility for how his products were used, saying, 'It is our province, as engineers to make the forces of matter obedient to the will of man; those who use the means we supply must be responsible for their legitimate application.'[6]

The grandfather of modern manufacturing, Henry Ford, was also driven by values. He believed that consumerism was the key to peace and social mobility and paid his workers well above standard rates. While he may have given the world the mass-produced automobile, he hated the idea of obsolescence, trying to build his cars to last. This strategy failed as GM under Alfred P. Sloan introduced the 'planned obsolescence' that drives the modern consumer society.[7] GM started to cut into Ford's market share, forcing a change of plan. Henry Ford also sought more sustainable solutions from agriculture, developing a prototype biopolymer-based car that ran on bioethanol.

Environmental concerns didn't become a focus of corporate ethics until the 1962 publication of *Silent Spring*, Rachel Carson's harrowing exposé of the damaged caused by the uncontrolled use of pesticides.[8] This began a counter-culture movement, producing the likes of the early green consumer guide *The Whole Earth Catalog* in 1968, but it took a long time to seep into the mainstream. The late Anita Roddick was one of the first eco-entrepreneurs, picking up on the rising environmental concerns and building a business empire, The Body Shop, to service them. The company is the breakthrough green brand of modern times, bringing a huge number of environmental and ethical issues to the general public's attention. It was one of the first to prohibit the use of ingredients tested on animals, one of the first to promote fair trade with developing countries and it pioneered the (modern) use of refillable containers.

Coming right up to date, Google, worth $23 billion, famously has the motto 'Don't Be Evil' and pumped more than $100 million into the Google.org foundation to fund renewable energy and low carbon vehicle projects.[9]

Personal Values

Ethics are personal. While they may be moulded by our parents, our peers, our teachers and our reading, each of us has our own personal ethical prism through which we view the world. This framework is applied quite differently on different occasions depending on the context. Many of those interviewed for this book talk about 'bringing their personal values to the workplace'. They found this liberating, empowering and exciting. The cognitive dissonance of spending eight or more hours a day doing something that clashes with our personal values is extremely wearing psychologically.

I can relate to this on a personal level. In my early 20s I worked in the defence industry and pursued green issues as a hobby. While I justified this career to myself for many years (every country has the right to defend itself etc., etc.), I was never fully comfortable. I remember sitting in one meeting where the discussion turned to the optimum size of missile cone fragment to cause damage to human flesh. I remember thinking, 'Is this what I get up in the morning to do?'. I quit not long afterwards to go travelling around the world. I ended up teaching English in the far north of Russia and on a weekend trip I saw the ecological devastation wreaked by acid rain from the nickel smelter at the town of Monchegorsk. At that point I swore that I would work to stop this kind of damage happening in the first place. That was a liberating moment and my career has been aligned to my values ever since, which has not just been fulfilling but inspiring.

To reheat the old cliché, will we lie on our deathbeds and say, 'Oh, I wish I'd just wrung out a few more dollars of shareholder value!', or would we like to say, 'I made a difference! The world is a slightly better place for me having been in it!'?

Corporate Values

Blasé statements of corporate values emblazoned over websites, reports and exhibition displays may have become something of a discredited cliché in recent years, but the influential book *Built to Last* found that 'visionary' companies who pursued their values rather than short-term profit, outperformed their more pedestrian competitors over the 1926–1990 timeframe by a factor of 15:2.[10]

In other words, having corporate values is not enough. You've got to eat, breathe and sleep them – the *Built To Last* authors describe it as creating a 'cult-like' adherence to those values.

So if we accept that we should bring personal values to work, how do we translate these into corporate values? This will depend on the business you are in, but the following questions should be considered:

- To what extent are you responsible for your staff?
- To what extent are you responsible for the well-being of people working in your supply chain?
- To what extent are you responsible for the environmental performance of your supply chain?
- To what extent are you responsible for the well-being of people using your product?
- To what extent are you responsible for the environmental or social impacts of your product in use?
- To what extent are you responsible for the safe disposal of your product?
- Are stakeholders in your product's lifecycle treated equally well irrespective of nationality, ethnicity, gender, disability or income?
- Is it acceptable to make a profit from the impacts of climate change?
- Is it acceptable to make a profit from tackling climate change?
- Is it acceptable to make a profit from the poor?
- How 'green' or 'ethical' does a product or service have to be before you can sell it as such?

We consider how to translate values into strategy and corporate culture in Part IV of this book.

The Ethical Tightrope

It is not easy being 'green' or 'ethical' in business. Anita Roddick's saintly image has been the target of detractors, in particular journalist Joe Entine who published a series of articles attacking what he perceived as 'greenwash'.[11] While Roddick may have dismissed Entine as 'a stalker',[12] the episode did result in the company publishing detailed social and environmental reports to back up their claims. The sale of The Body Shop, Whole Foods and Green & Blacks to larger rivals was seen as a mixture of sell-out by the smaller companies and greenwash by their new owners. Google's 'Don't Be Evil' idealism came unstuck when they cooperated with the Chinese Government to exclude dissident websites from searches on google.cn. At the time of writing, Google has removed search engine censorship in China.[13]

The issues can get even more emotive when businesses put themselves at the core of a social or environmental problem. US academic CK Prahalad has championed the idea of doing business 'at the bottom of the pyramid' – i.e. among the world's poor.[14] He found that the poor pay a 'poverty premium' over their richer countryman – staples such as rice can cost up to 1000 per cent more in a shantytown than a comfortable suburb in the same city. This locks those people into a poverty trap – they have little money and it doesn't buy much. A number of companies have made a fortune by undercutting those premiums, providing goods and services at a lower price, stimulating markets in poor communities and raising their standard of living.

This approach, of engaging extremely poor people in economic activity for profit, can make some people very uncomfortable. But the very same people are often happy to provide a charitable handout. It has been shown that in many cases, fragile local economies have been wiped out by having free Western donations dumped on them.[15] Ironically, our sense of ethics could be perpetuating global poverty.

The same is true with environmental issues – there is a perception that solutions providers shouldn't be making money. The press can sometimes take the line that altruism that makes a hefty return is somehow fake. US vice-president turned climate change campaigner Al Gore has invested millions of dollars of his own money in low carbon technologies. This investment is used against him by certain elements of the climate change denial brigade as evidence that he has a personal vested interest in climate change policies becoming law and therefore his views cannot be trusted.[16] Gore retorts that he is putting his money where his mouth is.

This is a difficult line to tread and to a certain extent you are 'damned if you do and damned if you don't'. Many of the interviewees in the book frame their motives carefully. InterfaceFLOR talks of 'doing well by doing good', Northern Foods calls it 'enlightened self-interest' and Marks & Spencer plays down the economic return on Plan A as they don't want to be seen to be mercenary.

The Bottom Line

Ultimately I believe the reasons for going green are much bigger than the hard nosed 'business case' we covered in Chapter 2. Bringing personal values and ethics to the workplace makes life more meaningful for everyone. Likewise I see no conflict between trying to do the right thing and making profit, but others may be more cynical about motives, as we shall see in Chapter 4. The key issue here is building trust and we consider trust in more detail in Chapter 17.

Chapter summary

1 Many market leaders are driven by the moral imperative – a feeling that their organization is there to do more than make profit;
2 Bringing values to the workplace makes life more meaningful for everyone;
3 Sticking to core values has been shown to make a business more profitable in the long run and can help avoid the pitfalls of short-term profit chasing;
4 Addressing ethical problems through business is necessary for a sustainable future but will bring cynicism from outside;
5 The moral imperative extends way beyond the factory fence – up and down the value chain and across all stakeholders.

The View from the Front Line: Paula Widdowson, Northern Foods

Northern Foods is a £1 billion food manufacturing business employing 11,000 people at 29 manufacturing sites across the UK and Ireland. The group produces ready meals, sandwiches, biscuits and puddings for major food retailers such as Asda, Marks & Spencer, Morrisons, Sainsbury's and Tesco as well as producing their own brands including Fox's and Dalepak. Paula Widdowson is the Director of Corporate Social Responsibility for the group and works across all the group's operations to catalyse and facilitate sustainable solutions.

Why and how did you get involved in this agenda?

I have a degree in biochemistry and was a science teacher for three years, so I understand the science of sustainability. My corporate background is in marketing and sales in major companies such as Mars, Esso and Bass. Then for three years I was operations director at Improve Ltd, a training and skills company focused on the food sector, which gave me a grasp of the skills agenda.

While I was at Improve, I was asked by the chief executive of Northern Foods to come in and take responsibility for CSR. They wanted somebody who wasn't just environmentally aware, but had a commercial understanding of the food industry. I love new challenges, so I thought 'Why not?'.

My new role was to determine what was going on currently and what was the best route forward for the company, then develop a strategy and get buy-in for that strategy. The first nine months of the job was 90 per cent internal, getting the strategy together. Now I spend 50 per cent of my time externally – starting projects off and facilitating their implementation.

I believe I've got the best job you could ever have. I get involved in everything, it is fascinating and I genuinely believe this agenda is here to stay. I want to ensure that our children have a world to play in and jobs to thrive in when they're our age.

What are the drivers for Northern Foods to engage in this agenda?

We've always done CSR, ever since the group was founded in the 1970s, but it was in a piecemeal manner. We don't use the term CSR internally – we call our sustainability programme 'The Northern Way'. Our approach is very simple and very straightforward – we call it 'enlightened self-interest'.

We approach CSR such that it has to make sense in the business case. Like Cadburys or Rowntree, we believe that you treat your people right, treat your customers right and treat your consumers right, then you will build yourself a business model which is more sustainable and which will bring profit into the company.

On top of that, we must also be doing the right thing. For example, energy efficiency will save us money, but those improvements will also motivate anyone with an altruistic side. We show people the knock-on effect of what they do – how many tonnes of carbon they are saving.

Reputation is a strong factor. If we have a good reputation we will recruit good people more easily, we will retain the best people, and we will sell more. This is a virtual circle – doing the right thing and making more money. We have delivered Plan A for Marks & Spencer on ready meals – reduction in packaging and cutting sugar and salt content.

Legislation is also a driver – legislation will never lead you, but it will push you.

What are the big challenges for your organization?

The biggest challenge is keeping the activity happening. We have to make sure that, once we kick a project off, everybody has accepted it and we keep doing it. We sometimes get asked 'Are we there yet?', and we say, 'We're never going to get there, we just keep on going.'

According to studies, 70 per cent of sustainability improvements in a factory are down to behavioural change. This is why we have such an emphasis on behaviour and people. It takes six weeks to change habits so we keep pressure on for six weeks after a change and then start checking it periodically.

We don't see legislation as a challenge as it will come along and we will deal with it. It's as simple as that.

What successes have you had?

The sustainability programme saved Northern Foods £2 million last financial year, and it will deliver £4 million in savings this year and even more in the following years. We have achieved 'Gold' status with Business In The Community and have been rated in the top eight companies for transparency in reporting CSR issues.

We have found the best solutions are about empowerment. For example, in our factories we have a colour-coded system of stickers on machines. Red means 'leave this machine running', amber means 'if this machine is doing nothing then ask before switching off' and green gives anyone permission to switch it off if it has been left on. This simple system has delivered between 4 and 6 per cent energy savings across the company and it costs about £22 per factory to implement.

What's your advice for others in your position?

I don't have a team of people and that is deliberate. We don't want anybody to think that this is someone else's job. We want to empower everyone to do their job in a better way, rather than tell them what to do. They're the experts in what they do, we just suggest how things could work and encourage them to move in that direction. We give people permission to act, give them confidence to move forward and allow them to fail until they get it right. You have to have the humility to accept that other people know more than you.

Green Business Risks

So far I have been unashamedly gung-ho about the reasons for becoming a sustainable business. The green/low carbon economy is coming and you should not only be prepared for it, but be ready to thrive in it. However, and this may be stating the obvious, you should never forget that you are running a business. I've seen a number of hard-nosed businesspeople catch the green bug, get carried away and lose their commercial sense.

As with any transition, there are risks involved. There is an analogy with the dotcom bubble at the end of the 20th century. Hoards of entrepreneurs jumped on the exciting new bandwagon of e-commerce, but far too many (and their investors) forgot to check that they had a viable business model underneath the hype. Only those who combined technological know-how and business sense survived the rather brutal market correction that occurred at the start of the 21st century. The same applies to the green/low carbon economy. It is not a matter of being green *or* being commercially minded. It is about being green *and* being commercially minded. In fact, as Vic Morgan of the Ethical Superstore says, 'If you are going down the [green] route, you actually have to *overcompensate* on the commercial side to make sure you still have a viable business.'

Managing these risks is a key element of green business success. On the one hand you have to learn by doing and be oriented towards action, but on the other it would be crazy not to learn from the mistakes of others. So we are going to consider three key external risks:

- Unrealistic views of markets: expecting your customers to take the pain – assuming customers will accept low quality products and services and/or a premium price or assuming customers will readily accept a radically different product to the one they are used to;
- Building on sand: investing in immature or ineffective technologies and/or not having the right supply chain in place;

- Greenwash: overstating your case and getting found out, or not being able to deliver on promises and having to back out.

Unrealistic View of Markets

Most green markets are still niche markets. While a small percentage (5–10 per cent[1]) of consumers will pay extra for a greener product, or accept some compromises on the quality front, virtually nobody will pay a premium for an expensive but poor quality product on green credentials alone. Again it is the question of 'and' rather than 'or'. Can you produce a green product or service *and* make it competitive on quality and price? For example, Procter & Gamble launched a green product range in the 1990s but it failed commercially. Now they take a hard line 'no trade-offs' approach and some of their greenest products are the best performing. The following paragraphs summarize some of the markets pitfalls.

Expecting your customers to take the pain

US marketing guru Jacquelyn Ottman talks about the 'green graveyard' of failed green products.[2] Her message is clear – don't expect your customers to take the pain. When Philips launched the compact fluorescent tube, it was big, ugly and cumbersome and called the 'Earth Light' – and it bombed. When it was redesigned to look like a traditional bulb and rebranded as the 'Marathon' it sold well.

This doesn't just apply to consumer markets. A common mistake is to expect public sector organizations to be obliged in some way to purchase an innovative and expensive green product or service. I have seen a number of businesspeople get obsessed with selling their green product to local authorities, assuming that because they are a public body, they should 'do the right thing' at any cost. They couldn't be more wrong. Given their high public profile, local authorities are naturally risk averse. A perceived waste of taxpayers' money will always make the headlines and local authorities are closer to the electorate than central governments. They are also under huge pressure to find cost savings.

The French company Utilicom shows how to approach local authorities effectively. Utilicom designs, installs and operates combined heat and power systems that deliver substantial savings on heat and electricity over a localized distribution system – with significant carbon savings as an added bonus. They have developed a model where the authority signs up to buy energy from the system for a number of years at a price set just under the market rate. Apart from that, the authority has no further commitment to make. They also have a 21-year old system working in Southampton, UK, which demonstrates the effectiveness and reliability of the approach. In other words they are de-risking a radical project for risk-averse customers.

Cultural differences

Markets around the world are subject to cultural differences, so you can't assume that what works in one country will work in another. District heating is the norm in much of Europe, but is viewed with suspicion in the UK, hence Utilicom's 'de-risking' business model above.

One of Jacquelyn Ottman's examples in the US green graveyard is the front-loading washing machine, which is much more water and energy efficient than top-loading models. Front loaders are the norm in Europe, but attempts to launch the product in the US, where consumers are used to top loaders, have floundered.

The same can happen in business-to-business products and services. In many countries across Europe and Australasia, compressed air is provided as a utility rather than as a capital investment, i.e. buying a compressor and taking on the maintenance of the system. In 2005, international compressor manufacturers CompAir launched a utility service called Airworx in the UK. Airworx was designed to provide a complete compressed air service, saving companies up to £100,000 per annum in energy costs. Despite this clear benefit, backed up with success stories from around the world, the service failed in the market. According to CompAir, the reluctance to take up such a service was due to the fact that UK industry prefers to make capital investments to add assets to their company, as businesses are sold so often.[3]

Not sticking to the knitting

Sudden diversifications into new markets have caught out a number of businesses and green markets are no different. If you are an established brand with a loyal customer base, you are better innovating within your area of competence rather than branching off in radical directions.

In the early days of Marks & Spencer's Plan A, they trialled selling 'green products' such as wormeries for composting food. They soon found that this was not the sort of product that the average person goes to M&S for and didn't pursue the idea any further. Recently I went to one of their stores because

I needed a new umbrella and was delighted to find they had a model made out of recycled polyester. By greening their mainstream stock, M&S took the pain out of looking for a green option for me.

Building on Sand

A substantial part of an organization's footprint lies in its supply chain. For example, the UK's National Health Service estimates that 60 per cent of its carbon footprint lies with suppliers.[4] The supply chain is also a limiting factor in developing greener processes, products and business models. We'll look at two major issues – weak supply chains and investing in immature technologies.

Weak supply chains

Weak supply chains present the following problems to a green business:

- Low volumes lead to high component or material prices that in turn drive up the price of the final product;
- Lack of competition can impact on product quality, reliability of supply and prices;
- Low demand leads to indifferent attitude from suppliers.

Many of the interviewees in this book have identified their supply chain as a key challenge. Smith's Electric Vehicles has found that the cost of the bought-in components for their electric vehicles is a limiting factor in allowing electric vehicles to compete on purchase price with conventional vehicles. National Express has not been able to source a low carbon coach that delivers on their wider requirements. InterfaceFLOR is much smaller than its main petrochemical suppliers, and finds its relative lack of firepower in that market makes it difficult to get the materials it wants. We'll be looking at how to strengthen supply chains in Chapter 11.

Immature technologies

With the demand for green products and services expanding rapidly, a significant number of charlatans and chancers has been attracted to the field. Some of these may be out and out conmen, while others are at the 'mad inventor' end of the spectrum – people who genuinely believe that they have developed a new technology but that it just needs a final few tweaks to get it working. They often have to sell their first system in order to finance the final stages of development. If you bite, then you end up financing that part of the product development cycle with no guarantee that the technology will ever work. Other developers want to sell large-scale systems but only have small-scale demonstration plants. While these can be impressive, there is no guarantee that the full-scale version will work.

Obviously, investing in capital equipment that doesn't deliver is a backward step, soaking up precious finance and spreading cynicism among your colleagues. So be very careful and be prepared to walk away. I would be particularly cautious with small-scale versions of technologies such as anaerobic digestion, gasification and biomass combined heat and power. There is nothing wrong with these technologies per se, but to date I have seen an example of each where the product never delivered what it promised.

Public Relations Disasters

The greatest sin in the eyes of the environmental movement is greenwash – trying to appear greener than you really are. In the words of green marketer John Grant, 'Green marketing is about making green seem normal, not about making the normal look green.'[5]

Patrolling the herds of green businesses are the 'green hyenas', waiting for a sign of weakness before they pounce. Green hyenas come in a number of guises including:

- The anti-capitalist end of the environmental movement that is intrinsically anti-business;
- Campaign groups who know that exposing wrongdoing in supposedly green businesses will raise huge amounts of publicity;
- Journalists who know that exposing greenwash will sell newspapers and magazines, for example Joe Entine's pursuit of The Body Shop;
- Anti-environmentalists who want to portray green efforts as ineffective as well as pointless;
- Regulators such as the UK's Advertising Standards Agency (ASA) who investigate green claims.

You may think I'm using the word hyena pejoratively against these types, but hyenas perform a very useful role in their ecosystem by keeping the herd strong and competitive. Joe Entine's campaign led to greater transparency and openness in The Body Shop and, as we shall see, the ASA pushed Lexus into producing better vehicles.

Overstating your case

In the UK, the ASA is taking an increasingly hard line on green claims, having ruled against Lexus, Shell and Ryanair in recent years. In the Lexus case, the company's 2009 model hybrid SUV was portrayed as planet-saving as it emitted 192 g/km CO_2, compared to the 302 g/km CO_2 of rival SUV models. The ASA ruled that this could not be portrayed as 'green' as it was still worse than the European average of 158 g/km CO_2 for all types of car.[6] The advert was banned. Lexus have since bounced back with the 2010 model SUV that emits 148 g/km CO_2. Likewise the ASA condemned Shell for claiming they used their CO_2 emissions to grow flowers when only 0.325 per cent of emissions were used in this way.

Some questions you must ask yourself are:

- Are you being truly objective in your comparisons? Lexus came unstuck as they thought they could compare SUV to SUV rather than car to car;
- Are you presenting the whole truth? Shell's problem was implying they were doing much more with their carbon emissions than they really were;
- Are you addressing the elephant in the room? There is no point in trying to present yourself as green if your business is intrinsically ungreen. Can an oil company or a producer of toxic paint stripper ever be sustainable?

John Hinton, operations manager of the Ethical Superstore, talks about '360° ethics'[7] – in other words you have to cover every issue, not just a selection. It is this kind of thinking that protects against the green hyenas.

Getting cold feet

If you are going to do the green thing, you need to do it properly. The worst thing you can do is make a big fanfare launching a new direction, then back-pedal rapidly when the going gets tough. Unlike, say, an unsuccessful joint business venture, backing out of green ventures will make the headlines and damage your reputation in the long term.

Probably the most infamous example of this was BP's flirtation with 'Beyond Petroleum'. BP had done a lot to cut the carbon emissions from their processes and decided to push this and some renewable energy investments into a marketing campaign in which they claimed that BP now stood for 'Beyond Petroleum'. But in an interview, a senior BP Manager, Bob Malone, had to admit they were decades away from that aspiration,[8] leading to a backlash from the environmental movement.

Likewise Shell invested in renewables, made a fuss about it, but then divested them when the returns didn't look so good.[9] While they present this as just normal business practice, they shouldn't have portrayed themselves as progressive and green before backing out when the going got tough. This further tarnished their reputation.

In the summer of 2009, Marks & Spencer ran ads poking fun at their rivals for cutting back on sustainability programmes in a recession. The ads show a model in a green dress with the slogan, 'For us, green is not just a fashion.'

Accidents and the unexpected

The other thing that can derail your green efforts is an environmental accident or another high profile incident. 'Green company causes pollution incident' is the most difficult position to recover from and the image of the company will take a huge hit. This is why 'compliance' is the base of the business case pyramid in Chapter 2.

Of course the obvious answer is that the truly green company will have divested itself of hazardous or toxic materials so is much less likely to suffer from a pollution incident. But when a substance as apparently benign as milk can have a devastating effect if spilt into a lake or river, it still pays to be meticulously careful to avoid environmental incidents of any kind.

Getting blamed for the sins of others

The globalization of supply chains presents many challenges to a green company. It has made traceability difficult and has been accused of creating a 'race to the bottom' in the developing world, encouraging a relaxation of environmental regulation and/or enforcement. For example, the Sony Playstation debacle was caused by a Chinese supplier of electrical cables. The supplier will never be remembered, but the embarrassment to Sony continues as it continues to be quoted as an example of an environmental incident in books like this one. Likewise when Greenpeace wanted to highlight the illegal logging of hardwoods from rainforest, instead of targeting the logging, they targeted retailers of the resulting products and high profile end-users. For example, Greenpeace found that 2 tonnes of illegally sourced plywood had been used in the UK Houses of Parliament in 2006,[10] embarrassing the government. It is therefore imperative that a green company actively de-risks their supply chain and is meticulous about the activities of their suppliers (see Chapter 11 for more details).

Chapter summary

1   Going green is not without risk;
2   Market reactions to green or low carbon products and services can be unpredictable;
3   As with any innovation, technologies and supply chains are likely to be immature, which can put the company at risk;
4   Public relations disasters can arise from not backing words with action, overstating your case, being seen to get cold feet or unexpected incidents;
5   If you're going to do it, you have to do it properly.

The View from the Front Line: Nigel Stansfield, InterfaceFLOR

InterfaceFLOR is the world's biggest supplier of modular flooring systems, supplying approximately 40 per cent of all carpet tiles globally – some 40 million square metres a year. The company has 5000 employees worldwide and a $1 billion turnover. In 1994 CEO Ray Anderson had an epiphany after reading *The Ecology of Commerce* by Paul Hawken, when he decided to make the company truly sustainable. The company now has made a commitment called 'Mission Zero' – the company will have a zero ecological footprint by 2020.

Nigel Stansfield is the Senior Director of Product and Design Innovation at InterfaceFLOR Europe. He is responsible for both continual incremental improvements in existing products and the strategic direction of the business in terms of future products and services.

Why and how did you get involved in this agenda?

I was originally a textile engineer. I did a seven-year apprenticeship and a textile technology degree at the same time, and then became a loom tuner, responsible for keeping the machines running. I moved into product development before the company I was working for was bought out by Interface in 1997. Under the new regime I discovered I was a 'closet environmentalist' and 2001/2002 I was given the opportunity to really learn about sustainability as it applies to the business. I was given a new role in the business with the freedom to investigate all the issues and talk to all the sustainability experts, like Forum for the Future, Amory Lovins and Janine Benyus.

What are the business drivers for InterfaceFLOR to engage in this agenda?

Originally it was 'because it was Ray's wish', but it has since proved to be the right way to do business – we call it 'doing well by doing good'. We are in the enviable position of being seen to be leaders in sustainability. We are engaging customers and exciting them. We have a very high staff retention rate – our average service is about 16 years – way above the industry norm. You can see what it does for our staff, and the innate confidence of our salespeople, in their swagger. You would not be able to talk to anyone in the business for more than five minutes without them mentioning sustainability.

What successes have you had?

When Ray Anderson had his epiphany back in 1994, we were a petrochemical-based company, using polyamide as a face material and bitumen or PVC as a backing material – all of it was virgin material and the process was energy intensive and quite wasteful. We have managed to substantially improve the environmental performance of our product across its entire lifecycle. We also look at the social impact of our product across that whole lifecycle. We have deliberately deleted products which are not going to progress us towards our Mission Zero goal – for example we have eliminated a number of products with certain flame retardants as we do not want to perpetuate a problem.

We have a whole range of innovative products like our random-installation tiles whose pattern means there is no wrong way to lay them. We have pioneered post-industrial material use and we were the first in the world to use post-consumer yarn.

We launched 31 new products during the recent recession, and in 2008 we launched a radical new product in an attempt to achieve true sustainability. It is made in India from local renewable and recycled materials, it uses local skills and everybody in the supply chain receives a fair price for their product. It would be a 'fair trade' product but the FairTrade movement doesn't have a floor covering category yet.

We have had many other successes. Our Quest programme has eliminated over $400 million of waste since 1994. We are the first carpet tile company in the world to launch products using post-consumer recycled yarn through our ReEntry 2.0 programme. We pioneered the first carbon neutral carpet programme.

We have also realized that we have influenced a broad spectrum of our competitors, demonstrating that sustainability is a business benefit. Now their products are improving from a sustainability point of view. We punch way above our weight on sustainability – we have topped the Globescan world sustainability rankings for the last three years in a row.

What are the big challenges for your organization?

We are a relatively small company and most of our suppliers are far bigger than us, like Shell, Esso and Invista, so it is difficult to build the supply chain we need.

We often take options which initially cost more. When we first bought 100 per cent renewable electricity for our factories in the UK it cost a premium, but we saw it as adding value to our product. Then renewable energy hit a tipping point and suddenly became a lot less expensive.

Another key challenge is product takeback as we know we need to recover materials for recycling to achieve our zero footprint goal. We have pioneered the ReEntry 2.0 programme for product takeback and we also launched the Evergreen flooring leasing service but the latter has proved difficult to market. End-users are happy to lease mobile products like photocopiers and forklift trucks, but flooring is still seen as a capital purchase, not a product to be leased.

Looking forward we would like to broaden our influence across the whole interiors sector – the ceramics industry, the timber industry and the furniture industry – and ultimately show that there is a different way of doing things.

What's your advice for others in your position?

Don't just look inside the business for radical innovation – you might not find it. We have put together a dream team of external thinkers to help us do radical innovation. And we mix internal and external thinkers together to get the medium—long-term projection of where we want to be.

On the other hand there are lots and lots of 'experts', but you have to be clear in your own mind what you want to achieve – what is your vision for the future. Then start your journey and don't be put off – you will go down dead ends and find many obstacles – but stick with it – stickability is the key.

Part II
The Global Context

The Global Context

In this section we look at the global context of the green business agenda. This is to give an idea of the scale of the challenges we are trying to tackle and the high-level solutions available to solve them. These macro-solutions translate into company-level solutions and opportunities, as we see in Part III.

Chapter 5 considers environmental problems, particularly the 'Big Three' of climate change, unsustainable resource use and the release of toxic and persistent materials into the environment. Other important issues, including acidification, ozone depletion and eutrophication, are discussed more briefly.

Chapter 6 looks at the various theories of sustainability and sustainable development, with a particular focus on environmental sustainability. In this chapter we introduce the two main environmental sustainability strategies: eco-efficiency and the ecosystem models that are broadly quantitative and qualitative respectively.

Chapter 7 translates these theories into potential future scenarios of sustainable economies. These scenarios can be used by businesses either to reactively respond to the emerging new business landscape, or, for cutting-edge businesses, to proactively rebuild their business, supply chain and markets to drive the agenda forwards.

Global Problems

Overview

In this chapter we look at global environmental issues. There are two different perspectives we can take on the environment: (1) anthropocentric (or 'selfish'): we need the Earth's resources and natural services to survive and indeed flourish; and (2) altruistic (or 'moral'): many believe that issues such as biodiversity (the number of species on the earth) are moral issues and we have no moral right to cause the extinction of another species.

The difference between these two perspectives can be a cause of conflict even between environmentalists. For example some will make the case that we must preserve biodiversity in the rainforests as one species may hold the cure to cancer; others would find that argument repugnant, saying we simply have no right to destroy species. We will be looking at different attitudes to the environment in detail in Chapter 17; in the meantime we take account of both perspectives in this section.

We look in some detail at the three most pressing environmental problems[1] and then more briefly at other environmental issues that need to be considered. The 'Big Three' are:

- Climate change;
- Resource depletion (including 'peak oil');
- Persistent toxic substances.

The differences between the Big Three and the other environmental issues are:

- Scale of impact: the predictions for climate change under a business as usual scenario are terrifying, with estimations of a million species extinct and surging sea levels. Likewise if oil production does peak, it could trigger major global insecurity and even resource wars. Virtually all of us have man-made persistent toxic substances in our bodies – these have been linked to many serious diseases and can devastate ecosystems.

- Time frame: the residence time for CO_2 in the atmosphere is 100 years and the other greenhouse gases, except methane, hang around even longer. If a non-renewable resource is gone, it is gone forever. Persistent toxic substances will exist in the environment for decades.
- Geographical scale: the 'other' environmental issues tend to have a local or regional impact, for example the ozone hole over Antarctica or the destruction of Scandinavian forests by UK sulphur emissions in the 1980s. While these are significant, the Big Three are truly global in scope. Climate change may be affecting polar bears, but it could also jeopardize the drinking water for half the world's population and destroy the world's coral reefs.
- Intractability: most of the 'other' environmental impacts are by-products of the processes that drive our economy (for example you can scrub sulphur emissions out of power station emissions), but the Big Three problems are intrinsic to the way we live today. If you burn fossil fuels, you get carbon emissions. You can try to capture and store them, but you can't eliminate them. If you have a high material standard of living, then by definition you will require a large amount of natural resources. With persistent toxic pollutants, it is often the 'problem' that we are utilizing as a 'feature' – DDT is an effective pesticide (in the short term) because it is very toxic and persistent.

Climate Change

In the last 20 years, climate change has risen from one of a number of environmental issues to the biggest environmental threat in the world today. The basics are well understood.[2] So-called greenhouse gases (most notably CO_2) trap the sun's heat, reflecting back off the Earth's surface. If they didn't do this, the world would be uninhabitable – the average surface temperature would be about 30°C cooler than it is today. However, since the industrial revolution, human activity has increased the concentration of these gases from 285 parts per million (ppm) CO_2 equivalent to 430ppm CO_2 equivalent. Average global temperatures are now 0.8°C above pre-industrial levels and are predicted to rise to 2–6°C by 2100. 2°C is regarded as the 'politically acceptable' level of temperature rise, but would still cause substantial human and environmental impacts. It would threaten the glacier system in the Himalayas that, via many of the world's greatest rivers such as the Ganges and the Yangtze, provides drinking water for 2.3–3.0 billion people. Overall the impacts are expected to hit the poor hardest. A 6°C rise is generally regarded as catastrophic – the last time the Earth was that warm it consisted of one large swamp.

The idea that emissions from our economic activities are changing global climates is now overwhelmingly accepted in scientific and political circles. There is, however, still something of a debate raging in the blogosphere and certain newspapers as to whether it is scientific fact, part of a natural cycle or even a huge socialist conspiracy to raise taxes. Most of the debate consists of non-climatologists cherry-picking or distorting apparently contradictory evidence and claiming that this disproves man-made climate change. These arguments have been thoroughly debunked time and time again yet they keep resurfacing. Some of these myths are deliberately circulated by organizations with a vested economic or political interest in trying to create a fake grassroots movement (aka 'astroturfing'), but much of it is repeated by individuals who simply don't want to accept the physical limitations of living on a single piece of rock. Hence the rather controversial term 'climate change denial'.

Nevertheless, there is a huge amount of genuine confusion among the general public over climate change. Most of this is because the majority of people don't understand the difference between weather (trends in temperature, precipitation, cloud cover etc. from day to day, year to year) and climate (the 20–30 year average of those weather patterns). In any period of less than about five years, the biggest effect on weather is caused by short-term weather systems, the most powerful being the El Niño Southern Oscillation, which has El Niño (warm) and La Niña (cool) phases. Greenhouse gases have a relatively small effect on weather month to month or even year to year, but it is a *persistent and cumulative* effect, slowly ramping up global temperatures over the medium to long term (i.e. in climatic terms). So you can still get short sharp wintery weather in any one year, but as time goes on, the likelihood of that cold weather will decrease. For example, 2008 (a La Niña year) may have been the coolest year in the 21st century, but it was still warmer than any year in the 20th century bar one, 1998 (a very strong El Niño year).

To have a chance of meeting the target of keeping temperature rises below 2°C, it has been estimated that the world must cut its carbon emissions by 50 per cent by 2050. As current emissions are dominated by Western nations, they will have to cut their emissions by 80 per cent by 2050 to allow some room for less developed nations to grow their economies.

Resource Depletion

We live on a single piece of rock floating through space. By definition, the resources contained within that rock are finite. By extension, the use of non-renewable resources, such as fossil fuels and mineral deposits, is unsustainable. In most cases before reserves are physically gone, their extraction will become economically and/or technically infeasible. Alternatives to these resources need to be found, otherwise there will be a significant drop in the standard of living.

'Peak oil' is the highest profile concern in resource depletion. Peak oil occurs when production hits its maximum and starts to decline. The idea was popularized by petrogeologist M. King Hubbert who developed the Hubbert curve model in the 1950s.[3] This model successfully predicted the peak in oil production in the US in 1970 – a fact that was driven home by the energy crisis of 1973/1974 when members of the Organization of the Petroleum Exporting Countries (OPEC) stopped supplying the US with oil. The sixty thousand dollar question is whether the same curve can be applied to global oil reserves given the number of interrelated variables involved. There is probably enough oil in existence to meet human needs for centuries, but the location of the remaining deposits, how accessible they are in terms of geology, local/regional/global politics, demand, taxation, exploration technology and drilling technology all affect the economics of the oil industry.

In 2008 Fatih Birol, chief economist of the International Energy Agency, announced that global oil reserves would probably peak in 2020.[4] A year later, two whistle-blowers declared to the press that this prediction had been influenced by pressure from the US government and that we were 'already in the peak zone'. Two independent European research bodies concurred with this view.[5] The most optimistic analysis around concludes that oil will peak in 2030, followed by a plateau rather than a sharp decline.[6] This scenario would require the extensive use of non-conventional and highly carbon intensive resources such as tar sands and coal for liquid transformation.

So there is huge uncertainty with widely different predictions coming from different sources. What we do know for sure is: non-OPEC oil reserves have already peaked; and OPEC countries do not meet internationally recognized standards for auditing and reporting oil reserves.[7]

In other words, we are relying on extremely unreliable data to plan for the future. Given the importance of oil to the modern global economy (fuel, plastics, pharmaceuticals), this is a terrifying position to be in. It appears that coal is unlikely to peak in the near future, but the processes for generating oils from coal are highly energy intensive.[8] Peak theory also appears to apply to other non-renewable resources including uranium,[9] which raises questions over the contribution that nuclear energy can make to long-term energy planning.

Many renewable resources, such as plants and animals, are still depletable – if they are overused they will be lost forever. To achieve the sustainable use of these resources, consumption cannot outstrip replenishment rates. Current examples of overuse include:

- Over fishing: according the United Nations Environment Programme, over 25 per cent of global fish stocks have 'crashed' and a further 40 per cent are being overexploited;[10]
- Over-hunting: the International Union for Conservation of Nature (IUCN) lists dozens of animals that are critically endangered due to the combined effects of hunting and habitat loss, including over 300 species of primate;[11]
- Unsustainable extraction of timber. An area of forest the size of Panama is lost every year through logging and clearance for agriculture.[12] Deforestation is also exacerbating climate change by decreasing the amount of CO_2 the planet can recycle back into oxygen.

A further complication of resource use is that 80 per cent of the world's resources are consumed by 15 per cent of the population.[13] This is obviously unfair, but there is a practical problem as well. As the quality of life of the populations of China, India and other fast developing countries improves, their resource use will increase, exacerbating the problem. Therefore efforts to make resource use sustainable must take into consideration a rapid increase in demand.

Persistent Bioaccumulative Toxic Compounds

Silent Spring,[14] Rachel Carson's seminal 1962 book on the effect of pesticides on ecosystems and human health, has been credited with launching the modern environmental movement. The book's title comes from the short, apocalyptic opening chapter that describes a fictional small American town where pesticides and herbicides have destroyed the natural environment – there are no birds to welcome spring. This vision was inspired by the after-effects that the blanket spraying of pests and weeds with insecticides and pesticides in the 1950s was having on the wildlife of vast tracts of America and much of the world. Carson points out that the simplistic safety tests for pesticides did not take into consideration the following key factors:

- Biomagnification: a 0.02ppm dose of chemicals into a lake can result in a fatal 1600ppm concentration in the blood of a grebe as the chemicals concentrate up the food chain;

- 'The cocktail effect': where combinations of chemicals can have a toxic effect many times the effect of either individually;
- Longer term effects on cells such as genetic damage and cancer.

Silent Spring became an unlikely bestseller and led to the banning of DDT in the US in 1972, which in turn can be linked to a revival in the fortunes of the national bird, the bald eagle.

Persistent bioaccumulative toxic (PBT) chemicals of most concern are known as persistent organic pollutants (POPs). They include:

- Pesticides such as aldrin, chlordane, DDT, dieldrin and endrin;
- Flame retardants such as polychlorinated biphenyls (PCBs);
- Products of incineration such as dioxins and furans.

Other similar chemicals of concern are:

- Polycyclic aromatic hydrocarbons (PAHs) that occur in tars and oils;
- Organometallic compounds such as tributyltin (TBT), which was used as an antifouling agent in ship paint.

POP exposure in humans can cause death and illnesses including disruption of the endocrine, reproductive and immune systems, neurobehavioral disorders and cancers.[15] They have also been linked to diabetes.[16] But these dangers are exacerbated by the persistence of these types of chemicals – most of these compounds take decades to decompose naturally so they can be passed up the food chain and from mother to child. The World Wildlife Fund tested 155 people and found traces of both DDT and PCBs in 99 per cent of them.[17] POPs can also travel long distances and have a tendency to move from warmer to cooler areas. POPs have never been used in either the Arctic and Antarctica yet they are found in the fat of animals in both environments.

The great irony of pesticide use is that insects can evolve resistance very rapidly so the effectiveness of the chemicals soon wears off. In 1948 in the US, 23 million kg of pesticides were used leading to a 7 per cent loss of crops to pests, in 2000, 20 times as much pesticide was used yet 13 per cent of crops were lost.[18] Species higher in the food chain (including humans) cannot evolve so quickly to develop immunity to their toxic effects.

The Stockholm Convention on Persistent Organic Pollutants has been ratified by 168 countries.[19] The convention commits signatories to banning nine of the so-called 'dirty dozen' POPs, limiting the use of DDT to malaria control, and minimizing the emission of dioxins and furans. A further list of nine chemicals was added to the Convention's lists in 2009, with another three under consideration at the time of writing.

Other Environmental Issues

The following environmental issues are important, but I've set them apart from the Big Three as they are more regional or local in geographical scale and/or temporary in terms of impact. Many of these problems can easily be solved through, for example, pollution control systems or substituting one chemical for another.

Ozone layer depletion

Ozone is a poisonous compound of oxygen and is a major pollutant at ground level. However, there is a layer of ozone in the upper atmosphere that filters out ultraviolet rays from the sun. These rays cause skin cancer in humans and other ecological damage. The release of certain man-made substances, most notably chlorofluorocarbons (CFCs), has caused a large hole to appear in this layer over Antarctica. The hole was discovered in 1984 and was found to be growing. In 1987 the Montreal protocol set out a programme for a phased banning of ozone depleting substances. This has been remarkably successful and the hole has stabilized and may soon start to shrink.[20]

Many people confuse ozone depletion and climate change. They are quite different, apart from the fact that CFCs and some related chemicals have a strong climate change effect as well. The ozone hole itself has something of a cooling effect over Antarctica, which counteracts climate change to a certain degree. Paradoxically, fixing the ozone layer problem could lead to more warming.

Acidification/acid rain

The most common form of acidification is known as 'acid rain'. Sulphurous and nitrous oxides (SOx and NOx) react with water vapour in the atmosphere to produce acids. These acids return to the surface though rain and other precipitation and cause significant ecological damage, in particular to forests, lakes and rivers, but also corrosive damage to buildings. Sulphur emissions have successfully been reduced by end-of-pipe pollution prevention systems such as flue gas desulphurization. Like the hole in the ozone layer, sulphur emissions have a cooling effect on the world, therefore fixing this problem is likely to make climate change worse.

There is another form of acidification that is less well known. The oceans absorb about 25 per cent of man-made carbon emissions where they acidify and damage sea life. Estimates suggest that ocean acidification could cause US shellfish revenues to drop by over one third by 2060.[21]

Air quality

As well as global and regional air pollution, certain environmental problems occur very locally, particularly in cities. It is estimated that up to 800,000 deaths per year are attributable to urban air pollution globally.[22] The main problems are:

- Particulates (PM10s): these are very small particles from incineration processes and can cause inflammation in the lungs of animals, making the blood thicken leading to potential heart and lung disease;
- Summer, or photochemical, smog, cause volatile organic compounds (VOCs) reacting in sunlight to create ground level ozone, which is poisonous;
- Winter smog, caused by dust and other pollutants such as SOx forming an acidic mist. Certain weather conditions can trap this mist over a locality. The infamous London 'pea-souper' of December 1952 was blamed for 12,000 deaths.[23]

Eutrophication

Eutrophication is a man-made increase in nutrients in rivers, lakes and seas. The microorganisms that feed on those nutrients can bloom, lowering the levels of dissolved oxygen, effectively suffocating other, larger aquatic creatures. The effect is caused by organic wastes such as sewage, agricultural and industrial effluents (for example brewery wastes), and other nutrients such as nitrates and phosphates, mainly from artificial fertilizers and detergents. Eutrophication can trigger a vicious circle. The increase in algae in particular can cut out light, killing oxygenating plants. The resulting decaying plant material stimulates an increase in bacteria, which further deplete the water of oxygen.

Other harmful substances

While POPs are the toxic chemicals of most concern, many other substances produced by man's activities have a toxic or harmful effect on humans and the environment. Examples include:

- Radioactive particles: large doses of radiation lead to radiation sickness and death. Smaller doses can cause cancers, sterility and genetic mutation;
- Heavy metals, such as arsenic, cadmium, mercury, lead and copper, have a toxic effect on plants and animals;
- Acids and alkalis are emitted from many industrial processes. These are toxic to most aquatic organisms;
- Oil is a major polluter of soil, rivers and seas. It is toxic to many creatures, suffocates fish by coating their gills and causes seabird feathers to lose buoyancy and insulation;
- Particulates from mining wastes, pulverized fuel ash, dredging spoils, drilling muds and atmospheric fallout can smother benthic (bottom dwelling) fauna. Litter, particularly plastics, can have a major effect on river and marine animals through choking and entanglement;
- Cooling water and other industrial effluents can introduce heat into aquatic environments. The temperature of the water can exceed the thermal death point of certain organisms. However, it should be noted that certain bivalves and fish thrive on this heat.

Land issues

There is a raft of important issues relating to land use, for example:

- Soil erosion/desertification/salination: we depend on soil for virtually all our food supply, yet its importance is rarely appreciated. Soil damage can occur through poor agricultural techniques, over-extraction of water and the use of heavy vehicles;
- Contaminated land tends to have a much more localized effect than pollution of air and water, unless of course the contamination gets washed into rivers and streams. But even if there is no run-off, toxic substances in soil can cause effects to users of that land, enter the food chain via crops and animals, and can contaminate aquifers that are often used as a source of drinking water;

- Deforestation, land clearance and drainage of wetlands for agricultural and industrial/residential development can lead to loss of habitat and extinction of species as discussed under 'resource depletion' above;
- The loss of important natural services such as slope stabilization and water management.

Chapter summary

1   We are exceeding Earth's carrying capacity – the definition of being unsustainable.
2   The Big Three environmental issues, climate change, resource depletion and persistent toxic substances, must be tackled as a priority.
3   These problems are huge challenges – in scale of impact, time frame, geographical spread and their intractable nature in relation to modern lifestyles.
4   The root cause of these problems is consumption in rich, industrialized nations, yet the impacts may be most keenly felt in poorer countries.
5   There is a whole raft of other important considerations such as ozone depletion and acid rain, which must not be forgotten.

The View from the Front Line: Sally Hancox, Gentoo Housing Group

The Gentoo Housing Group manages 30,000 homes in Sunderland, UK and develops new private and social housing schemes. The Group has won many accolades for its environmental performance including being named twice in the Times' 50 Greenest Companies and the Developer of the Year at the Rosenblatt New Energy Awards 2009. Sally Hancox is the Director of Gentoo Green, the Group's 'internal environmental consultancy', and is responsible for integrating green thinking across all its operations.

Why did you personally get involved in this role?

I care about the environment and I am concerned about climate change. I don't have children so it's a moral response rather than an emotional one. I've had a good time on the planet and I don't want the place to be messed up for generations who come later. There's no need for environmental destruction either – much of it seems so senseless to me. Between us we should be able to work out what to do. We have the technology and we have the money – it's just not in the right place. We could put it in the right place but the politics get in the way.

From a business point of view, I am very interested in the behavioural change aspect of sustainability. We as a nation are very disconnected from the consequences of our actions. I would very much like to be part of the required reconnection by having an influence both inside and outside the organization.

What are the drivers for Gentoo to engage in this agenda?

We describe ourselves as a 'people and property business' where people are put first. We are an organization with a very strong conscience, and we know that the sustainability of our neighbourhoods is not just about collecting the rent and doing the repairs, it's about engaging with the people who live there and nurture their potential. That social conscience leads us to ask 'what is our environmental impact and how can we reduce it?'.

There are also big business drivers such as cutting costs through reduced waste, making buildings easier and cheaper to build and an increased resale value.

Regulation plays a part too – as a social landlord we are obliged to build new homes to meet Level 3 on the UK's Code for Sustainable Homes. Some of our current buildings reach Level 4 and we're in the process of building one to Level 6 (the top level). We like to stretch ourselves and stay ahead of the curve.

But the bottom line is – it's the right thing to do.

What are the big challenges for you at Gentoo?

Getting people to make connections between their behaviour and the environment. That includes our residents and we also need to motivate and mobilize decision makers. While many trade bodies and architects are ahead of the game, the construction industry lags behind and we want to help with that.

We also need to make sure that our staff make these connections so it doesn't just become a case of 'ticking boxes', but that everyone has an understanding of the link between actions and consequences. Whether it is simply someone switching off lights or putting waste in the right skip, through procurement decisions and up to designing new buildings, I would like to see everyone understanding how this contributes to sustainability.

In terms of the built environment, we manage 30,000 existing buildings which need to be improved in terms of energy efficiency – we've made some improvements, but more needs to be done to hit the government's 80 per cent carbon reduction target. It's not a problem of technology – we have all the technology – it's a matter of financing. This is an issue that cannot be ignored for much longer.

What successes have you had?

In just two years, and from a standing start, we've got a good percentage of staff who are aware of the issues, we've built good connections both inside and outside which allow us to look at different things and look at things in a different way. We've got a good baseline, a good carbon and ecological footprint and two years of key performance indicator data. I've got a great team working for me, and we've got about 40 self-selected champions throughout the business who are dedicated to making this agenda work.

In terms of our property, we've built a development of bungalows that we believe will be the first in the UK accredited to the German PassivHaus standard, we're building our 'Pea Pod' development which meets UK Code for Sustainable Homes Level 6 (zero carbon). We've launched our 'Retrofit Reality Programme' to tackle 120 existing buildings and we're modelling behavioural change and building performance.

What's your top tip for others in your position?

Give responsibility for sustainability to someone with a real passion for it, otherwise it will just disappear into a spreadsheet.

Global Solutions

Sustainability

We saw in Chapter 5 that we are exceeding the carrying capacity of the Earth, and a minority of the world's population are responsible for the excess. While the majority's impact on the planet is relatively small per person, this can be attributed to poverty rather than 'green living'. This situation is clearly unsustainable: keeping the majority of the world's population in poverty is immoral, but if they follow the industrialized nations' model of development, the Earth will not be able to cope. So we need a completely different solution: sustainability.

A sustainable world would be one in which everyone had at least a decent quality of life while living within the natural limits of the Earth. Jonathon Porritt, former chair of the UK's Sustainable Development Commission, says 'sustainability is non-negotiable as the opposite of sustainability is extinction'.[1] The terms 'sustainability' and 'sustainable development' are often used interchangeably, but I believe there is a clear difference between the two. Sustainability is the endpoint we are aiming for and sustainable development is how we get there (see Figure 6.1).

Sustainable Development

The most quoted of the hundreds of definitions of sustainable development is that of the United Nation's Brundtland Commission in 1987: 'Development that meets the needs of the present without compromising the abilities of future generations to meet their own needs.'[2] This is known as the principle of intergenerational equity – that people not born yet have as much right to quality of life as those who are alive today. While this is important, it is isn't specific as to what the needs are – although it has become generally accepted that they are

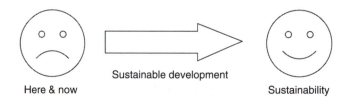

Figure 6.1 *Sustainable development and sustainability for dummies*

material/economic needs, social/ethical needs and environmental needs. My own definition makes it clear specifically what we are trying to achieve:

Saving the planet and solving world poverty.

This definition makes the scale of the challenge clear, makes it explicit that sustainability is the morally right thing to do, and gives a glimpse of benefits of success.

Models of Sustainability

The most popular way of visualizing sustainability is three interlocking circles representing economy, society and environment. The overlapping point in the middle is regarded as sustainability. This is a very weak definition as it implies some sort of balance between the three rather than a radical rethinking of how the world works – if tweaking would save the planet and solve world poverty we would have made those tweaks long ago. The lack of any constraints or scale on the model means you can identify societal, environmental and economic issues in pretty much anything and claim it is compatible with sustainable development (see Figure 6.2).

I prefer the less well-known but much more meaningful 'fried egg' model (see Figure 6.3). Here sustainability is defined as the situation where the economy operates within the limits set on it by societal values such as equity, justice and liberty, and where that society flourishes within the hard ecological limits placed on it by the natural world. This provides us with a much more robust framework within which to manage and measure progress to sustainability. Of course the simple circle labelled 'environment' belies the many dozens of environmental issues we considered in Chapter 5, while the definition of an equitable and just society is arguably even more complex. This book is primarily concerned with environmental considerations, but we will inevitably touch on societal issues as the two cannot be isolated.

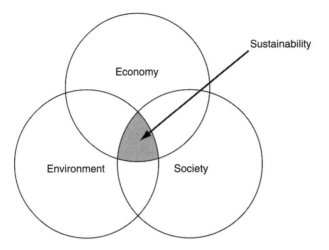

Figure 6.2 *Traditional model of sustainability*

Other Sustainability Principles

Two other key principles in sustainability theory are the 'precautionary principle' and the 'polluter pays' principle.

The precautionary principle has existed in various forms for several decades and was explicitly included in the Rio Declaration resulting from the first Earth Summit in 1992. In simple terms the principle states that, given the exceedingly high levels of uncertainty in predicting environmental damage, the prudent approach is to avoid risk and abandon or reject policies or practices that may have unsustainable outcomes or substantial negative environmental impacts.

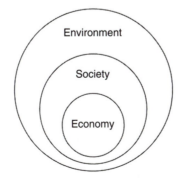

Figure 6.3 *'Fried egg' model of sustainability*

It also means that suitable margins of error should be applied to all potentially environmentally damaging projects or activities.

'Polluter pays' is self-explanatory – if you cause damage, you are responsible for fixing it. Expanding on this slightly, the principle also requires that those carrying out potentially damaging practices have a 'duty of care'. European legislation is starting to reflect these principles, for example:

- Duty of care is embedded into waste management regulations. The producer of waste is responsible for its safe disposal – transferring it to a waste contractor does not remove that duty;
- Producer takeback legislation requires the producers and users of electrical goods, packaging and batteries to pay for their recovery and recycling;
- Purchasers of sites with contaminated land can require the organization who contaminated that land to pay to remediate it.

Environmental Sustainability Models

This book is concerned primarily with environmental sustainability in industry and the economy. In this section we consider the two main models of environmental sustainability:

- Eco-efficiency, which is concerned with reducing the amount of materials and energy flowing through the economy. In less technical terms, eco-efficiency is about using less stuff;
- The ecosystem model, which is largely concerned with the type of materials and energy and how we use them. In simple terms, it is about using better stuff in a better way.

So eco-efficiency is about quantities and ecosystem models are more concerned with qualities. There is plenty of synergy between the two approaches, but they have different mindsets so we explore each in more detail.

Eco-efficiency theory

Eco-efficiency is the most prevalent environmental strategy. It is defined as getting more utility (i.e. more use) from each unit of natural resource. An everyday measure of eco-efficiency is fuel consumption expressed in miles per gallon (mpg). 'Miles' is the measure of utility – the amount of distance the vehicle moves – and 'gallon' is the unit of resource required to deliver that utility.

Eco-efficiency is very business friendly as it often delivers economic benefits. Utility is what your customers pay for (for example miles travelled), resources are costs incurred to deliver that function (for example the cost of fuel), so a company with a high eco-efficiency will tend to be a more profitable company, and efficient products have obvious appeal in the marketplace. It is no surprise that the eco-efficiency concept was formalized and promoted by the World Business Council for Sustainable Development as a business response to the Earth Summit in 1992.[3]

Improvements and sustainability targets for eco-efficiency are expressed as 'factor x', so a factor 2 improvement would be a doubling of eco-efficiency, either by doubling utility, halving resource use, or a combination of both. The first proposed target for sustainability was factor 4, which aimed to deliver sustainability as the world is now by 'doubling wealth and halving resource use'.[4] However, with so much of the world's population currently living in poverty, factor 4 does not allow for rising consumption in developing countries, as we are currently seeing in very populous countries such as China and India. A global eco-efficiency of factor 10 would be required to allow the world's poor to achieve an equitable standard of living while staying within natural limits.[5]

Good examples of eco-efficiency include:

- Light emitting diode (LED) bulbs that are 90 per cent more efficient than a conventional incandescent bulb (factor 10);[6]
- PassivHaus standard houses are 80–90 per cent more efficient than standard new build houses (factor 5–10);[7]
- 'Virtualization' techniques in data centres have improved the utilization of each server from 10–20 per cent to 50–70 per cent (factor 3.5–7);[8]
- Air filled bags as protective packaging as opposed to polystyrene chips (at least factor 10).

Eco-efficiency problems

So eco-efficiency sounds great – easy to understand and cost-effective, but unfortunately delivering such huge efficiency improvements is not simple.

While there are some great examples of high eco-efficiency solutions (see above), many technologies have been more difficult to improve. The Toyota Prius is regarded as a technologically advanced eco-friendly car, with its hybrid engine, regenerative braking and aerodynamic profile. Yet it barely out performs a good diesel car of the same size in fuel efficiency stakes. In carbon terms, the Prius does a bit better having 66 per cent of the average emissions of a car on the UK roads[9] (i.e. factor 1.5), but this is still a long way off our targets of factor 4 or factor 10. Likewise, Boeing describes its 787 Dreamliner as 'a super-efficient airplane',[10] but the fuel saving over similar aircraft is only 20 per cent (factor 1.25) per passenger.

The second big problem with eco-efficiency is known as 'the rebound effect' – when expected benefits are swallowed up by unexpected side effects. To take an example, government campaigns to encourage people to install insulation in their home will often say 'cut carbon emissions and save £200 per year!'. The rebound effect can complicate this idea in two different ways:

1   direct rebound effect: if you make something cheaper, people will use more of it (i.e. extract more utility). In this example, they may turn up the thermostat and enjoy more heat for the same cost;
2   indirect rebound effect: someone may keep their thermostat steady and pocket the £200. But what do they spend it on? If they buy cheap flights, the extra carbon emissions will outweigh those from their house in the first place.

Essentially the rebound effect means that the environmental success of eco-efficiency depends on consumer/user behaviour, which is usually outside your control, unless you cleverly design the product or service you provide to avoid it. Governments can help combat the effect by making, say, high carbon activities much more expensive than low carbon equivalents.

Ecosystem model theory

Earth is about 4.5 billion years old. For the first 1–2 billion years, it was chaotic – a volcanic primordial wasteland where life struggled to evolve. Then at some point (the timing of which is much debated by scientists) blue-green algae started absorbing CO_2 and producing oxygen through photosynthesis – and a crucial natural cycle was born, leading to the development of ecosystems.[11] These natural systems became self-regulating, levelling out wild swings in conditions in the biosphere – the part of Earth and its atmosphere where life exists.

Ecologists have a three-level model for the maturity of ecosystems:[12]

• Type I: invasive species enter a void and use up as much resource as they can, spread as quickly as possible, and do not form symbiotic relationships;

- Type II: as resources get scarce, the ecosystem starts to recycle 'wastes' internally and organisms form symbiotic relationships to survive;
- Type III: mature ecosystems, like ancient woodlands, recycle all resources internally. Change is evolutionary and symbiosis overtakes competition.

The ecosystem model of sustainability basically says that the post-industrial revolution human race is at the Type I level (or perhaps just entering the Type II level) and this is unsustainable. If we are to survive, we need to emulate the Type III model and act like a mature ecosystem.

A number of slightly different ecosystem models have been developed to guide us towards that Type III ecosystem target. The simplest is the 'BioThinking'[13] approach by the sustainability consultant Edwin Datchefski, which has three requirements:

- Solar: all energy is renewable;
- Cyclic: all materials move in cycles;
- Safe: the concentrations of all materials are at 'safe' levels.

Eco-design gurus McDonough and Braungart have a slightly more complex set of principles that they call 'Eco-Effectiveness':[14]

- Use solar income: as opposed to fossil fuels that are stored solar energy;
- Waste = food: nothing goes to waste, all material flows should be useful or designed out;
- Respect diversity: be compatible with the natural world.

The main practical difference between these ecosystem models and eco-efficiency is the strictness of the rules. In eco-efficiency, the use of toxic materials and fossil fuels is minimized, in the ecosystem model they are prohibited. In eco-efficiency, recycling of materials is pursued where there are efficiency savings in doing so; in the ecosystem model you have to make the recycling work or eliminate the material concerned.

McDonough and Braungart describe two types of 'nutrient' that can endlessly be cycled through the economy:

1 Biological nutrients are natural materials such as wood, fibres and food that can either be recovered and recycled in the economy, or recycled in nature, for example by composting;

2   'Technical nutrients' are man-made materials that can be recycled ad
    infinitum in the economy. Certain polymers, glass and metals can all be
    technical nutrients.

Other examples of the ecosystem model in practice include:

- Sheep's wool building insulation;
- Sustainably sourced timber products;
- Biodiesel fuel made from waste vegetable oil;
- Passive biological treatment plants for water.

Ecosystem model problems

The main problem with the ecosystem model is whether such principles can be
applied to the huge volumes of material and energy used in the modern economy.
For example, the production of supposedly sustainable materials such as palm
oil and bioethanol has been accused of driving up food prices and causing
deforestation and other habitat destruction.[15]

Energy is the limiting factor in both natural and man-made systems. While
the ecosystem model will lead to some efficiency improvements, for example the
recycling of some materials requires substantially less energy than extracting raw
materials (for example aluminium, steel), it is difficult to see how the ecosystem
model could function without also implementing factor 10 scale efficiency
improvements.

A strategy for sustainability

Nature has given us a model of sustainability, proven over several billion years of
trials, but, as we have seen, it will be a real challenge to adopt it and maintain
current standards of living. Eco-efficiency can help deliver that ecosystem model,
but, to paraphrase management guru Peter Drucker, 'There is nothing so useless
as doing efficiently that which should not be done at all.'[16] In other words, we need
to be clear about what we are not going to do as well as what we are going to do.

This gives us an environmental sustainability strategy as follows:

- Pursue the ecosystem model (solar, cyclic, safe) as the ultimate strategy;
- Implement large-scale (i.e. factor 10) eco-efficiency improvements in
  activities compatible with the ecosystem model (for example the energy
  efficiency of devices);

- Rapidly phase out activities that are incompatible with the ecosystem model (use of toxic materials, oil exploration, oil shale and tar sands exploitation, rainforest destruction).

Governmental Options

Overview

Governments around the world are responding to the challenges of the Big Three environmental challenges. While the Copenhagen climate change conference in December 2009 may have ended without agreement, the sight of 192 world leaders huddled in groups trying to hammer out a deal demonstrated how seriously the issue is being taken. Here we look at two different approaches to governmental action: (1) environmental economics: restructuring the economy to encourage more sustainable industrial activity and consumer behaviour; and (2) stronger interventions to deliberately design a sustainable economy. These are not either/or options, but need to be used together to give the required end result.

Environmental economics

This approach to delivering sustainability involves restructuring global, national and local economies to reward green behaviour and penalize polluting activity to a degree where economic activity evolves to sit within natural limits, as per the fried egg model. The choice between eco-efficiency and ecosystem models is then made by the markets, not by active design. This section covers some key concepts in environmental economics to give you a flavour for how the economy may change in the next few decades.

The essential concept of environmental economics is to ensure that costs of 'externalities' (uncosted environmental and social impacts) are internalized (costed) into the economy. The price of products and services should reflect the wider costs that those products and services have on the 'global commons' – all the life support systems that we need as a society. This would help combat the rebound effect as any financial savings from efficiency would effectively purchase less pollution when spent on other products and services.

To take an example, we have traditionally treated the atmosphere as a free repository for carbon emissions. The price of the fuel burnt rarely if ever covers the cost of the resulting climate change impacts. By introducing, say, carbon taxes, the price of fossil fuels comes closer to their true cost. Renewable energy would not attract such taxes, so the market would start to favour low carbon energy.

The main problem with such an approach is citizens' reaction to green taxes. In most countries income tax is the main form of raising public revenues and other forms of tax are often regarded as 'stealth taxes'. 'Family holiday abroad could cost £300 in tax' was one newspaper's headline following the UK government's proposals to reform aviation taxes.[17] In Australia, the government changed and then the new prime minister, Kevin Rudd, was forced to step down over controversies relating to a cap and trade system for carbon emissions.[18]

A practical problem with this approach is how do you put an economic value on, say, the existence of a species of butterfly? How do you value an area of outstanding natural beauty? There are a number of methods of estimating these economic values, such as surveying how much people are willing to pay to maintain such 'natural capital'. All of these methods have limitations as economics cannot include moral absolutes and values.

Another issue is the use of gross domestic product (GDP) as the dominant quality of life indicator by governments and other organizations. An undesirable event such as a major pollution incident will increase GDP through emergency response and clean-up costs, whereas much desirable activity such as voluntarily looking after an elderly relative or friend is not recognized. Analysis suggests that, globally, GDP and quality of life indicators such as life expectancy are only directly related up to a relatively low level (approximately $7500 per capita) and then increases of GDP have little or no effect. Paradoxically, falling GDP does appear to bring down quality of life as we have seen in recent years in countries such as Zimbabwe.[19]

There have been a number of attempts to develop alternatives to GDP that better reflect actual quality of life, including gross domestic happiness, the Index of Sustainable Economic Welfare (ISEW) and the Global Happiness Index. These indicators take into consideration non-economic quality of life factors including environmental parameters and measures of social equity and cohesion. All of these indicators suggest that quality of life has been more or less constant in recent decades, while GDP and environmental degradation have risen.

Which leads us on to another problem: to date we have not been able to decouple economic growth and, say, carbon emissions at a global level. At present, more growth equals more climate change. To address this failure, the concept of a 'steady state' economy has been championed by environmental economists such as Herman Daly and more recently by the UK's Sustainable Development Commission.[20] Such an economy would not grow as such, but would evolve within limits to meet human needs, but the concept has largely been ignored by governments. So we are left with the challenge of making that decoupling happen.

Another key controversy is economists' discounting of future costs to take into consideration time preferences – people like jam today rather than jam tomorrow. There is a strong argument that discounting the future is incompatible with the Brundtland definition of sustainable development and its call for intergenerational equity. We cannot respect future generations if we treat environmental impacts that will impact on them as less important than those occurring today. The Stern Review on the economics of climate change used a very low discount rate (1.4 per cent compared to a typical 3–5 per cent for public policy analyses) on the economic impacts of climate change for this very reason,[21] causing some controversy among other economists.[22]

Governmental interventions

While environmental economics has a role to play, governments around the world are using a number of more active interventions to encourage a shift to a sustainable economy. These can include:

- Prohibiting certain activities (for example oil production in wilderness reserves) or materials (for example banning DDT or phasing out CFCs);
- Putting the duty of care on companies (for example the EU's REACH regulations that require chemical companies to prove their products are safe);
- Implementing product stewardship policies (for example the EU's WEEE directive that makes producers of electrical equipment pay for its recycling);
- Stimulating demand for green products and services through public sector procurement policies;
- Providing greener infrastructure (for example electric vehicle charging infrastructure, smart grids);
- Funding R&D programmes to accelerate the commercialization of green technologies;
- Setting sectoral standards (for example building standards, vehicle emissions standards);
- Introducing cap and trade schemes such as the EU's Emissions Trading Scheme or the US Acid Rain Program;
- Developing labelling standards and requirements, such as the EU Energy Label or the US EnergyStar standard;
- Publishing environmental data on companies, for example the US Toxic Release Inventory.

Technological optimism vs. behaviour change

There are many debates within the field of sustainability, but one of the most prevalent is the technology vs. behavioural debate. This is often driven by the rebound effect problem associated with eco-efficiency strategies – sustainable production must be matched by sustainable consumption.

Politicians favour the technological approach as it is optimistic and exciting – providing a bright new future, 'clean tech' innovations, green jobs etc. In industrialized countries, selling frugal lifestyle choices, however satisfying they may be in reality, is not part of current political narratives. Green pressure groups do the sums and say 'we can't keep living the way we do and just put a solar panel on the roof, it isn't enough!'. They berate politicians for not showing 'leadership', conveniently forgetting the constraints of the democratic system within which politicians work.

I believe that this 'technology *or* behaviour' argument is over-simplistic. There are technological solutions that enable behavioural change. Telecommuting, or working from home, is one of the most sustainable behavioural options – cutting the daily commute *and* strengthening local amenities *and* improving quality of life – yet the ability to do so is, outside of certain crafts, almost entirely down to recent technological advances – broadband internet, teleconferencing, mobile phones etc. Finding and facilitating such '*and*' solutions is the holy grail of a sustainable business.

Chapter summary

1   Sustainability is not negotiable;
2   The 'fried egg' model of sustainability gives a clear vision of the overall goal: the economy delivering for a society that thrives within the planet's natural limits;
3   There are two models of environmental sustainability: eco-efficiency and the ecosystem model (solar, cyclic, safe);
4   To deliver the 'fried egg' model, we will have to shift to the ecosystem model, however, this will require eco-efficiency to be feasible;
5   Government options include environmental economics policies and legislative interventions;
6   There is an ongoing debate between whether technology or behavioural change will deliver sustainability – the answer is to find 'and' solutions.

The View from the Front Line: Richard Gillies, Marks & Spencer

Marks & Spencer is a retail legend. Growing from a single penny bazaar in Leeds, UK in 1894, the company now operates in 43 countries, turning over £9 billion and employing 78,000 people. In 2007, Marks & Spencer Executive Chairman Sir Stuart Rose launched Plan A ('because there is no plan B'), making 100 commitments on environmental, social and ethical issues. Richard Gillies is the Director of CSR, Plan A and Sustainable Business, leading a team of 11 and working with many other specialists throughout the organization.

Why and how did you get involved in this agenda?

I had one of those strange little moments that make you stop and reassess things. I left the house one morning drinking a bottle of yoghurt. While in my car, I tried to throw the empty bottle into the recycling bin, but missed. I undid the seat belt, got out of the car, picked the bottle up and put it in the bin. When I got to work, someone put an electricity bill in front of me to sign off. I almost signed it without thinking about the implications of our energy use. It hit me then that I wasn't bringing my personal values to work with me the way I should.

In my previous role of Construction Director we started to take a long-term view of our buildings. I instigated a review of our property portfolio with a view to future proofing, and energy efficiency became a key focus for us.

In 2008 I was appointed to my current role. The recession was just starting to bite and I was given the job of making sure the economic situation did not undermine Plan A.

What are the drivers for Marks & Spencer to engage in this agenda?

The most important driver is to protect and enhance our brand. Marks & Spencer is one of the most trusted brands in the world and the environmental and ethical issues are important aspects of the modern view of 'trust'.

But, we shouldn't underestimate the importance of 'doing the right thing'. Plan A came about because Sir Stuart watched Al Gore's climate change documentary 'An Inconvenient Truth' and was inspired to act.

We originally put £200m into Plan A over five years as a pump primer but so far it has delivered more in savings than it cost. While this is excellent, we see it as a secondary driver to the other factors – we didn't get involved in this for mercenary reasons.

What are the big challenges for your organization?

Behavioural change and education of individuals is always a challenge. We treat Plan A just like any other change management programme, but it has to be said that this is the easiest one I've worked on – people are very motivated to act. There is, however, a language barrier between the 'CSR junkies' and the 'economic animals' – while their aims are aligned, it can be difficult to get them on the same wavelength.

There are many external challenges. As a society there is a strong trend of 'disposable fashion', which means competing with very low cost competitors. Supply chains are another challenge. For example, cotton is our biggest raw material and has all sorts of environmental issues associated with its production. We are working with our suppliers to improve their performance.

In our annual reports on Plan A, we are very honest about admitting our mistakes. We have appointed Jonathon Porritt (founder of Friends of the Earth and Forum for the Future) as an independent advisor and overseer of our work. He's not one to gloss over any shortcomings.

What successes have you had?

We have met 39 of the original 100 commitments in Plan A and have added 24 new commitments that stretch us even further. Some examples include:

- Our arrangement with Oxfam to accept used clothes, which has helped the charity earn £1.9 million and keep 1500 tonnes of clothes out of landfill;
- We have started using recycled polyester in many products including umbrellas and school uniforms although the finished fibre is expensive. In order to strengthen the supply chain, we have started using cheaper lower grade recycled polyester as cushion filling. This gives economies of scale in the whole polyester 'loop' and makes the higher grade material more competitive in price;
- We have developed an eco-factory in Sri Lanka to produce lingerie. It emits 96 per cent less carbon than a standard factory;
- We've reduced the number of plastic carrier bags we give out by 400 million per annum;
- We are recycling 325 million clothes hangers per annum;
- We've cut our energy use by 10 per cent and our carbon footprint by 15 per cent.

Looking to the future, we want to get to a position where Plan A and the Plan A way of doing things is ingrained in how we do everything within our business.

What's your advice for others in your position?

While you should stretch your brand to include greener products, don't diversify too far. For example we experimented with selling wormeries, but we soon realized that people do not come to Marks & Spencer to buy this kind of product.

Seeing is believing – if you want to bring people on board, show them how it works in practice. Finally, devolve responsibility, get everyone involved.

Visions of a Sustainable Economy

Overview

In this chapter we apply the two models of sustainability, eco-efficiency and the ecosystem model, to the economy to develop more detailed scenarios of what the future may look like. This will provide an insight into emerging landscapes into which your organization can position itself in the future. For more proactive green businesses, these models can be deliberately brought into existence by redesigning supply chains, creating new markets and influencing the legislative and policy frameworks within which the company operates. As pioneering computer scientist Alan Kay famously said 'The best way to predict the future is to invent it.'[1] We will be considering these issues further when we look at green business strategy in Chapter 16.

Industry and the Environment

Figure 7.1 shows a simple model of one company. All the arrows in and out represent a cost and an environmental impact, except for the product/service emanating from the end.

Figure 7.2 shows how a large number of the companies modelled in Figure 7.1 add up to form a model for the traditional value chain for a product or service. This is the classic, linear 'take, make, waste' product lifecycle that corresponds to the Type I ecosystem we discussed in the last chapter.

The most environmentally destructive industries tend to be early in the chain, such as oil production, mining, forestry, farming, fisheries – primary industries. For example, the mining of ores requires all the 'overburden' of soil and rock to be removed first – this is usually several times as much material as the ore deposit itself. Extracting useable materials from ore is difficult and dirty – producing 1kg of pure copper from ore results in 50–200kg of waste and requires 50–100MJ of energy, which in turn will release about 13kg of CO_2 into the atmosphere.[2]

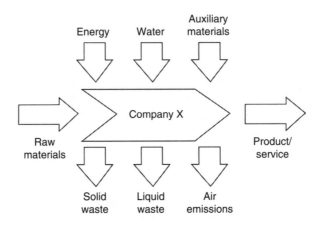

Figure 7.1 *One business's impact on the environment*

The supply and distribution chain can extend across the whole globe. The aluminium for a soft drinks can may be mined as bauxite in Australia, smelted in Sweden, rolled into sheets in Germany and made into cans in the UK.[3]

In reality, this linear model is slightly simplistic – some materials are recycled back into the system – metals, precious metals, jewels and even whole products such as Rolls Royce cars and Rolex watches are rarely thrown away, but are repaired and maintained for as long as possible. There is a whole industry selling second-hand goods, whether through thrift shops or online auction services such as eBay.

Eco-efficiency in Industry

We saw in Chapter 6 that the main focus to date on greening the economy has been to improve its eco-efficiency – getting more from each unit of resource entering the economy. Under eco-efficiency, the linear model of the economy does not change shape – instead the whole chain becomes leaner.

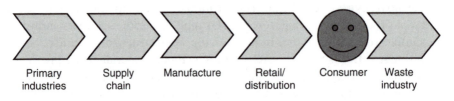

Figure 7.2 *Linear product lifecycle*

The global economy is hugely inefficient – of all the raw materials extracted every year, only 6 per cent ends up as final product, the other 94 per cent is waste. And of those final products, only 20 per cent have a lifespan of more than six months.[4] In other words 98.8 per cent of raw materials extracted from the Earth becomes waste in the short term. Many products are also incredibly inefficient, for example only 1 per cent of the energy going into the tank of a petrol car is used to move the driver.[5] The rest is lost as heat in the engine, used to overcome resistance or is used to move the vehicle itself. Likewise, most industries can be substantially improved by redesigning processes and products, switching to cleaner technologies and ruthlessly cutting waste in all its forms.

In the eco-efficiency model, in contrast to the ecosystem model, recycling is only undertaken where there is a clear quantitative environmental and economic benefit, for example in the case of aluminium, steel and precious metals. Similarly, renewable energy has to compete against energy efficiency for cost-effectiveness in reducing carbon emissions.

Due to the rebound effect, eco-efficient production of eco-efficient products must be combined with sustainable consumption patterns, either through behavioural change or economic instruments. We consider the production side and consumption side in turn.

Sustainable production

Sustainable production in this section includes all the supply side elements of the economy – i.e. the delivery of products and services and the design of those products and services themselves. This section gives a strategic overview – we look at cleaner production and operational options for a range of sectors in Chapter 10 and product design in more detail in Chapter 12.

We saw in the last chapter that eco-efficiency can be limited by technological constraints. For example, even the most efficient production hybrid car is not even twice as efficient as the average car, well short of the factor 10 improvements we need. There are two ways of addressing this problem: exploiting cumulative benefits and radically rethinking how we do things.

The cumulative approach uses the fact that efficiency gains accumulate through manufacturing processes and indeed through supply chains. For example if every process in a linear ten step supply chain from raw material to product managed a 20 per cent cut in resource use, the cumulative reduction in resources would be 89 per cent[6] – almost factor 10. So lots of modest and achievable improvements can add up to one very large one.

The other way of delivering breakthrough eco-efficiency changes is to develop new ways of delivering products and services. For example, information technology allows us to consume the service we desire (for example music, films, literature) with little or no product involved (i.e. CDs, DVDs, books) by delivering those services electronically. Moving away from selling 'stuff' to selling a service, goes some way to decoupling the link between economic activity and environmental damage that we discussed in Chapter 6. Similarly we can transform our transport patterns by eliminating the need to travel – teleconferencing, telecommuting, online shopping or providing transport services, for example car clubs and door to door public transport systems. We discuss the development and delivery of such innovative services in Chapter 13.

Sustainable consumption

For a soap powder manufacturer such as Procter & Gamble, there are two opportunities to make significant improvements in the eco-efficiency of clothes washing – reduce the amount of powder required for each wash (and thus the raw materials, packaging and distribution logistics per wash) and enable consumers to wash at a lower temperature. Both strategies require the consumer to play their part – the individual must actually use less powder (and refrain from throwing in a little extra for luck) and to actually choose the lower temperature option on their washing machine (the dial on my own washing machine seems to creep magically upwards over time). If consumer behaviour doesn't change, then the innovations fail. Some soap manufacturers have tried to combat these direct rebound effects by, say, packaging their powder as tablets and providing information. Procter & Gamble's Ariel Excel Gel is designed to encourage smaller doses.

Raising this up to a macroeconomic level, we have seen that the indirect rebound effect can lead to the environmental benefits from resource efficiency being wiped out or worse by consumers spending the economic savings on high carbon alternatives. This can be achieved through taxing carbon, so each dollar spent buys less pollution but, as we discussed in Chapter 6, politicians often fear a voter backlash against such taxes and their introduction has been slow.

Another option is to encourage consumers to change behaviour through education. Attempts to raise public perception of major environmental issues have had a mixed success. This is partially due to the appalling quality of most campaigns,[7] but there is a large inertia in the general public. Many people are concerned about the environment but do not relate impacts to their own lifestyle choices. In fact some studies have shown that, paradoxically, people who are concerned most about the environmental often have a higher carbon footprint than average.[8] Businesses have attempted to help educate consumers with some success, for example Marks & Spencer have a 'wash at 30°C' campaign to encourage lower temperature clothes washing.

Trends in consumer behaviour are complex. On the one hand, it appears that additional discretionary spending is tending to go towards low carbon purchases such as digital products (mobile phone tariffs, music on MP3) rather than high carbon purchases such as cheap flights.[9] On the other hand, for many sectors, consumption is shifting towards cheaper, low quality, almost disposal products (for example clothing, furniture) rather than expensive, high quality products.[10] Product lifespans are determined predominantly by fashion, with many people upgrading their mobile phones every six months or even more frequently. As products get cheaper, there is also little incentive for consumers to maintain and repair products – repair costs often exceed the initial purchase price.

Sustainable consumption is the ultimate challenge if eco-efficiency is to be successful. Businesses can, as we have seen, present their products in a way that encourages sustainable behaviour (for example washing powder tablets or gels), educate the consumer (for example wash at 30°C), develop innovative low carbon products and services that are more desirable than their high carbon equivalent (for example MP3s for music) or develop products and services that cut environmental impacts in use (for example efficient lighting and vehicles). Governments can help by green taxation, leadership and education, but ultimately the decision rests with the individual consumer.

The Ecosystem Model in Industry

The application of the ecosystem model to the industrial system is known as industrial ecology.[11] Industrial ecology requires four changes to the current status quo:

- The linear model in Figure 7.2 is bent into a closed loop (see Figure 7.3);
- All other waste materials are recycled/composted, or designed out of the system;
- Toxic materials are eliminated by design;
- All energy used is renewable.

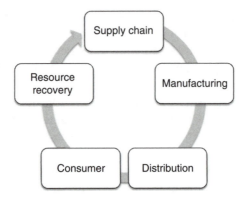

Figure 7.3 *Closed loop economy*

Closed loop product systems

The cyclic requirement of the ecosystem model requires us to 'close the loop' on material flows. This means ensuring that products are made from recoverable, recyclable or compostable materials (see Chapter 12 for how to do this), and that there is a mechanism for products and/or materials to be recovered and returned to the manufacturing process after use, or composted and returned to nature.

There are two approaches to closing the loop:

1   Sourcing material from the general pool of recovered material, for example purchasing scrap steel or aluminium from the general market. This works for metals, paper, cardboard, glass and certain plastics where there is a competitive market in secondary materials, but for many products and materials the supply chain for recovered materials is weak (we'll be looking at how to strengthen supply chains in Chapter 11);
2   Recovering the actual products that your company produces. This is known as product stewardship and the practical recovery task is known as reverse logistics. Options include takeback schemes (either voluntary or via a financial incentive) or maintaining ownership of the product and leasing it as a service to customers (see Chapter 13 for examples).

Zero waste manufacturing: Industrial symbiosis

Nature is not quite as red in tooth and claw as the more lurid TV programmes about predators would have us believe. For example, all organisms live in symbiosis with others – i.e. in relationships where both parties benefit. For example humans could not survive without certain bacteria in our gut that help us digest food. They eat and we eat and both are happy. Industrial symbiosis is the concept of one company's waste becoming the raw material for another. By adopting industrial symbiosis, the neat model of Figure 7.3 becomes a messy web of symbiotic interactions involving completely different industrial sectors.

The most famous instance of industrial symbiosis is found at Kalundborg, a small industrial town on the western coast of the Danish island of Zealand. A simplified diagram of the main interactions between the industries at Kalundborg is shown in Figure 7.4. There is a shortage of fresh water in the region, so water is cascaded from one process to another, starting where it has to be cleanest and working its way down through the less fussy processes, and recycling it wherever possible. Excess steam from the power station is piped to the other plants and to the town where it heats all the buildings. A plasterboard company takes the gypsum from the power station's pollution control equipment to incorporate into its products. The fish farm uses (and cools) some of the warm wastewater. A pharmaceutical plant produces a fertilizer product made from its process substrate. This is produced to strict standards, trademarked, but given away free to local farmers.

The initial symbiotic relationships were uncovered by a group of students doing a school project. This led to the setting up of a small institute to coordinate

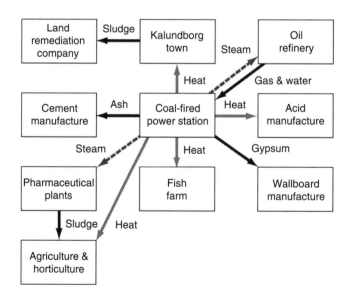

Figure 7.4 *Simplified diagram of industrial symbiosis at Kalundborg*[12]

the relationships and investment in further synergies. Links have come and gone, but with the habit ingrained and the benefits proven, the infrastructure has simply been adapted to exploit new opportunities.

Industrial symbiosis is a key part of industrial ecology, but it also delivers eco-efficiency benefits by extracting maximum utility out of the resources entering the system.

Renewable energy

The ecosystem model requires a shift to 100 per cent renewable energy. Renewable energy has many advantages over conventional fossil fuels. For example, for most forms of renewables (for example solar, hydro, wind), renewable energy will not run out, energy security is not a problem as each country owns its own resources, and prices are more stable. The main disadvantages are current costs and intermittency – the dependency on weather conditions. Bioenergy (for example liquid biofuels and solid biomass) does not suffer from intermittency, but it does often compete for available land with food supplies and natural habitats.

Renewable energy is quite different from fossil energy and it is a mistake to simply try to replace one with the other. Fossil fuels come in a highly concentrated form – one of the reasons why they are so popular. They must be located, extracted, often converted into other forms of energy for example electricity, and distributed to the end-user via national and international networks.

By contrast renewable energy is distributed across the globe. It is very inefficient to treat such energy like conventional energy sources by concentrating that energy into a centralized distribution system and redistributing it back to the user. In most cases it makes much more sense to store and use that energy close to where it is captured. A good everyday example of this is a solar powered calculator – it would be crazy to export and re-import the electricity from its tiny solar panel rather than store and use it on the device when required. So renewable energy requires a localized system of generating, storing, distributing and using electricity to optimize efficiency and smooth out intermittency. For example, EAE Ltd uses electricity from its wind turbine to power its factory by day and to charge its forklift truck by night when very little electricity is required elsewhere on site. The forklift is effectively acting as a storage device, levelling out demand on the turbine over 24 hours.

This approach can be scaled up into 'smart grids' that use intelligent control systems to optimize energy management between a cluster of organizations and/or residences. Users connected to the grid would generate, buy, store, use and sell energy depending on availability, need and prices. Householders with solar photovoltaic (PV) on their roofs could sell electricity to the grid by day when the houses are often empty, and buy some back at night. Electric vehicle owners connected to the same grid could charge their batteries when energy is plentiful and sell it back when demand is high. Smart control systems would optimize these trades and manage the flow of cash.

Localized generation of electricity from biomass means power stations can be located much closer to concentrations of population. This opens up opportunities for co-generation (heat and power) and tri-generation (heat, cooling and power) and district heating/cooling systems, which makes much more efficient use of the fuel.

The exception to this shift to local systems is where renewable energy can be harvested in large quantities but is far from potential users, for example, offshore wind and concentrated solar energy in desert locations. These sources would require national and international distribution systems, compatible with local smart grids.

Eliminating toxic materials

The ecosystem approach has a zero tolerance of persistent toxic materials, particularly POPs. In eco-efficiency the use of toxins is minimized; in industrial ecology they are eliminated. In the words of eco-designers McDonough and Braungart 'Take the filters out of the pipes and put them where they belong, in the designers' heads.'[13]

For example, InterfaceFLOR have been ruthless about abandoning product lines that require toxic flame retardants. But elimination can be difficult where the material's toxicity is its selling point – new ways of working must be found. For example TBT was commonly used as antifouling on boats until it was banned in the UK in 1987 and globally in 2008. Fouling can increase the drag on a ship's hull by up to 60 per cent and increase fuel consumption by 40 per cent so on the face of it there is a trade-off. Innovative thinking can give the best of both worlds and in this case, the US Office of Naval Research has developed an alternative coating inspired by shark skin to which marine animals and plants find it difficult to adhere.[14]

In Part III we examine how to eliminate toxic materials by redesigning processes (Chapter 10), eliminating them from suppliers (Chapter 11) and, best of all, removing them from the whole lifecycle of products and services (Chapters 12 and 13).

Chapter summary

1 This chapter has translated the high level environmental sustainability models (eco-efficiency and ecosystem model) into potential future industrial scenarios;

2 The reality will be a mixture of both models, but care needs to be taken not to block the route to the endpoint (ecosystem model) when pursuing eco-efficiency;

3 Eco-efficiency requires eco-efficient products to be produced in an eco-efficient manner. Consumers must then use these products in an efficient way for them to be effective;

4 The ecosystem model requires a more radical change: closing the economic loop, using industrial waste as a resource, designing out toxic material and switching to 100 per cent renewable energy.

The View from the Front Line: James Hagan, GlaxoSmithKline

GlaxoSmithKline is the world's second largest pharmaceutical company, employing over 90,000 people worldwide and with a turnover in excess of £22 billion. The company is currently broadening its activities from simply developing and manufacturing pharmaceuticals to the wider healthcare agenda, particularly in the developing world.

Dr James Hagan is the company's Vice President of Sustainability and Environment, responsible for providing leadership and guidance on sustainability and environmental issues across the breadth of GlaxoSmithKline's activities from research and development through to commercial operations.

Why and how did you get involved in this agenda?

I grew up in Pittsburgh, Pennsylvania amongst the city's steel mills with their classic environmental problems. For me they were a test case of being clearly non-sustainable. My father worked in the mills and so did many of his friends, and many of them came home in ambulances maimed from accidents – my father died from a work related injury. Obviously the environment was polluted, the air was grey and the rivers ran in colours. But the real issue for companies was that they failed to innovate and failed to evolve – now they no longer exist and that's put the whole community in jeopardy. They lost out in competition with the Japanese, who despite having a higher labour cost and no raw materials to speak of, managed to compete on cost, occupational safety and environmental grounds.

As a result I wanted to get an understanding of how things are made. I studied as a chemical engineer and did a masters degree in environmental health and another in management science. My PhD is in environmental engineering and science with a strong minor in environmental planning and management. I've since worked in the chemical industry and for the US Environmental Protection Agency.

What are the business drivers for GlaxoSmithKline to engage in this agenda?

The main driver is that, historically, we've had a situation where we take a huge risk in discovering the molecule that improved human health, but after that, there is a reluctance to innovate. We tend to make things the same way and we tend to market and sell things the same way. And throughout the industry there is an empirical approach – trial and error. So the level of science application to operations hasn't been profound. My responsibility when I started 26 years ago was not to provide end-of-pipe controls, but to improve the process itself. For example traditional pharmaceutical manufacturing is relatively inefficient. It typically consumes about 100 tonnes of raw material for each tonne of active pharmaceutical ingredient, because we all use processes which were optimized in the late 1800s.

Initially, to get the company to accept what I was doing we made it a cost reduction effort, but I think they also realized there would be environmental benefits. If I reduced the raw materials we buy in there would a cost–benefit both from those raw materials costs and reduced waste, and there's a reduction in the level of risk we have from dealing with those materials.

The real complexity for us now is that people within the industry feel we should be doing the right thing – a positive force for good. Any negative response from the public and our reputation would suffer. Reputation has become a much more important part of the corporate structure than it was in the past.

What successes have you had?

We have a long-term sustainability plan which emerged in 2000, was escalated in 2005 and is being escalated again now in 2010. When I say long term, it is a specific plan for ten years with an aspiration of 20 years beyond that. We now have the ability to capture the data we need and the platform to talk to people about how the business can be transformed. We now have sustainability targets that R&D aims to meet when they generate a new product.

In practical terms, we have reduced that 100 tonnes of raw material per tonne product down to 37 tonnes – and our goal is 20 tonnes. We've had a climate change programme underway since 1995 when the first International Panel on Climate Change (IPCC) report came out. We have exceeded our targets – in 2001 we set a four year target of 8 per cent and achieved 13 per cent. We've now got a further target of 20 per cent energy reduction per dollar sales by 2010 and 45 per cent by 2020. For example we've shifted from air to sea in our logistics and we want to develop our distribution networks to improve efficiency there. We are working to eliminate bioaccumulative, persistent and toxic (BPT) compounds.

Eco-efficiency improvement is just one step on the path towards our desired endpoint of industrial ecology. For example, in India we have a facility that captures and uses rainwater. The wastewater is treated within the facility and used to irrigate crops for the staff cafeteria. We anaerobically decompose the sludge from the wastewater plant to generate methane to cook the food. So even on an industrial site we can approximate a natural cycle.

What are the big challenges for your organization?

The big challenge is the recognition of the need to move away from the status quo, to accept that there may be some risks in making those changes and being willing to accept those. We would like to adopt a model of industrial ecology and part of that is we're not going to produce any waste. That as a concept is difficult to comprehend, so we're trying to get to a point where we understand that changing the chemistry or changing the processes allows us to produce by-products which have value.

We have a huge amount of sunk cost in existing technologies – not just the capital sunk cost in physical plant, but also the personal sunk cost – many people in the organization have developed expertise in the technologies that define the company. If we move into innovative approaches, their expertise may no longer be useful and may become obsolete which can make people anxious. In terms of the physical infrastructure we have to invest in new technology which may not be justified in a traditional business case so we have recognize that it is an investment for the future and how the company is going to evolve.

There are enormous social challenges for us in terms of equity in the wider world – in terms of gender, in terms of inter-generational and intra-generational equity. We would like income levels not to be a fundamental impediment to healthcare. Women's rights are a huge issue when it comes to the population debate – and a fundamental right is having control over reproduction.

What's your advice for others in your position?

You need an understanding of the technology, because without that appreciation and understanding of the alternatives, you can never envisage the future. Anyone can understand the problem, but the key question is 'what's the solution?'.

Traditional environmental programmes are not sustainability programmes, but bolt-ons designed to control emissions. What we need to do is build in changes to the essence of the business as that's where sustainability lives.

Part III
Practical Action

Practical Green Business Techniques

Chapter 7 covered potential sustainable business models at the macro level. In the following chapters we look at the practical actions that a business can take to make its activities sustainable. They are described in order of rising potential benefit, risk, cost and disruption from the simple, low cost, low risk options up to the entire transformation of the underlying business model. The steps are:

- Chapter 8 Outreach: contributing to sustainability externally through volunteering, donating to charity, sponsoring R&D and carbon offsetting;
- Chapter 9 Good Housekeeping: simple low cost options to improve internal performance;
- Chapter 10 Greener Operations: more radical approaches to redesigning internal operations to deliver products and services in a much more environmentally friendly way;
- Chapter 11 Greening the Supply Chain: for most organizations, the bulk of their environmental impact will occur in their supply chain, therefore it is imperative to build the supply chain required;
- Chapter 12 Greening the Product Portfolio: changing the product on the drawing board allows the designer to control environmental impacts over the entire product lifespan;
- Chapter 13 Green Business Models: developing and delivering radically new business models and enabling products and services.

In each chapter, the practical actions are placed in a strategic context to maximize their impact and to give an insight into how a company's wider strategy should be formulated to make them happen.

Outreach

Overview

Traditionally most corporate social responsibility (CSR) activity revolved around charity and handouts, usually involving local good causes such as sponsoring shirts for the local kids' soccer team. CSR is now widely understood to cover environmental factors and all company activities, including those up and down the company's value chain. However, as we will see in this chapter, there are still a number of ways that businesses can make a real difference by reaching outside their factory fence.

Of course such outreach won't improve the environmental performance of your business per se, and care is required not to exaggerate the benefits of such activities as overblown claims will be labelled as greenwash. Observers will expect to see progress within the organization as well as outside.

Charitable Donations

Donating to a charitable organization operating in the green arena is simplest way of making a difference as your involvement begins and ends with writing a cheque.

Options include donations to:

- Practical conservation organizations or projects;
- Supporting community projects in your company's field (for example an energy company could provide renewable energy educational kits to schools);
- Philosophical and educational charities that promote environmental awareness;
- Campaign groups (note that these are usually not charities as 'political' activities are precluded under charity law).

Donations can be a simple handout, or they can even be used as a staff incentive. For example KPMG donates a certain amount to charity for every sheet of paper saved in their offices, incentivizing staff to act in a green manner without the pitfalls of personal financial rewards.[1]

Volunteering

Giving staff time to carry out environmental and social tasks is a popular outreach method. For example, your staff could take part in local practical conservation tasks, such as tree planting, pond digging and using traditional skills such as hedge laying or dry stone walling. Such activities can form an ice breaker in terms of engaging staff in the green agenda by literally getting employees' hands dirty, and of course they can also double up as a form of team building. It also gives the green executive an opportunity to be seen to be committed and willing to 'muck in'.

Education is another opportunity to make a difference through volunteering. Many large organizations allow staff time off to educate or mentor young people from deprived backgrounds. Others support environmental education in schools and universities. It can also involve bringing people on site for educational activities. For example, Glen Bennett of EAE Ltd brings classes of school children on site to see EAE's wind turbine, biodiversity garden and recycling systems to demonstrate what companies can and should be doing. Glen then challenges the kids to pick one green thing to do back at home. This kind of activity forges close links with local communities that can reduce local sensitivities to, say, wind turbines.

Research and Development (R&D)

Investing in R&D programmes can accelerate the introduction of new technologies and innovative practices in your business, in your sector or in the wider world. Universities are always looking for industrial collaborations and/or financial contributions to research programmes. This can take the form of funding part of a particular project, sponsoring a professorial 'chair' or even a whole research department. However, there are ethical pitfalls in this type of arrangement and both sides need to ensure that academic objectivity is not compromised, or seen to be compromised, by the sponsorship.

As an example of this kind of support, the carbon footprint of the internet has attracted a lot of attention recently. Google's for-profit but philanthropic arm Google.org has chosen climate change as an area to focus on for this very reason and it is making big investments in relevant projects. Its RE < C project aims to develop renewable energy technologies that can deliver electricity cheaper than that produced from coal. The goal is to produce one gigawatt of renewable energy capacity, enough to power a city the size of San Francisco, within years, not decades. At the time of writing, Google has invested $36 million into schemes to make this happen.[2] They have also, among many smaller projects, invested $4 million in developing low carbon vehicles and $2 million to create a Centre on Energy Efficiency Standards to help the US and China develop voluntary and mandatory efficiency standards for buildings, equipment and appliances. This scale of investment is a genuine case of Google putting its money where its mouth is.

Trade and Professional Bodies

Other external contributions can be made within new or existing trade and professional bodies. The World Business Council for Sustainable Development was established in 1992 to present a proactive business response to the first Earth Summit. The organization now has over 200 members including General Motors, DuPont, 3M, Deutsche Bank, Coca-Cola, Sony, Oracle, BP, Walmart and Shell. It continues to promote the business case for sustainable development within businesses and works with governments to help shape the future agenda.[3] There is a raft of similar organizations across the world, for example the UK's Business in the Community and the US Business for Innovative Climate and Energy Policy (BICEP) group. Joining and actively participating in such an organization will not only provide a forum for the exchange of ideas, but also makes a public statement of intent.

Professional bodies represent another avenue for contribution. I remember the furore when my own body, The Institute of Engineering and Technology whose roots go back to 1871, created the 'Engineering for a Sustainable Future network' in 2001, as many less enlightened members saw 'the environment' as a purely political problem and nothing to do with engineering. In 2003 I wrote an article on engineering and sustainability for the Institute's journal, but I had to wait for a special edition on the environment to get it published. A few years later and things have changed – every edition of the journal has several pieces relating to sustainability. A similar transformation is taking place in other professional and trade bodies, and taking a role in such networks again demonstrates leadership and provides opportunities for exchanging best practice and experience.

Voluntary standards and agreements

A number of business organizations have gone further and established standards and agreements for their sector. This kind of engagement is extremely proactive and clearly demonstrates that participants are on the right side of the argument. Examples include:

- US Green Building Council's LEED green building standard and the UK Building Research Establishment's BREEAM standard for non-residential buildings;
- The UK's Courtauld Commitment between retailers to reduce packaging, packaging waste and food waste;[4]
- ResponsibleCare is an environmental initiative for chemical companies operating via national associations in 53 different countries. The initiative puts requirements on those companies to improve sustainability performance and reporting.[5]

Deliberate disassociation

The flip side of joining positive organizations is true – if you want to appear environmentally enlightened, you need to distance yourself from bad company. Ever since Rachel Carson's groundbreaking book, *Silent Spring*, catalogued the effect of pesticides and herbicides on ecosystems, there has been a coordinated attack on the green movement by certain sections of industry. Whether the issue is persistent organic pollutants, the health effects of passive smoking or, more recently, climate change, there have always been elements who would prefer to invest in dubious tactics to maintain the status quo rather than change their ways. For example, the industry-backed and disingenuously named Global Climate Coalition spent 13 years feeding exaggerated accounts of the uncertainties in climate change science to the press, despite their own scientific advisors protesting to the contrary.[6] The Coalition eventually withered and died in 2002 as members such as Shell, BP and GM decided to disassociate themselves. Associating with any such organizations will backfire on green efforts. The hyenas mentioned in Chapter 4 are particularly hard on any organization perceived to have be saying one thing while doing another.

Having a zero tolerance to industrial resistance to sustainability can be used to demonstrate commitment. In 2009 a number of high profile companies including Nike and Apple left the US Chamber of Commerce in protest at the Chamber's stance on President Obama's climate change bill.[7] By doing so they sent out a message to their customers, their peers and the government that they were taking the green agenda seriously.

Carbon Offsetting

Reducing your organization's carbon footprint to a sustainable level internally can be extremely difficult. For example you may not have control over your building, or the low carbon options open to you may simply be unaffordable. In the late 1990s a number of companies and charities proposed a new model called offsetting, where individuals and organizations could calculate their carbon emissions and 'neutralize' them by investing in projects that would reduce global carbon emissions by the same amount.

The earliest offsetting projects involved tree planting (relying on the new trees to remove CO_2 from the atmosphere through photosynthesis) but soon other projects involving energy efficiency and renewables emerged.

Controversy

Carbon offsetting is probably the single most controversial tactic in the environmental field. The environmentalist George Monbiot likened offsetting to the 15th century Dutch practice of buying indulgences – paying for God's pardon for crimes such as incest, lying or murder.[8] In July 2007 the campaigning magazine *New Internationalist* dedicated a whole issue, entitled 'CO2NNED!', to attacking the offsetting industry.[9] CheatNeutral.com, a joke website, satirized offsetting by purporting to let people offset their infidelity by paying other people to be faithful.[10] A high profile public blow came when the rock band Coldplay announced it would offset the emissions caused by the release of its second album in 2002 by planting 10,000 mango trees in southern India – but many of the trees died within a year to the great embarrassment of the band.[11]

There is another way of looking at offsetting: as a voluntary carbon tax ring-fenced for projects to tackle climate change. The sticking point seems to be the economic mechanism – the buying of carbon credits – which seems to offend the hardcore environmentalists, whether or not it works. This ideological aversion to trading as a potential force for good is, in my opinion, short-sighted.

There are two main factors that determine the robustness of a carbon offsetting method: (1) effectiveness – will the scheme actually reduce carbon?; and (2) additionality – does your money make the difference between carbon being reduced or not? We look at each of these in turn.

Effectiveness

The initial criticisms of carbon offsetting focused on whether the investment schemes would actually cut carbon. This was predominantly due to the complex issues around planting trees for carbon sequestration. There are three questions you need to ask and I illustrate them using tree planting:

- Technical effectiveness: does the offset project actually cut carbon, and, if so, how much? For example how much carbon do trees sequester? (The answer depends on local conditions);
- Carbon leakage: will the project inadvertently cause an emissions increase elsewhere? For example will the tree planting process release carbon from the soil? (It can do, depends on the soil.) Or would the tree planting in one area lead to tree felling elsewhere due to land use pressures? (More difficult to answer);
- Permanence: is the carbon removed forever? For example will the trees be cut down for fuel or development sometime in the future? (They would need legal protection.)

Similar uncertainties will apply to any offset project and you will have to ensure that they have been minimized as much as possible through good governance by the offsetting organization.

Additionality

This is the more complex issue. At first glance it appears simple: if you are investing in a project that would have occurred anyway without your money, then you are being ripped off. But it is the definition of 'anyway' that gets complicated. At the highest level, some people consider that any emissions cuts in Kyoto signatory countries would have happened 'anyway' as the countries' governments had signed up to that cut. This argument would restrict offset projects to non-Kyoto countries. Personally I think this is stretching the additionality definition too far – to me there is no problem with companies using offsetting to contribute to national and international targets.

Types of offsetting schemes

There are a number of different offset schemes:

- Voluntary projects, some of which comply with one of the variety of quality protocols. Examples include community renewables, insulating homes, and of course, tree planting;
- Credits from certified sources, such as projects certified by the Kyoto Clean Development Mechanism (CDM) or the Kyoto Joint Implementation Mechanism;
- Purchasing allowances from cap and trade schemes such at the EU Emissions Trading Scheme and 'retiring' them (i.e. tearing them up) so the companies in the scheme will be forced to collectively cut their emissions by that amount.

In terms of which type of scheme to go for, it is a matter of what suits you or your organization. If you simply want to offset your carbon in as robust a manner as possible but don't care how it is actually done, then go for CDM-type schemes or purchase and retire allowances. If you see offsetting as more of a CSR-type activity and that the investment in a specific project (for example a local project or one that also meets a societal need related to your sphere of business) is more important than the robustness of the offset, then find a voluntary scheme that suits you and do your homework on its effectiveness and additionality. Of course, you may have to loosen your additionality criteria or take a chance on effectiveness to get the project you want.

Chapter summary

1 Traditional CSR has focused on sponsoring other organizations to undertake social and environmental activities;

2 While the CSR agenda now requires radical internal change, 'outreach' activities still have a role to play;

3 Outreach options include charitable donations, volunteering and sponsoring relevant R&D;

4 You can associate with positive moves to green business but you must disassociate from reactionary organizations;

5 Carbon offsetting is a highly controversial topic, but can have a role to play if done properly.

The View from the Front Line: Roy Stanley, Tanfield Group

Roy Stanley is the chairman of the Tanfield Group, which owns Smith's Electric Vehicles – the oldest electric vehicle manufacturer in the world. Smith's was incorporated in 1929 and produced their first vehicle in 1935. The company's business model is to purchase the chassis and cabs of conventional commercial vehicles and fit electric drive trains. The company turned over £38.6 million in 2007 and employs about 230 people.

Why and how did you get involved in this agenda?

In the early 1990s I was given the opportunity by Sunderland City Council to develop a strip of land by the River Wear. Part of the project was to identify a number of companies who could be acquired who were capable of being grown and moving into an expanding market. One of those companies I came across was Smith's Electric Vehicles.

I wasn't an environmentalist and I'm still not to a degree. So I didn't come at it from a green perspective, I came at it from a commercial opportunity.

What are the drivers for the Tanfield Group to engage in this agenda?

When we looked at Smith's we felt it was underperforming. At the time, there was a huge interest in reducing local air pollution – as opposed to tackling climate change. Our angle was very much health driven – the statistics showed that 1000 people were dying early every year due to air pollution. We saw the latent technology in Smith's and then looked at where we thought the world would go.

The technology at the time was pretty basic – milk float technology like lead acid batteries and normal electric motors giving a range of 24 miles at a maximum speed of 25mph. We found some improved technologies which took us up to a 50–60 mile range and 35mph. For a commercial van in a closed urban environment, that's all you need. So we made a bid for Smith's – it took us ten years to close the deal, but we managed it in 2004.

What are the big challenges for your organization?

Our vehicles have a higher capital cost than conventional equivalents, but they have much lower running costs so the overall through life costs are reduced. We could reduce this up front cost by simply increasing the volume in our supply chain – an extra 1000 vehicles a year would reduce the cost of our bill of materials by 40 per cent. Batteries represent about 45 per cent of the total bill of material costs. There are a number of ways of getting around this including leasing charged batteries instead of selling them as part of the vehicle.

There is a lack of knowledge and some fear from our customers about the range and repair facilities for electric vehicles. The owners have a learning curve as electric vehicles do need to operate in a different manner. But there are many benefits – they are cheaper to run, their silent nature means they can operate in sensitive environments and outside daytime hours and driver stress is massively reduced. In fact our customers find that once they put a driver in an electric vehicle, they refuse to come out again.

What successes have you had?

We are the only manufacturer of electric commercial vehicles in the world where you can pick up a phone, put in an order and have your vehicle in five working days.

We have incrementally improved the technology to produce vans with an 80 mile range and speeds of over 50mph. Most commercial vehicles in urban environments do less than 100 miles per day, in fact the average distance covered by a courier vehicle in Manhattan in a day is just seven miles.

We are also the only electric vehicle manufacturer in the world to have invested in the supply chain. We have worked to de-risk the supply chain so we have a diversity of suppliers.

Internally, we have reduced our energy demand by 60 per cent. I don't think about waste minimization so much as efficient production. We work with our suppliers to reduce weight, making the components fit for our needs and using less resources – in some cases by 15–20 per cent. This also has a knock-on effect of improving the vehicle performance.

Looking to the future, we would like to see multinational manufacturing sites delivering 100,000 vehicles per year. We currently have the supply chain capacity to produce 5000 globally and we've got plans afoot to scale that up rapidly.

What's your advice for others in your position?

The rules of green business are just the same as any other business – you need a scalable business model in an expanding market. You either have to be able to do it quicker, smarter or better than everyone else or own some intellectual property. You have to have a passion for what you do and believe in what you are doing. The single most important quality for anyone in this game is perseverance.

Good Housekeeping

Many organizations start making changes by seeking out and implementing 'quick wins' internally. These measures are the archetypal incremental improvements in environmental performance, i.e. those that don't require any major changes to the way the business operates. In this chapter we look at:

- Compliance and risk management;
- Resource management (materials, energy and water);
- Green travel planning;
- Capital investments to add greener technologies;
- Biodiversity projects.

Staff buy-in for these actions is essential as many of them are dependent on behavioural change. Conversely, such initiatives also provide opportunities for gaining staff buy-in for more fundamental changes. We examine this in more detail in Chapter 17.

Compliance and Risk Management

We saw in Chapters 1 and 2 that compliance and avoiding pollution incidences is imperative. Pollution incidents can be highly damaging to the environment and the business responsible. The release of hazardous material into watercourses or the atmosphere can have a devastating effect on the surrounding area. In 1984 the Union Carbide plant in Bhopal, India released methyl isocyanide (MIC) leading to the deaths of 15,000–20,000 people and a legacy of injuries, contaminated groundwater and birth defects.[1] And it is not just 'toxic' materials – accidentally releasing milk into a river or lake can have a huge impact on that ecosystem.

From an economic point of view, fines, clean-up costs and, most of all, damage to reputation, can cost a company dearly.

Being aware

As we saw in Chapter 1, ignorance of environmental legislation is shockingly high, putting businesses at risk of prosecution for activities they have never dreamed could be a legal problem. Therefore it is imperative that businesses identify and understand all the legislation that applies to them. Critical pieces of legislation must be understood properly by senior management so the appropriate resources can be allocated to compliance.

One ethical question for transnational corporations is how they manage different standards in different countries. Do they merely meet the standard in each host country or do they apply the highest standards across the whole company? Showing a commitment to the highest standards around the world is an opportunity to show true commitment to CSR and reduces the risk of embarrassing incident undermining other achievements.

Reducing risk

Risk is commonly defined as the product of probability of an event happening and the impact of that event. So in the case of environmental incidents, risk can be reduced by: (1) reducing the probability of an incident, for example by monitoring and inspection, staff training, contractor and visitor awareness, maintenance, safety processes in place, tidy sites, proper signage and warnings, and failsafe systems; and (2) reducing the impact of an incident if it occurs, for example by storing the minimum possible quantities of dangerous materials, providing bunds and containment tanks, monitoring, sensors and alarms, and staff training.

Of course under the ecosystem model, toxic materials will all be eliminated from the company's operations – obviating the impact of any incident before it happens. We consider how to do this in Chapters 10–13.

Resource Management

There are many low or no cost actions you can take immediately to save energy, waste and water. I frequently walk around industrial sites and hear the hiss of escaping compressed air, or see a hose pouring water into a drain, needlessly costing the business money. The solutions to these problems are often very low or zero cost, for example improving maintenance, improving awareness and discipline, or fitting simple equipment such as trigger nozzles on hoses. There is usually a swift economic return on these actions as they cut operating costs with minimal investment.

Materials and waste

We looked at the true cost of waste in Chapter 2 – typically it is ten times the cost of disposal, which for many companies turns it from a minor issue into a medium-sized one. In order to get people to develop a better attitude to waste I have a simple little saying:

> *Waste is a verb, not a noun.*

The thinking behind this is that by designating a material as 'waste', we are instantly designating it as a problem rather than a resource. By using the verb 'waste', we are prejudiced against the *action of wasting* rather than the *resource* itself.

Reducing waste going to landfill has a number of environmental benefits:

- Organic material decomposes in landfill to produce a 50:50 mix of CO_2 and methane, the latter being 23 times more powerful in terms of the greenhouse effect than CO_2;[2]
- Without proper management, methane can build up in landfills causing an explosion risk. Other materials can catch fire in landfills – an underground fire in a Welsh tyre dump was thought to have burned for 15 years;[3]
- Toxic materials can leach out of landfills and poison watercourses. Modern landfill developers claim to have eradicated this problem, but only time will tell if they are correct;
- Avoidance of pollution from raw material extraction and production of the wasted material. As we saw in Chapter 7, primary industries tend to be the most environmentally damaging across the value chain.

One of the most widely used tools for waste management is the waste hierarchy (see Figure 9.1). This sets out waste options in order of preference, with the avoidance of waste in the first place being the ultimate goal.

Figure 9.1 *The waste hierarchy*

Running through the steps of the hierarchy in order:

- Energy from waste: this effectively avoids releasing methane into the atmosphere by converting all the carbon in the material to CO_2, while producing heat and/or electricity. Critics point to the loss of resources and pollution from incomplete combustion – including POPs such as dioxins and furans;
- Recycling: this is the process of recovering material to be used again inside or outside the business. By providing relatively 'clean' material, those 'dirty' primary industry processes can be avoided, for example recycling 1kg of aluminium only requires 5 per cent of the energy of extracting material from ore;[4]
- Reusing: this is the process of recovering products or substantial components of products to be used again, for example pallets. This not only avoids environmental damage from primary industries but also some of the pollution from the rest of the supply chain. Reuse can be internal (for example using pallets from suppliers for moving work in progress) or external (returning packaging to a supplier for them to use again);
- Waste minimization: reducing waste at source, whether paper in an office or damaged product in a factory, can be achieved through better maintenance of equipment, better control systems and better employee performance;
- Waste avoidance: to avoid waste in the first place you may have to use different ways of working, some of which may come down to better working practices, but may require a new production or operating process, which are covered in the next chapter.

While the hierarchy is a useful rule of thumb, it is an eco-efficiency tool and is less useful for the ecosystem model. It does not encourage substitution of materials and it can even lead to a 'waste' stream being reduced to a level where it is not economically viable to recycle and the material ends up being landfilled. It includes landfill as an option, which is not part of the ecosystem model. The equivalent ecosystem principle to the hierarchy would be 'reuse/recycle or design it out of the system'.

Most office-based businesses start their green journey by trying to cut paper use as this is the most tangible environmental impact of office work. For example, the lawyers Muckle LLP managed to cut their paper use from 3000 sheets per lawyer per month down to 1000. Manufacturing businesses should concentrate efforts at the end of their production process. Waste generated from damaged or off-spec products at 'goods out' is the most expensive form of waste as this is where maximum value has been added.

Energy efficiency

For most businesses, waste costs only become significant when the true cost of waste is considered. Energy costs, however, are usually significant, up front and explicit, and the benefits from energy efficiency can be felt almost immediately. In cost and environmental terms, different forms of energy have quite different characteristics:

- Fossil fuels such as coal, gas and oil are relatively cheap and have a relatively low carbon intensity (kilogram CO_2 per unit energy);
- Mains electricity is more expensive and has a much higher carbon intensity as it is predominantly produced inefficiently from fossil fuels;
- Renewable energy is generally more expensive again, but has a much lower, near zero carbon intensity;
- Compressed air is the most expensive and carbon intensive form of energy on most industrial sites as it is produced inefficiently from electricity. This combined with its ability to escape easily from its network of pipes and appliances makes it a priority for energy efficiency efforts;
- Steam is usually cheaper and less carbon intensive than compressed air, but it can also be lost through leaks so it is another candidate for close inspection.

Manufacturing companies can often make significant improvements in energy efficiency for very small investments. For example, Northern Foods managed to cut the energy bill in one factory by 6 per cent by annotating equipment with colour coded stickers. A green sticker means 'if this machine appears to be doing nothing useful, switch it off'. An amber sticker means 'if this one appears to be doing nothing, ask your supervisor'. Red means 'leave this machine on, whatever'. This saves tens of thousands of pounds per year, yet the stickers cost just £22. Other common energy efficiency opportunities include maintaining compressed air and steam facilities to avoid leaks, zoning factories' heating and lighting systems to reflect shift patterns and ensuring proper ventilation of refrigeration compressors.

Service companies can find it more difficult to implement energy efficiency measures. Office accommodation is very carbon intensive – the average office worker is responsible for more carbon emissions every year just while at work than the average person's domestic emissions.[5] Much of this can be blamed on air conditioning – an office with aircon has twice the carbon footprint of one that hasn't. The problem that most service sector businesses face is they rarely own their properties. It is usually the landlord who has to pay for upgrades to heating and cooling systems, or effective building management systems. These can cut heating bills (and carbon), but as landlords don't pay those bills, they don't get a return on investment. This means that options are often limited to educating staff in energy efficient behaviour, for example switch it off campaigns and how to operate a thermostat etc.

Water conservation

Water use is often neglected from both an economic and environmental perspective, yet water comes with a significant cost in both terms. In many parts of the world, water is a scarce resource – this includes South East England and South West USA as well as sub-Saharan Africa. Even where water is plentiful, it must be treated and pumped to your site and most wastewater requires treatment as well. All of this has a cost in terms of carbon and money.

The main opportunities for water conservation through better housekeeping are:

- Identification and elimination of leaks using observation or, for underground pipes, ultrasonic leak detectors;
- Provision of equipment such as trigger nozzles on hoses to prevent loss through bad practice;
- Elimination of wasteful water practices by staff through training and enforcement of rules;
- Reusing water, for example cascading water from a high purity use down to lower grade uses.

Tools for resource management

The basic tools for the different types of resource management – waste minimization, energy efficiency and water conservation – are identical and can be combined into a single resource management programme. They are:

- Auditing: gathering data, observing operations and behaviour, and using tools such as mass balances to identify opportunities for improvements;
- Maintenance: a good maintenance regime can eliminate resource loss through, for example, leaks of compressed air, steam and water, loss of product from faulty machinery, and loss of efficiency through suboptimal settings on machinery;
- Culture change and staff engagement is vital as many of the potential quick wins in an organization require different behaviour from employees (we cover this in Chapter 17);
- Use of key performance indicators and monitoring equipment/systems for monitoring resource use (covered in Chapter 18). These can identify sudden changes in resource use or inexplicably high consumption (for example energy or water use when the site is not operating).

Greening Transport

Transportation is responsible for over 14 per cent of global greenhouse gas emissions,[6] so logistics, work journeys and staff commuting will form a major part of the environmental impact of most companies. Figure 9.2 gives data on the carbon intensity (the amount of CO_2 produced per passenger per kilometre) for various modes of transport.

Business travel

Business travel is seen by some as a glamorous part of doing the job, but to others it is a chore and to be avoided at all costs. Business travel is thought to be responsible for 30 per cent of all transport-related emissions[8] – or about 4.2 per cent of all carbon emissions. Much travel can be avoided – probably the most infamous case of recent years was when the chairman of a London-based company ordered a member of staff to fly to Dublin to fetch his Blackberry that he had left behind on a business trip.[9] The story later appeared as front page news after a court case over the redundancy of the company's environmental manager.

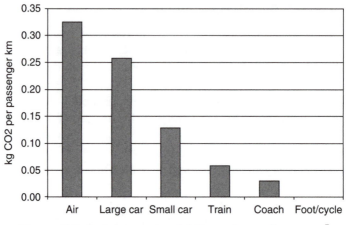

Figure 9.2 *Carbon intensity of different forms of transport*[7]

Methods for reducing business travel include clamping down on unwarranted or unnecessary meetings through the management approval system, and using teleconferencing. It has been estimated that teleconferencing could avoid 30 per cent of global business travel.[10] This would save the equivalent carbon emissions to that of the carbon footprint of the whole population of London.

If transport is necessary, then a modal shift to lower carbon forms of transport is the biggest opportunity for cutting carbon. There can be other benefits too, for example many short haul flights take more time than their rail equivalent if the time from door to door is counted rather than the advertised journey time as railway stations tend to be at the centres of towns and cities while airports are usually on the outskirts. In addition, it is often easier to work on a train than a plane.

If your organization owns or rents its own fleet of vehicles for business travel then low carbon options can be chosen, for example hybrid cars, diesel cars or, simplest of all, smaller cars. Eco-driving training can also cut emissions by up to 20 per cent.[11]

Logistics

Leaflet distribution firm EAE Ltd is shifting to electric vehicles for short range deliveries. While mains powered electric vehicles have less of a carbon footprint than their fossil fuelled equivalents, EAE takes this a step further by using renewable energy from their wind turbine to charge the delivery vehicle and an electric forklift truck overnight, making them near-zero carbon. On its conventional vehicles, the company has fitted trackers to cut unauthorized use and uses software to design efficient rounds. All drivers have gone through eco-driving training.

EAE's actions demonstrate a number of opportunities: use of low carbon vehicles – other examples include the aerodynamic 'teardrop' trucks being used by Marks & Spencer to cut emissions; minimizing emissions using trackers and route design; and training drivers in good driving techniques. Another example is GlaxoSmithKline's shift away from air and to low carbon modes of transport such as rail, inland waterway or sea.

Staff commuting

The third area for cutting emissions from travel is staff commuting. While some staff will enthusiastically switch to, say, cycling if facilities are provided, others are wedded to their cars. Parking seems to be a touch paper issue for many individuals, therefore arrangements must be made carefully to avoid insurrection in the ranks. Potential solutions include:

- Making commuting by car more difficult, for example by limiting parking permits, or increasing parking charges;
- Avoiding locking staff into inflexible routines, for example annual permits that discentivize staff from alternating, say, cycling and private car;
- Making lower carbon options more attractive, for example providing cycle racks, showers and lockers, subsidizing and/or improving key public transport links;
- Engaging staff in the process, for example BOSS Paints provides free cycle maintenance courses to encourage people to bring their bikes to work and create a cycling culture in the company;
- The biggest opportunity is allowing staff to work remotely – we examine this in the next chapter.

Many local authorities now require a 'green travel plan' for major developments, requiring organizations to demonstrate how they are promoting green travel. Such plans are produced by auditing staff commuting patterns and identifying opportunities to introduce modal shifts, for example by organizing bus routes or encouraging cycling.

Capital Investments

Sitting somewhere between the 'housekeeping' suggestions in this chapter and the more radical process redesigns covered in the next chapter are capital investments. These fall into two categories: (1) 'green' investments such as micro-renewables, rainwater harvesting or skimmers to remove fats and oils from effluent for recycling; and (2) standard improvements and upgrades to plant, for example replacing motors or IT equipment with more efficient models.

Green investments can range from very small projects – BOSS Paint's first venture into solar energy comprised just 64 small panels (they now have 1477), up to huge projects such as Diageo's £65 million investment in anaerobic digestion in Scotland.[12] The latter will turn a problem – wastewater with a high organic content – into a solution – the biggest renewable energy system in the UK outside the energy sector.

We look at how to green the investment decision process in Chapter 18, but in brief the following tips apply:

- Consider the wider system when making investments, for example when upgrading a motor, would a variable speed drive be more appropriate for the application than a motor and valve?
- Choose new systems on the basis of through life costs rather than capital costs alone;
- If an investment has wider benefits (for example good PR for the company), this should be factored into the cost–benefit assessment rather than restricting it to pure return on investment.

Site Biodiversity

Many companies have developed wildlife areas on site. For example, despite being restricted to a strip of grass a couple of metres wide, EAE Ltd has developed a wildlife trail around the inside of its factory fence. While this may have a small effect on biodiversity on the global scale, wildlife areas have a number of advantages:

- They contribute to the environmental quality of the surrounding area;
- They engage staff directly in environmental issues and provide a more pleasant working environment;

- They make a clear and tangible statement to staff, local communities and visitors that the company takes environmental issues seriously;
- Being able to demonstrate commitment to, say, a rare orchid or butterfly is often a much more engaging way to communicate environmental issues, than, say, saving the polar bear from climate change;
- They can cut maintenance costs, for example by eliminating grass cutting or even sewerage costs by providing space for surface water to soak away rather than draining to sewer.

Chapter summary

1 There are plenty of quick wins that can be secured without changing anything radically – but they will only deliver incremental improvements;
2 Compliance is the first place to start – as we saw in Chapter 2, compliance underpins all other efforts;
3 Improved resource management – waste minimization, energy efficiency and water conservation – can deliver good financial returns at low or no cost interventions;
4 Travel is a key environmental aspect of almost every business, whether staff commuting, business travel or logistics;
5 Capital projects can improve the environmental performance of your site by adding green energy sources or improving efficiency of plant;
6 On-site biodiversity projects can provide a tangible commitment and improve staff morale.

The View from the Front Line: Chris Tuppen, BT

BT is the largest communications services company in the UK and one of the largest in the world. BT's UK network has 128 million km of copper wire and 11 million km of optical fibre. The company's international network provides coverage to more than 170 countries and their customers include more than 25 per cent of Fortune 500 companies.

Dr Chris Tuppen is BT's Chief Sustainability Officer.[*] His job is to lead the development of BT's sustainability strategy. He is also involved in public policy development for climate change and he heads up BT's role as a sustainability partner for the London 2012 Olympics. In January 2008 he was named by *The Guardian* newspaper as 'one of the 50 people who could save the planet' alongside Al Gore and Angela Merkel.

Why and how did you get involved in this agenda?

I was originally a BT research scientist investigating advanced semiconductor fabrication technologies. Twenty years ago I could see that area of research starting to wane and I had a choice to make, either to become a software engineer or to carry out an environmental analysis of the company. I chose the latter as it was a topic I've always been interested in, and it gave me the opportunity to try something completely different and it has evolved from there. It was quite a culture change moving from an almost academic environment into the commercial PR/communications department. But I made a home for myself there and if you ask anyone they'll say I've become really passionate about it.

What are the business drivers for BT to engage in this agenda?

The business case for us consists of risk management, reputational management, cost savings through eco-efficiency and employee motivation – recruitment and retention. On risk management, we are interested in how individual issues (climate change, diversity, ethics etc.) could impact on our business. Finally there is the innovation area – winning more business based on our sustainability credentials and on the development of new products and services.

What successes have you had?

The thing that I am most pleased about is the way that the values of sustainability are now embedded into the business so it becomes part of the way business is done around the company. That manifests itself in people getting in contact to ask what's the right thing to do in certain circumstances while others have been motivated to get on and do stuff on their own volition.

Internally, we have reduced our UK carbon emissions by 58 per cent against our 1997 base year. Forty-one per cent of our energy now comes from renewable sources. We have launched 120 'Carbon Clubs' with 400 members to encourage our staff to adopt carbon cutting behaviour. Between 2005 and 2009 our environmental programmes saved £400 million and supported bids worth a potential £1.9 billion in 2009.

We have received many awards for reporting, diversity and for specific sustainability projects. The one I'm most proud of is topping the Dow Jones sustainability index for eight consecutive years. We started reporting in 1992 and we've received award after award ever since.

I initiated the Smart 2020 report (www.smart2020.org) which plotted reductions in the ICT sector's carbon footprint to 2020 and also looked at the potential for the sector to decarbonize other parts of the economy. The potential emissions savings are five times the necessary increase in ICT carbon emissions to deliver this transformation.

What are the big challenges for your organization?

Short-termism is the biggest problem. Investors are looking for a payback of less than a year, but these issues cannot be fixed in a year, so it is hard to show the kind of return on investment that is normal in business.

Customer pull is a little weak at present, although we have plenty of employee pull. At the minute our employee's expectations are rather higher than we can deliver against.

There are some technological issues to overcome like driving energy efficiency of networks and data centres. In particular, we have invested a huge amount of money in existing infrastructure and we can't just write that off.

Things aren't just black and white – it is often difficult to decide what is the best thing to do. For example, on the social side of sustainability, in internet content there is a triangle of issues: national security, privacy and freedom of expression. As an internet service provider, we get caught in the middle of that, getting pulled in all sorts of different directions by different people. There is often no 'right' answer – we just have to make a collective, informed decision.

What's your advice for others in your position?

You've really got to understand the business case as it applies to your company and deliver clear business benefits. Too often companies have jumped in without really understanding the connection to their core business. They receive plaudits from the outside world but sustainability hasn't become properly embedded and it will fail. At the same time you have to hold your company firm to a set of core principles.

Note

* Since giving this interview, Chris has left BT and now operates as an independent consultant.

Greener Operations

At the next level of sustainability, a business realigns its internal processes, equipment and/or buildings to its green objectives. For many businesses, particularly those in manufacturing, this will require investment, disruption and thus risk, but done properly it is possible to cut capital and operating costs. Greening operations is highly sector specific, so we'll look at a number of sectoral examples before drawing up some generic principles.

Information and Communications Technologies

The world is fast becoming digital. Music, films, news and books are being freed from their physical forms and are delivered over data networks instead. This is a good thing from an environmental point of view (as we shall see in Chapter 13), provided the benefits are not wiped out by the additional energy required to power and cool the vast data centres dotted across the globe. The ICT industry is currently responsible for 2 per cent of global carbon emissions.

Incredibly the typical server in a data centre uses only 10–20 per cent of its capacity, which is hugely inefficient. A technique called 'virtualization' can be used to increase this to 50–70 per cent – a massive improvement that can cut hundreds of servers down to dozens.[1] Virtualization fools each individual server into thinking it is actually several servers, so one machine does the job of many with a negligible extra energy requirement.

Currently a third of the carbon footprint of data centres is caused by cooling. New technologies allow microprocessors to run at a higher temperature. Fresh air can often be used for cooling through clever design of server rooms, and smart systems allow cooling to be directed to areas where temperatures are running high. These measures can reduce the cooling load by an estimated 18 per cent.[2] Obviously virtualization reduces the need for cooling by decreasing the number of servers producing heat.

Telecoms giant BT has reduced its UK carbon emissions by 58 per cent against a 1997 base year; 41 per cent of their energy now comes from renewable sources. This has had clear business benefits – between 2005 and 2009 their environmental programmes saved £400 million.

Construction

The construction industry is highly resource intensive. In the UK, the construction industry consumes 90 per cent of non-energy minerals extracted in the country each year. Concrete is second only to water in terms of the amount of materials used by humanity and cement production accounts for about 6 per cent of global carbon emissions, with other construction materials accounting for a further 4 per cent.[3] It has been estimated that 13 per cent of materials going onto a construction site are wasted without ever becoming part of the fabric of the building.[4]

Given the nature of construction, it is difficult to green operations on a construction site without changes to the design process (Chapter 12) and/or procurement practices (Chapter 11), but some techniques to improve environmental performance in operations include:

- Four dimensional planning systems that ensure that the right material is delivered to the right part of the building at the right time;
- Careful planning of ground works to minimize the need to shift soil and rock;
- Optimizing the use of materials through careful planning, for example minimizing offcuts from wallboards;
- Prefabricating building components offsite under better controlled conditions (for example steel work, hotel bathrooms);
- Smarter ordering systems (see Chapter 11) to ensure the correct quantities and sizes of material are purchased in the first place.

Manufacturing

Manufacturing is responsible for about 30 per cent of global carbon emissions.[5] There are some very specific cleaner production opportunities available to manufacturing businesses, for example:

- Chemicals: the process intensification movement has long had a target of reducing chemical plant size by a factor of 100. In practice it has been demonstrated to deliver energy efficiencies of 70 per cent (factor 3.33).[6] Bioprocessing techniques are helping to bring ecosystem model principles to this industry;

- Steel making: switching from a basic oxygen furnace to an electric arc furnace can deliver a factor 4 improvement, which can be further improved to factor 10 with the latest technology. Steel is infinitely recyclable and 37 per cent of global production is already from scrap steel;[7]
- Cement production: energy use can be reduced by 30 per cent by shifting from wet to dry manufacturing processes. An 80 per cent (factor 5) improvement can be achieved by switching to geopolymer cement (sourced from, say, fly ash) but that is the realm of green product development – see Chapter 12;[8]
- Pharmaceuticals: GlaxoSmithKline has reduced its raw material to product ratio from 100:1 to 37:1 (almost a factor 3 improvement) and has an ambition to hit factor 5. GlaxoSmithKline is also shifting towards an industrial ecology approach to manufacture as their long-term ambition.

Some generic opportunities in the manufacturing sector include:

- Implementing better control systems to cut overproduction, off-spec product and start-up losses;
- Optimizing pipework: short fat straight pipes requires less energy than a spaghetti of long thin pipes to pump the same amount of material from place to place;
- Investing in efficient motors and installing variable speed drives in pumps rather than using energy to push fluids against a valve;
- Using systems engineering to optimize process designs at the system level rather than component by component (in the two examples above you can use smaller motors and pumps);
- Waste heat recovery: waste heat from a number of sources can be used to heat water, air or chemical reactants;
- Using lean manufacturing techniques to eliminate work in progress (which is vulnerable to wastage due to changing orders or damage).

Retail

The retail sector had until recently only come under the environmental spotlight for the products sold (for example fur, hardwoods) rather than their in-store performance. But this is fast changing with major chains such as Walmart, Marks & Spencer and Tesco leading the charge. Marks & Spencer has implemented a number of greener operations including shifting from HCFC and HFC refrigerants (which have a high global warming potential) to CO_2. They have cut energy consumption per square foot of sales floor by 10 per cent between 2006/2007 and 2008/2009, 7 per cent per square foot in warehouses and cut fuel use in delivery fleet by 20 per cent.[9]

There are some conflicts between good energy management and conventional retail theory. For example, retailers prefer having the main doors of their stores open and don't like putting barriers between the consumer and goods for sale, such as doors on freezer and chiller units. In the UK, Aldi and Lidl have implemented freezer doors across their stores, but ASDA (a Walmart subsidiary) trialled doors and rejected them due to 'customer protest'.[10]

More substantial benefits will come from shifting from traditional store-based retail to e-commerce. It has been estimated that every delivery van takes three cars off the roads. Warehouses use about a third of the energy per square metre as shops and can hold a lot more stock as there is less space required for displays, check-outs etc.[11] The Ethical Superstore concept was developed to exploit these environmental opportunities.

But undoubtedly the biggest effect that major retailers can have is to use their buying power to reduce the environmental impacts of their supply chain. We'll be looking at how to green the supply chain in the next chapter, but retailers have an extra weapon in their armoury – 'choice editing'. In order words they can simply refuse to stock items that they believe are unsustainable. UK home improvement giant B&Q hit the headlines when it stopped selling patio heaters in 2008.[12] Patio heaters were a popular product, so discontinuing them sent a clear signal about B&Q's commitment to sustainability. Ethical Superstore has taken this a step further by only offering products with an ethical or environmental benefit over mainstream products.

Office-based Businesses

Office-based organizations will find it more difficult to manage their environmental footprint as many do not own the buildings they operate from. This means that, while they pay their utility bills, they have little or no control over the hardware that consumes those utilities. Choosing an eco-friendly building in the first place is the only way to overcome this problem effectively. Fortunately there are a range of well-established green building standards such as

LEED in the US (and increasingly elsewhere) and BREEAM in the UK to guide you on this choice.

Other operational changes include the use of teleconferencing (see Chapter 9) in place of business travel, changing from paper-based to electronic documentation, and the virtualization of IT servers, which we discussed earlier in this chapter. For example, lawyers Muckle LLP have cut their servers from 13 down to 3 using virtualization.

But the biggest opportunity to reduce the impact of office-based businesses is telecommuting – working from home either part-time or full-time. There are two potential environmental benefits from telecommuting: (1) reduction in CO_2, local air pollutants and congestion from commuting; and (2) reduction in CO_2 from carbon-intensive office accommodation by hot-desking telecommuters.

Research has shown that organizations allowing telecommuting make significant carbon reductions – studies have suggested it can cut commuting emissions and office emissions by 20 per cent.[13] There is the wider social benefit that telecommuters tend to use local facilities, strengthening local communities. While telecommuting requires good management, delegation and trust, it can provide better quality of life for staff as well as environmental benefits.

Generic Principles

The sector specific examples above have given a flavour of the opportunities to align processes to sustainability. Here are some generic principles for greening your operations, whatever sector you operate in:

- Be prepared to invest to save: make your investment decisions on lower lifecycle costs (aka through life costs) instead of simply optimizing capital costs;
- Don't do what you always do: challenge every assumption – use the 'toddler test', i.e. keep asking 'but, why?' until the question can't be answered, and check out what works in other sectors to see if the idea is applicable to yours;
- Optimize at the system level before optimizing individual elements (for example fatter, shorter, straighter pipes can mean smaller pumps);
- Replace physical resources (energy, materials, water) with information: better control systems in manufacturing to avoid wasting energy, building management systems for offices and other buildings to manage heating and cooling, route planning systems to increase the efficiency of transport etc.

Of course, these process improvements need to be made in the context of any the changes to the product and business models, as we describe in Chapters 12 and 13. Investments at this stage should not preclude those more fundamental changes – we look at how to avoid any clashes in Chapter 16.

Chapter summary

1   The first opportunity to really make a difference is to align the operations of your organization to sustainability;
2   The capital investment and risk is commensurately higher than simple housekeeping measures;
3   Many opportunities are highly sector specific, for example changing from one chemical process to another;
4   There are a number of generic principles: base investments on through life costs, use systems thinking and replace resources with information;
5   More significant sustainability benefits will come from redesigning products and business models. Changes to operations should be carefully chosen to avoid conflicts with future redesigns.

The View from the Front Line: Roberta Barbieri, Diageo

Diageo is the largest wine, beer and spirits manufacturer in the world with more than 20,000 employees operating in 180 different countries with a turnover of £12 billion in 2009. The company's brands include Guinness, Gordon's Gin, Bell's Whiskey, Bailey's Liqueur and Piat D'Or wine.

Roberta Barbieri is the Global Environmental Project Manager for the company, responsible for setting the environmental/sustainability agenda worldwide and for helping implement that agenda.

Why and how did you get involved in this agenda?

I've being doing corporate environmental work for 20 years – my entire career. I have a bachelors degree in environmental science and two masters degrees in environmental science and engineering. I started my career at Pitney Bowes and then moved to Joseph E. Seagram and Sons where I was the global environmental, health and safety manager. While I was with Seagram, the company was purchased by Vivendi Universal. Several years later, Diageo purchased some of the Seagram liquor part of the business and I moved over to Diageo as Director of Environmental Health and Safety for North America.

Where my previous positions were predominantly about ensuring compliance with Environment, Health and Safety regulations, my current role is all about strategy, embedding environment into long-term business thinking and driving target achievement.

What are the business drivers for Diageo to engage in this agenda?

There is a combination of factors. One is the cost-efficiencies inherent in environmental sustainability. Improving environmental performance and improving cost-efficiency go hand in hand. Another is the set of marketplace drivers out there today – the influence of customers and consumers, the expectations of investors, not to mention the needs of employees.

We have also been driven by the personal passion of several senior executives. David Gosnell, Managing Director Diageo Global Supply, is the executive level environmental champion for the company. He is passionate about sustainability and has actively sponsored the environmental agenda across the company.

What successes have you had?

We've always had a solid environmental programme at Diageo. We've been setting public targets for greenhouse gas emissions, energy efficiency, waste and water for years, but the big change occurred a few years ago when we decided that, instead of trying to get incremental improvements in our performance, we would take the leap to make step change improvements. Whereas before we simply had incremental year on year targets like 2 per cent a year, in 2008 we published aggressive targets for 2015 of 50 per cent reduction in absolute carbon, 30 per cent improvement in water efficiency and the 100 per cent elimination of all waste sent to landfill.

We have several of what I call 'rock star' projects at Diageo – bioenergy facilities at two of our distilleries in Scotland. One is amongst the largest single investments in renewable energy by a non-utility in the history of the UK. In both, the facility takes wastewater heavily laden with spent grains and instead of discharging it, we will be anaerobically digesting it to provide the primary energy source for the distillery in terms of heat and steam – 85 per cent of the plant's needs. It also has a large water reuse component and significantly reduces the discharge of organics into the wastewater.

We have many more projects that might seem a little more mundane. In Africa we've improved water treatment plants, which along with the Scottish projects, will take us a long way toward achieving our pollution reduction target for 2015. We've put in solar panels at a packaging plant in South Korea (which halved the site's carbon footprint), at a bottling plant in Sydney, Australia and at a winery at Napa Valley in California. In the latter, visiting tourists take a solar powered gondola onto the site.

What are the big challenges for your organization?

Many of the improvements we want to make require capital investment. Securing cash for such investments is always difficult. Fortunately our boss sees environmental projects as a priority and many of the projects are delivering a good return on investment, so we do get many approved.

Driving a cultural change into the employee mindset is a big priority. We're making a lot of progress but it certainly doesn't happen overnight. We have a competitive culture, so we use contests to engage our staff – each site can compete for a bronze, silver and gold Olympic medal for the programmes their site implements. Our next challenge is to operationalize environmental thinking into decision making, everywhere from operations to human resources to the executive office.

From an external perspective, we have not yet seen a strong pull within our industry from consumers. Rather it is the retailers that are providing the pull, particularly in the US and UK.

What's your advice for others in your position?

Three things:

1   Senior management commitment is essential – so build your senior executive relationships.
2   Be passionate, balanced with a good understanding of what's right for the business. The worst thing that you could do is push for something that is good for the environment but not good for the business or you lose credibility.
3   Recognize that it is a marathon, not a sprint. You will have moments of disappointment, but you've got to keep moving forward.

Greening the Supply Chain

Don't Buy Trouble

For most organizations, much of their carbon footprint is in their supply chain rather than within the factory fence/office walls. For example, for Canon products, the supply chain represents 47 per cent of lifecycle carbon emissions, or 66 per cent of emissions from 'cradle to gate'.[1] In the UK's National Health Service (the third largest organization in the world), the supply chain accounts for 59 per cent of carbon emissions, predominantly due to pharmaceutical production.[2]

It is obvious from these statistics that a truly green company must improve the environmental performance of its supply chain. As well as reducing the overall footprint of the company, greening the supply chain avoids potential problems on your site, for example, phasing out the purchase of hazardous materials reduces the risk of a pollution incident. It is also important to reduce the risk of environmental and social problems from your supply chain being attributed to your business. In the broader sense, you will also strengthen markets for greener products and services, helping to green the wider economy.

In this chapter we look at the basic principles before moving on to some advanced techniques.

Basic Principles

Fundamentally, you have three basic options to green your supply chain:

1 Purchase less stuff;
2 Purchase 'better' stuff;
3 Purchase stuff from better suppliers.

The sections below describe each of these in turn.

Buy less stuff

This is the easiest of the three, as less of the same thing is always better. Techniques include:

- Checking you really do need the product (you'd be surprised how much stuff gets bought and never used);
- Ensuring dimensions and quantities match your needs;
- Carefully managing stocks of perishable items;
- Keeping stocks as low as possible (for example using lean manufacturing techniques).

For example I have worked with several companies who were purchasing components too long for their needs and cutting them to length every time. By buying smarter, in this case buying the correct length of component, less material was being bought in the first place, the cutting was eliminated and less waste was produced, saving time, money and resources.

Over-purchasing goods, particularly those with a limited shelf life, is a prime cause of 'hidden' waste. Buying material simply to throw it away is bad business.

Your procurement staff should always ask the following questions of procurement decisions:

- Do we need it at all?
- Can we do with less?
- Can we buy it in quantities that better match our needs?
- Will we use it within its shelf life?

Buy 'better' stuff

'Better' in this sense means solar, cyclic, safe or where production or use is more eco-efficient. Examples include:

- Sheep's wool insulation has 9 per cent of the embodied energy of rockwool;
- Recycled aluminium has 5 per cent of the embodied energy of virgin material;
- An efficient variable speed drive pump in place of a traditional pump plus valve set up;
- A solar powered internet services provider;
- A cycle courier in place of a motorcycle courier;

- Local food, cutting 'food miles';
- Non-toxic paint stripper.

The car manufacturer Volvo pioneered the use of 'grey' and 'black' lists to filter out materials and chemicals that are not safe.[3] Black list substances should never be purchased and those on the grey list should only be used where no alternative exits. Black and grey lists are highly industry specific, so you will need to research toxic materials in your business and determine which can and can't be replaced. Other companies put minimum requirements on purchases, for example IKEA has a set of requirements ruling out illegally harvested wood or wood from areas of high conservation value, with a long-term goal to require all wood to come from certified sources.[4]

Purchase from 'better' suppliers

The press, NGOs, clients and customers and the general public will hold you responsible for the performance of your suppliers. This has been particularly noticeable in the human rights field (for example sweatshops producing clothing or electronic goods), but environmental problems in the supply chain can also embarrass high profile businesses.

For example, the Toyota Prius has been attacked as the nickel required for its battery comes from a smelter in Sudbury, Canada that has had pollution problems in the past. Never mind that the ecological damage was caused decades before the Prius ever went on sale, or that the factory concerned has won awards for restoration since, Toyota has been unfairly tarred with this brush.

For this reason if you are going to present yourself as a green business you need to be careful about who you do business with, and indeed who they do business with.

There are a number of ways to identify potential problems:

- Monitor the environmental press, both at the business end of the market (for example the *ENDS Report*) and the activist end (for example *New Internationalist*);
- There are many books, websites and reports available that list the 'ethical' performance of companies against set criteria;
- Audit potential suppliers using short supplier questionnaires and visit their main sites if possible;

- Implement a ranking system for suppliers. For example, Sharp ranks its suppliers from A to D; A rated suppliers are given preference and the default position is not to purchase from a supplier ranked D.[5]

Advanced Techniques

The basic techniques described above will deliver incremental improvements to supply chain environmental performance. Making more radical improvements can be difficult – we saw in Chapter 4 that immature supply chains are a key limiting factor in going green. Leading companies are rising to this challenge by taking a much more proactive approach to rethinking, developing and shaping the supply chain they require to meet their sustainability targets. Here we examine a number of examples.

Buy a service rather than a product

One of the most powerful methods of reducing the impact of procurement is to buy services rather than products. For example Xerox does not sell photocopiers per se, rather it provides a copying service. Its machines have been developed to be long-lasting and easily upgradeable. You pay per copy you make, which discourages you from being wasteful. This is known as a 'product-service system' as you are buying the service required rather than the physical product. This puts an incentive on both buyer and supplier to be efficient in terms of materials and/or energy.

The idea of the product-service system is described in more detail in Chapter 13 as an option for your own business model, but the concept can be used in purchasing as well. Well established examples include solvent management services where the supplier keeps ownership of the solvents, advises on how best to use them and removes them for recycling, and vehicle leasing where the supplier provides and maintains the vehicles to best effect.

Engaging your existing supply chain

You may find your suppliers can change their product to suit both parties. When the UK's Carbon Trust carried out a carbon footprint of Walker's Crisps, they found that potato suppliers were keeping the potatoes hydrated as they were bought by gross weight – but the water needed to be driven off during frying.[6]

Walker's talked to their suppliers and agreed to buy potatoes by dry weight instead. As a result the hydration stopped, saving energy and water, and the frying took less energy too.

Marks & Spencer went into collaboration with one of their lingerie suppliers in Sri Lanka to produce an 'eco-factory' that requires only 4 per cent of the energy of a traditional factory. The use of natural light and ventilation makes working conditions as far from a sweatshop as could be imagined.

Smith's Electric Vehicles have also worked to strengthen and diversify their supply chains for electric vehicle components. The higher cost of electric vehicles relative to petrol/diesel equivalents is largely due to the supply chain. Smith's believe if they could increase their throughput by another 1000 vehicles a year, they could cut a third of their bill of material costs through economies of scale.

Building a new supply chain

But what if there is no viable supply chain for the materials and/or products you need? The really cutting-edge companies are proactively building new supply chains to meet their needs.

As a major clothing retailer, Marks & Spencer is keen to get as much recycled fibre into their products as possible, starting with school uniforms and umbrellas. However, the cost of high grade recycled polyester fibre was prohibitive due to low volumes and a virtually non-existent supply chain. The company found that by developing products such as cushions with a large amount of low grade recycled fibre (where the cost differential is smaller) as fill, it is bringing economies of scale to the collection, sorting and processing links in the polyester loop, in turn bringing down the price of high grade recycled polyester fibre. The company hopes that the recycled fibre can soon be produced at a price that is competitive with the virgin equivalent.

Even the largest organizations can expand their buying power through collaboration. As a responsible logistics company, Royal Mail wants to improve the environmental performance of its fleet, but radical new solutions are emerging very slowly. By joining forces with other postal services across Europe through the PostEurop organization, the company has persuaded the motor industry to bring forward the commercial production of hydrogen vehicles by a decade to 2014.

The following generic strategies can be used to help build new supply chains:

- Lateral thinking to improve the economies of scale (for example the Marks & Spencer example above);

- Working in collaboration with suppliers to innovate new products and services, for example Renault-Nissan is working with A Better Place to develop battery leasing services for electric vehicles;[7]
- Working in collaboration with other purchasers to bring buying power and economies of scale to new supply chains (for example Royal Mail);
- Funding the commercialization of innovative new technologies (for example Google's investment in solar energy technologies).

Implementing industrial symbiosis

In Chapter 7, we saw how industrial symbiosis turns the whole idea of a supply chain on its head. Instead of a simple linear flow of materials from extraction through manufacturing use and to disposal, industrial symbiosis creates a tangled web of material and energy flows where 'waste' and 'raw materials' become synonymous.

To implement industrial symbiosis, by definition, you must build or join a wider network of organizations in order to uncover synergies between your business and others. As in nature, the more diverse the actors in the system, the more opportunities for symbiotic relationships can be exploited. There are a number of 'honest brokers' who provide this networking service. The World Business Council for Sustainable Development (WBCSD) has initiated a number of projects in the US, Mexico and the UK, although those in the UK have since evolved into the government-funded National Industrial Symbiosis Programme (NISP).

These projects are much bigger than simple 'waste exchanges' that allow companies to swap unwanted products on a small scale, for example three drums of unwanted solvent. Industrial symbiosis is about building large-scale, semi-permanent supply relationships. There is a proximity principle to industrial symbiosis. Many of the players in the Kalundborg symbiosis exist cheek by jowl, which minimizes the need for expensive logistics. So it is best to start looking for local symbiotic opportunities before moving further afield.

Product takeback

Also in Chapter 7, we saw how product takeback is the tightest example of 'closing the loop' – your own products become your own supply of raw material. InterfaceFLOR has decided that product takeback is the only way they will meet its target of having a zero-footprint by 2020. The company has implemented two different approaches to product takeback:[8]

1   the ReEntry 2.0 takeback system, which is taking back and reprocessing almost 1 million pounds of carpet per week. Once the material is recovered, the face and the backing of the carpet are separated and recycled back into carpet components;

2   the Evergreen flooring service – a product-service system that we consider in more detail Chapter 13, but the basic principle is that by retaining ownership over the product, it is relatively simple to recover and recycle it.

Chapter summary

1   For most organizations, the bulk of their environmental footprint is in their supply chain rather than within the factory fence;

2   There are three basic principles for greening the supply chain: buy less stuff, buy better stuff and buy from a better supplier;

3   Many green supply chains are weak, so you may have to work with existing or new suppliers to strengthen them;

4   Other advanced techniques include buying a service rather than a product, implementing industrial symbiosis and developing product takeback systems so your own products become your raw materials.

The View from the Front Line: Stephen Little, The Sage Gateshead

The North Music Trust operates The Sage Gateshead Music Centre, which, in addition to being one of the best music venues in the UK, provides conference facilities and an extensive musical outreach programme. Stephen Little is the Director of Building Services for the Trust and is responsible for the maintenance and operation of its iconic, Norman Foster-designed building on the south bank of the River Tyne at Gateshead.

Why and how did you get involved in this agenda?

I've always been in the energy business – my first job was as a National Coal Board electrician at Lambton Cokeworks. I've worked for many energy and energy management companies since including BP Energy, Elyo and the National Health Service. For me sustainability just makes good business sense.

What are the drivers for The Sage Gateshead to engage in this agenda?

Sustainability is a great marketing tool. While we only get occasional inquiries about our environmental performance at present, we are expecting this to increase over the next few years. At the minute it is more about positive association. If, say, we have an accredited environmental standard, then people are reassured and don't have to ask any more questions.

Obviously reducing our energy and water bills is another key driver.

What successes have you had?

We are now committed to achieve the BS 8901 Sustainable Event Management standard and we aim for The Sage Gateshead to be the first venue in the northeast of England to achieve the standard.

We have achieved a C ranking with a score of 75 on our display energy certificate (DEC) – the average building of this kind would get a D and 100 and we would probably have received an F when we started. We purchase our electricity from a green tariff – it costs us an extra 0.006p per kWh.

We recycle all the material we can – about 65–70 per cent by weight as much of our waste is glass from the bars. We recycle cardboard, plastics, cans and paper too, but there's more that we could do.

We have signed up to the 10:10 national campaign in which individuals, business and organizations of all kinds try to cut carbon emissions by 10 per cent in 2010

What are the big challenges for your organization?

When we moved into the building, it was not optimized for energy efficiency. We don't own the building so we have to apply for permission to make any major changes, but fortunately Gateshead Council is a very good landlord so there are rarely any major problems. Unfortunately we are unlikely to achieve an A or B on our DEC as we would need renewable energy and that is impossible due to our location. We're getting to the stage where we're doing small projects to make incremental improvements. Generally we look for a two to two and a half year payback.

We've been focusing on energy so far, but our next big challenge is water. We have kitchens, which are notorious for using a lot of water, and our water bills are almost as big as our energy bills. The legal requirements on water supply to a building like this are a huge challenge in themselves.

Running conferences and events is all about the customer experience – the whole thing has to work together and that includes the sustainability issues. Nothing can detract from the quality of our product and that is always a challenge in everything we do. Being a public building, a huge amount of our effort goes into basic maintenance – keeping the building clean, tidy and repairing damage very quickly.

We're also trying to bring all our systems into a single framework – including sustainability, risk assessment, health and safety, so the whole organization is working as one.

What's your advice for others in your position?

Get the right staff and get the right balance between in-house staff and contracted staff. If you contract everything out, you lose ownership of the situation. We have a small staff of core skills and bring in the specialists as and when we need them.

You should always plan for succession – I try to bring someone younger along with me so when I move on there is someone to take my place.

Greening the Product Portfolio

Starting Afresh

It is often said that 80 per cent of a product's environmental impact is decided on the drawing board.[1] Whether there is any empirical evidence for that claim is unclear – I suspect it is a read across from the rule of thumb that 80 per cent of through life costs of a product are determined at the design stage. But there is little doubt that product design is the most cost-effective way of reducing the environmental impact of your business. A designer has the opportunity to eliminate problems and exploit opportunities across the whole product lifecycle (raw materials extraction, manufacturing supply chain, distribution, use, disposal) without leaving their desk. Eco-design gurus Bill McDonough and Michael Braungart have a great saying: 'take the filters out of the pipes and put them where they belong – in the designers' heads'.

This chapter considers the development of green products and services (but without changing the underlying business model, which we examine in the next chapter). First we look at how to develop green products and then consider the strategic and commercial context within which product innovation lies.

How to Develop Green Products

What is a green product?

A green product is one that, over its entire lifecycle, fulfils the sustainability targets we developed in Chapter 6. It should:

* Follow the ecosystem model (solar, cyclic, safe) in the first instance and, where this is not possible ...

- ... Be efficient (with a target of factor 10) in activities compatible with the ecosystem model;
- Eradicate activities and materials incompatible with that model.

The classic 'cradle to grave' lifecycle is shown in Figure 12.1. It is largely linear like the status quo model in Chapter 7 (Figure 7.2) but with a number of subsidiary loops. To comply with the ecosystem model, we need to strengthen those loops to form the closed loop model we saw in Figure 7.3.

Figure 12.2 shows lifecycle carbon emissions for some typical products. While different products have different profiles, the most significant phases in the lifecycle tend to be materials production in the supply chain and, for energy consuming products, the use phase.

Many companies spend a huge amount of time and money on Life Cycle Assessments (LCAs) to map every environmental implication of their products. While they can provide useful insights, LCAs are expensive, time-consuming and the results are often highly dependent on uncertain predictions such as the lifespan of the product. This means they can be overly swayed by assumptions taken by the analyst – in fact it has been said that most LCAs comparing two products favour the product of the organization sponsoring the study (aka WYNIWYG or 'what you need is what you get).[3] So, while some form of LCA may be necessary and/or useful, you shouldn't get bogged down in detail – the emphasis should be on identifying the big issues and making substantial improvements to address them.

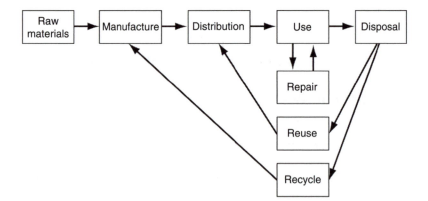

Figure 12.1 *The product lifecycle*

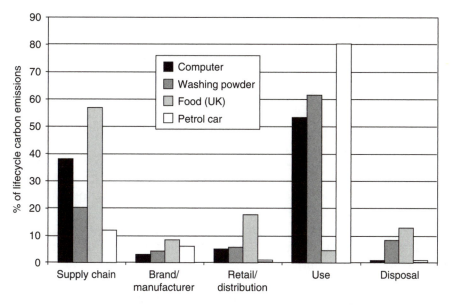

Figure 12.2 *Example lifecycle carbon emissions[2]*

Ecosystem compatible products

A product that is compatible with the ecosystem model has the following characteristics:

- All toxic materials are designed out of the system from cradle to grave;
- All materials are either technical nutrients (for example steel, aluminium, certain polymers) or biological nutrients (for example wood, natural fibres);
- All the energy consumed over the lifecycle is renewable.

While this may seem daunting, don't forget that a spider produces silk that, pound for pound, is stronger than Kevlar or steel, yet it is produced at atmospheric pressure and ambient temperature using dead flies as a raw material and energy source. A famous example of an ecosystem compatible product is the Climatex fabric produced by Rohner Textil AG.[4] The developers tested 1600 available dye chemicals for toxicity and only 16 passed muster. However, these 16 chemicals allow the fabric to be any colour except black. The fibres of the material itself are both natural and compostable.

Eco-efficient products

Eco-efficient products reduce the resources they consume over their lifecycle by a factor of 10 or more. Generic principles for eco-efficient design include:

- Dematerialization – design material out of the product (for example use stronger, lighter materials or exploit stronger shapes);
- Use energy efficient components (for example motors, lights, integrated circuits);
- Reduce friction, electrical and other forms of resistance (for example aerodynamic vehicles);
- Improve utility either by extending the lifecycle, improving performance or providing multifunctional capability (more on this later);
- Replace resources with information (for example engine management systems in a car, washing machines that judge the weight of their load and adjust water use to suit);
- Reduce carbon from transport and distribution (for example local distribution networks, smarter route planning, multi-skilled operatives);
- Use systems thinking to multiply up the benefits of these principles (for example dematerialization of moving parts can allow the use of smaller, more efficient motors, which in turn can lead to dematerialization of supporting structures).

There are many examples of eco-efficient products, some of which meet our factor 10 target. For example, a PassivHaus standard home only requires 10 per cent of the energy of a standard house[5] and a LED bulb uses 10 per cent of the energy of an incandescent bulb to produce the same light.[6]

Wider Considerations

Consumer behaviour

In Chapters 6 and 7 we saw that eco-efficiency in production needs to be matched by sustainable consumption patterns. The direct rebound effect and other aspects of consumer/operator behaviour may impair the expected environmental performance of your product in use. Examples of tactics to influence consumer behaviour include:

- Providing information, for example Marks & Spencer's 'Wash at 30°C' campaign;

- Making green behaviour simple, for example easily accessible on/off switches on televisions and DVD players;
- Designing the product to reinforce green behaviour, for example providing washing powder in tablets to encourage the user to use the optimum quantity;
- Pricing products and product options to incentivize green behaviour, for example making upgrades cheaper than buying a new product.

As we saw above, one approach that is often used to improve eco-efficiency is to expand its utility either through making the product multifunctional or extending its lifespan. However, multifunctional products are only environmentally friendly if consumers refrain from buying other products. For example, my Apple iPhone has a camera on it, but I already had a digital camera, so that didn't deliver material efficiency in this case. However, I did refrain from buying a voice recorder for the interviews in this book as I could download an App onto the phone instead – so the picture is complex.

Likewise, product lifespans are usually determined by fashion rather than mechanical wearout, so extending the lifespan of, say, a cell phone is unlikely to improve its actual eco-efficiency as it will probably be replaced long before it breaks. There is a dilemma here for companies in sectors whose economic sustainability depends on planned obsolescence (personal computers, mobile phones, motor vehicles, high street fashion) as the constant requirement to buy/sell the latest model couples economic performance directly to higher material and energy consumption, a link we need to break.[7]

Don't forget the supply chain

Figure 12.2 demonstrated that, in most cases, much of the environmental impact of a product occurs early in the supply chain. Existing supply chains have been developed to cater for conventional products, so materials and components for green products can be of poor quality, expensive, single sourced, or all three. Over time, as greener processes and materials become the norm, this problem will diminish, but at present it is a serious risk to innovative green products and services and one that cannot be ignored.

So, supply chain development must go hand in hand with product development. We saw in Chapter 11 how companies such as Walkers, Marks & Spencer and Smith's Electric Vehicles have worked proactively outside the factory fence to build the supply chain they need to produce and sell greener products.

Designing for product stewardship

The ecosystem model requires a closed loop approach to materials. We covered product takeback schemes in Chapter 11, but whether your product is going to be recycled by your organization or recovered by another organization for recycling in the wider market, you must design your product to be easily recyclable. For example, InterfaceFLOR has redesigned its products to be easily dismantled in its ReEntry 2.0 product takeback process. This is known as 'design for disassembly'. Considerations include:

- The number and type of materials: for example McDonough and Braungart's book *Cradle to Cradle* is made of compatible polymers so it can simply be melted down as one and recycled;[8]
- Types of fastening: gluing incompatible materials together makes recycling almost impossible; snap fittings are easier to dismantle;
- Innovative approaches: for example the use of 'smart materials' in fastenings. These change shape at high temperatures, for example screws can be designed to lose their threads, to produce self-dismantling products;
- Labelling of materials so they can be identified and recycled properly.

The Product Portfolio

Niche or mainstream?

In the 1990s, Procter & Gamble launched a range of green products to sit along side its conventional ranges. Unfortunately the consumer assumed that those products would be inferior to the others because they were 'green' and the products failed in the marketplace. Now P&G is greening its entire product range with a strict 'no trade-offs' rule – all products have to compete on price, performance and sustainability. More recently, Marks & Spencer flirted with the idea of selling a range of 'green lifestyle' products such as wormeries, but then realized that people did not come to its stores for such products. So it shifted its emphasis, embedding 'green' into its mainstream products instead, for example recycled polyester cushions, umbrellas and school uniforms.

This move from niche products to the mainstream is a general trend in green product portfolio development. And rightly so – to deliver the kind of global transformation described in Chapters 6 and 7, all products will need to be aligned to sustainability principles, not just a few green exemplars.

Creative destruction

The next question is whether you will complement the launch of new greener products by deleting unsustainable products from your portfolio. This can be a big dilemma when it comes to existing cash cows, but killing off unsustainable product lines, no matter how popular they are, is a key step on the journey to sustainability.

Keeping unsustainable products on the books can leave businesses wide open to accusations of greenwash from green hyenas. Ford received a 'greenwash award' from the NGO CorpWatch in 2000 for declaring a green motoring revolution when the average fuel efficiency of its cars was rising due to the popularity of its SUVs.[9] A couple of years later, Ford killed off its electric vehicle programme, citing consumer indifference and focused on trying to improve the mileage of its SUVs instead – a futile goal given the inherent size, weight and poor aerodynamics of such vehicles. Interestingly, when SUVs fell out of favour with the American public in 2006, Ford, along with rivals GM, was ill-prepared and its market share fell.[10]

In contrast, InterfaceFLOR has deleted almost 30 products that were deemed to be holding the company back from its sustainability targets. 'We do not want to perpetuate a problem', says Senior Director of Product and Design Innovation, Nigel Stansfield. It is significant that one of GM's key moves in its 2009 'green rebirth' was to sell off the gas guzzling Hummer brand. To keep such vehicles in its product portfolio would have made a mockery of its investments in electric vehicles.

Difficult products

There is a particular problem where the qualities that make a product effective are the very qualities that make a product an environmental liability. DDT is an excellent insecticide (at least until the insects build up immunity), but it is that very effectiveness that decimates other wildlife. On a smaller scale, there is a constant debate in my household over the use of green washing up liquids. There is no doubt that their performance is weaker than conventional equivalents, but this is the whole point. The strong surfactants in mainstream products cause damage to fish and frog skins. The green alternative requires more elbow grease but the frogs live. It is unlikely that a powerful detergent that didn't damage aquatic life can be developed.

In these cases, more innovation is required to attack the problem from a different, less aggressive angle. For example, biological controls, crop breeding and different agricultural techniques can replace POP-based chemical pesticides. We saw in Chapter 7 how mimicking the non-stick properties of sharkskin can produce non-toxic antifouling coatings for boats and ships.

Markets and Marketing

Green product development is the point at which that we start making really significant moves towards sustainability, but as we saw in Chapter 4, the risk of a new product failing in the market place is very real – Jacquelyn Ottman's 'green graveyard' has many claimed many victims over the years. In terms of green markets and marketing, the traps are:

- Overestimating the market for green products;
- Assuming customers will accept low quality products and services and/or a premium price in exchange for 'green';
- Assuming customers will readily accept a radically different product to the one they are used to;
- Overstating your case and being accused of greenwash.

We consider these issues for both consumer and business-to-business markets.

Consumer markets

There have been numerous attempts to segment and re-segment green consumers, but as a crude rule of thumb:[11]

- One third of consumers have no interest in environmental issues whatsoever;
- One third could be tempted to buy green but won't pay extra or compromise on quality;
- One third will consider environmental considerations important in their buying decisions and a quarter of those (i.e. approx 8 per cent overall) will actively seek out green products and are less sensitive to price.

This gives us three strategies:

- Aim for the green niche and hope it expands with time;
- Aim for the two thirds of consumers to whom environmental performance is a factor in purchasing decisions;
- Present the product as a normal product (i.e. to the whole market).

Niche products can get away with compromises on performance, quality and price, but mainstream consumers will not be so tolerant. Addressing the wider market is much more complicated as public understanding of green issues can be inconsistent and many consumers still perceive 'green' as 'inferior'. There is an added complication – according to the three consumer goods manufacturers interviewed for this book, it is the retail sector that is driving sustainability rather than the consumer. Effectively the large retailers such as Walmart, Tesco and Marks & Spencer are acting as 'gatekeepers' for their customers, demanding and assessing price, quality and sustainability performance on their behalf. So, whether your product's green credentials are being targeted at the consumer or a major retailer, the critical green marketing goal is to get the product right. A mass market product must hit those buttons of performance, price, quality *and* sustainability.

The second issue is how to present 'green'. If you portray it as a moral obligation on the part of the consumer to purchase your product, you will simply switch people off. The actual approach depends on the product and its target audience, but here are some good examples:

- Philips rebranding their 'Earth Light' compact fluorescent lamp bulbs as 'Marathon' to promote their long life and quoting financial savings from the efficiency – in other words 'selling the sizzle';
- Innocent Drinks using a logo of a carton face with a halo – it is smart, funky and cool – just like their target market;
- BOSS Paints pushing a 'bundle of benefits' to the users of their water-based paints – the products are marketed as eco-friendly, low odour and quick drying;
- Communicating the issues in an engaging way, for example Blackfriars café in Newcastle upon Tyne, UK has a map on its place mats showing the range of local farms, some organic, that the company buys its supplies from – no preaching, just information.

Lastly, to avoid accusations of greenwash, you will need to provide evidence to back up any green claims. This can be done in several different ways:

- Utilizing one of the many third party eco-labels, for example the EU energy label, the EU eco-label or the US Energy Star;
- Getting a trusted third party to assess performance and endorse green claims;
- Providing detailed background information online that the user can refer to if they are interested and/or concerned.

Business-to-business markets

Business-to-business markets are generally much clearer cut than consumer markets. As we saw in Chapter 2, many of the world's biggest private and public sector organizations are making sustainability a key issue in purchasing decisions. If you are in the supply chain of these organizations then you are part of their environmental footprint, so they will make increasing demands of you and your products' environmental performance.

But, like consumers (or even more so), these organizations are highly unlikely to buy poor products and services in exchange for green credentials. It is a matter of quality, cost *and* green rather than quality, cost *or* green. As Chris Jofeh of ARUP says 'focus on enhancing the client's business, helping them do what they want to do, but do it better. Use this as the route to delivering green solutions.'

Again it is essential that you do not try and pressurize customers to purchase your product as some sort of moral imperative. Business-to-business clients will be impressed by:

- Facts and figures, preferably endorsed by third parties whether government regulators or non-governmental organizations;
- Testimonials from satisfied customers;
- Risk reduction, for example if your product eliminates the need to store toxic materials on the customer's premises, it cuts their health, safety and environmental liabilities;
- Public relations opportunities: if your product is photogenic, novel and/or quirky then it can be used to promote the sustainability efforts of your client as well as your organization.

Chapter summary

1 Design is the engine room of good environmental practice;
2 Environmental problems across the product lifecycle can be eradicated at the drawing board;
3 The basic principles are to apply our sustainability criteria, the ecosystem model and eco-efficiency, across the lifecycle;
4 The two lifecycle phases that tend to be most significant are materials extraction and the use phase;
5 From a strategic point of view there is a need to consider the supply chain, consumer behaviour and product stewardship;
6 Marketing is a key issue that must be considered during product design to avoid 'the green graveyard';
7 Leading companies are greening their entire product portfolio, not just a 'green' subset;
8 Deleting unsustainable products is a key demonstration of commitment and a spur to innovation.

The View from the Front Line: Martin Blake, Royal Mail

The Royal Mail is the UK's national postal service and operates as a limited company owned by the government. Its history goes back to the time of Henry VIII, but it lost its monopoly on letters in 2006 and is now subject to competition. However, it is still subject to a universal service obligation, which means it has one price for mail across the whole country.

The company has over 180,000 employees and delivers 85 million pieces of mail to 27 million addresses covering 2 million miles a night. It also has one of the largest fleet of vehicles in Europe – 35,000 vehicles and growing – and 14,000 Post Office branches, of which Royal Mail owns 500.

Martin Blake is the Head of Sustainability at Royal Mail, responsible for implementing strategy across the whole organization – the letters business, ParcelForce and Post Offices. He also holds posts as an Associate Professor of Sustainable Business Development at the University of Southern Queensland and is on the Strategic Board of Henley Business School, developing sustainable business courses.

Why and how did you get involved in this agenda?

I've always worked in an area helping people and the planet. I started off working to improve public health and preventative medicine in Abu Dhabi. I then worked for the Saudi national oil company Aramco developing infrastructure projects in Saudi Arabia building schools, hospitals, clinics, roads and universities. The company generated 98 per cent of the country's GDP and our CSR agenda was effectively to build an entire country's infrastructure. I joined Royal Mail in 2004 and was asked to establish a CSR framework as the company had only previously managed elements of the CSR agenda, taking a compliance-based approach. Initially the focus was on social policy, but once we had that structure in place, I moved on to tackling wider sustainability issues, in particular carbon management.

What are the business drivers for Royal Mail to engage in this agenda?

The new framework was developed to engage employees, improve the way we did business and bring in the brand/reputational issues that going 'beyond compliance' can do.

There is a growing recognition of the power and influence of the supply chain. To take carbon as an example, our scope 1 (internal) emissions are someone else's scope 3 (supply chain) emissions. Our customers are now asking the question, 'You are now contributing to our carbon footprint, what are you doing to reduce it?'. We have both won and lost eight figure contracts where carbon performance was a significant factor in the final decision.

Another driver is cost. We obviously want to mitigate against rising energy costs and maintain security of energy supply for business continuity. But we also want to avoid depreciation of the book value of our built estate. So when we get to 2019 and everybody is looking for low carbon buildings because it will be financially punitive to occupy ones that aren't, what will be the effect on the yield values, rental values and capital values of our estate, which is worth billions? How does that affect our balance sheet?

From a regulatory point of view, we're going to be caught up in the UK Government's new CRC. We also look at future regulation, such as the government's zero carbon building by 2016 policy – so what will we build today? What other levers of control will governments use?

What successes have you had?

The CSR strategy we created seven years ago is perceived as being one of the best in the world. We have won about 40 national and international awards for our CSR performance. We were one of the first companies in the UK to achieve the Carbon Trust standard – demonstrating we're committed to measuring, managing and working continuously to reduce our carbon footprint.

Our carbon management programme is in place – it's gaining more and more traction, it's embedded into the company and the buy-in is there. A carbon management board has been established along with targets, KPIs, milestones and all the footprinting work has been done. The programme has been broken down into projects with people owning those projects. We've cut carbon emissions by about 11 per cent. Our ambition is to cut that footprint to 50 per cent by 2015 – one of the most stretching targets in Europe.

We have been instrumental in the development of hydrogen fuel cell vehicles. We got together with postal services across Europe to create enough demand to sign agreements with the motor manufacturers to bring mass produced fuel cell vehicles to market by 2014 – a decade ahead of schedule – that's the legacy I'm most proud of. We've already got the first hydrogen post vans outside California. In Stornoway in the Hebrides we're powering an internal combustion hydrogen vehicle using biogas from an anaerobic digestion plant.

What are the big challenges for your organization?

As a government owned company we are not cash rich – we have a high turnover but a relatively low profit margin. This means that, to make a substantial investment in modernization or sustainability, the business case has to stack up. We use McKinsley's marginal abatement cost (MAC) curves to inform what we invest in. This means we avoid whimsical trends and fads in favour of what gives us most bang for our buck.

Another challenge is the changing nature of our business. The 'postie' is no longer carrying many letters as fewer people write to each other, but they are struggling with bags of CDs and books. This means we are having to deploy more vans and fewer bicycles due to the weight and bulk of the parcels – which pushes up our carbon footprint.

What's your advice for others in your position?

Tenacity. Don't take no for an answer and don't ever give up.

You have to be creative, for example in joining forces with other organizations as we did with fuel cells, or by innovative financial agreements with banks.

People will often tell you that things are not possible when they actually are. You need to be a fifth columnist and get in there and shake it about a bit.

Green Business Models

New Ways of Doing Business

The most radical green business option is to develop innovative new business models that are intrinsically green, either to replace a conventional product/service or to facilitate greener behaviour in your customer base. For example, the rise of the MP3 player and online music sales has slashed the carbon involved in creating and distributing (and wasting) CDs.[1] Car clubs reduce the numbers of cars on the road and shift the cost away from the purchase price and towards a 'per km' basis.

Such new business models have the potential to cut the customer's carbon emissions by a degree that is often many times the carbon footprint of the business itself. For example the Smart 2020 report estimated that the ICT sector has the potential to save five times its own carbon footprint by the year 2020 by providing low carbon services to consumers, energy infrastructure and business.[2]

Three key opportunities for new green business models are:

- Replacing products with services (for example car clubs, leasing equipment and facilities, chemical management services);
- Replacing products with information (for example MP3s, movies on demand, ebooks);
- Developing novel enabling products (for example renewable energy systems, low carbon fuels, smart meters, control systems) and services (for example eBay, telecommuting technology, videoconferencing).

From Products to Services

A product-service system replaces a physical product with the intangible service the product delivers instead. Is an automobile an automobile, or is it a way to get

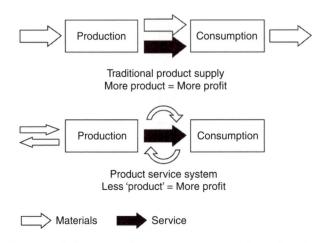

Figure 13.1 *Product-service system vs. a traditional product*

from A to B? Then again, do you really need to get to B, or can you access it remotely from A, via, for example, videoconferencing?

Figure 13.1 shows how, in the traditional take-make-waste linear economy we considered back in Chapter 7, profit is made from the number of products sold. More profit means more material flowing through the economy, so environmental damage is coupled to economic growth, as we discussed in Chapter 6. In a product-service system, profit comes only from the service, whereas any material is a cost borne by the service provider, cutting into their profit margins, so there is a disincentive to use 'stuff'. Therefore environmental impacts are largely decoupled from economic activity.

Product-service systems aren't new and there are many examples of in business and everyday life:

- Libraries lending books, CDs or DVDs – the customer gets the service (story, music, film) and returns the physical artefact to be used by the next customer;
- Demand side management (DSM) was introduced in parts of the US following the 1973 energy crisis. Energy companies were mandated to work with customers to conserve energy, so they were effectively providing an energy service rather than simply selling kilowatt hours;
- Chemical management services (CMS): a complete service for supplying, optimizing the use of and disposing of chemicals. A review of CMS in companies such as GM and Delta Airlines found an average saving of 30 per cent of chemicals;[3]

- Xerox provides a 'per page' copying service in lieu of selling a photocopier. As a result it designs its copiers for remanufacturing and upgrade, saving 1 million tonnes of waste between 1991 and 2007.[4]

Business benefits

The business benefits of product-service systems are:

- The customer avoids capital costs and pays for the service as a revenue instead (as we see below, this benefit is not always appreciated by customers);
- The provider is assured an income stream into the future rather than a single purchase from each customer, building a long-term relationship;
- The service can be continually updated, refined and improved without the expense of upgrading the physical product;
- The provider keeps control over any physical product, which facilitates product takeback (see Chapter 11).

Business risks

In practice, some attempts at delivering product-service systems have failed. We saw in Chapter 11 that InterfaceFLOR developed an innovative floor covering service called 'Evergreen' where they would supply, maintain and dispose of a customer's carpet. Carpet tiles in heavy use areas would be replaced more frequently than those in corners or under furniture. Unfortunately InterfaceFLOR ran up against customer indifference. It appears that businesses are happy to lease mobile equipment such as forklift trucks, but leasing something that is perceived to be a fixture such as carpet is just not on the radar. As we saw in Chapter 4, the Airworx compressed air service failed in the UK, not because it wasn't a great service with lots of benefits, but because UK businesses like to add capital assets to their business to increase their book value.

The risks can be summarized as:

- Customer perception: customers may be used to paying for a product as a capital investment (for example carpets) or see a purchase as a capital investment rather than a cost (for example air compressors). Your customer may simply be unwilling to rearrange their budgets to match the shift from capital to revenue;

- Lack of ownership: in the consumer market many purchases are seen as a lifestyle choice, providing intangible benefits such as prestige, identity and status. A successful businessman may want his executive car to demonstrate his success and a car club will not deliver the same kudos;
- Financial risk: the product-service system transfers financial risk from the user to the provider. The latter must make the investment and take the risk that the long-term revenue streams remain profitable.

Replacing Products with Information

The product-service concept still includes a product, but one that is leased as part of a wider service. The next step is to remove the physical product altogether, by shifting from atoms to bytes. As we have seen, the digital economy gives a huge opportunity for such dematerialization, in the process saving up to five times the carbon that it uses, but also eliminating raw material use and the need for hazardous materials in product production. Examples include:

- Apple's iTunes sells music in an MP3 format without that music ever becoming embedded in a physical object such as a vinyl record or a CD;
- Most cable TV companies now offer 'movies on demand' – the entertainment is provided without becoming a physical product such as a video tape or DVD;
- eBooks give you the information stored in a book without the paper, card and glue. On Christmas Day 2009, eBooks outsold paper books on Amazon.com for the first time;[5]
- Digital cameras remove the need to produce and distribute film and processing prints and slides. The user decides which pictures, if any, are worth printing. This eliminates materials for the film itself, photographic paper and hazardous printing chemicals;
- Smartphones and downloadable Apps are allowing users to buy many functions without purchasing new products. For example, the interviews in this book were recorded using an iPhone App, iTalk, rather than a physical Dictaphone.

The nature of the digital economy means that many of the risks we saw in product-service systems are minimized for digital products. Investment in capital is minimal and many modern physical products (CDs, DVDs, books) go through a digital stage in any case, so the digital product has little or no marginal cost to produce. Customer pull is strong given the hip image of the digital product (for example Apple products), the emergence of the portable multi-functional digital lifestyle device (iPhone and iPad) and the undoubted convenience of purchasing by downloading.

Enabling Products and Services

The shift to a sustainable, low carbon economy is generating demand and opportunities for innovative products and services that enable others to become more sustainable. For example, in Germany the introduction of a Feed in Tariff (FIT), which guarantees householders and businesses a premium price for generating renewable energy, in 1996 has created a renewable energy industry employing 250,000 people.

It's not just the green products/services themselves that present growing opportunities – every new technology requires a raft of supporting services. For example, for electric transport, it is envisaged that the vehicles will interact with a smart charging infrastructure to advise the driver when it is best for them to charge and where they can get the best price (which will vary through the day). As well as delivering that service, someone has to produce, maintain and upgrade the hardware and software. Demand will also grow for specialized breakdown services, emergency service training and servicing for the vehicles themselves. Even legal services companies are finding specialist niches in, say, contracts for renewable energy projects.[6]

There has also been a boom in services that allow individuals or organizations to follow a greener lifestyle or business process. Green consultancy and even low carbon life coaches are flourishing. eBay has created a huge market for second-hand goods – along with its free equivalent, Freecycle. Home shopping takes traffic off the roads (but smarter systems are required to facilitate deliveries as a huge number fail). IT systems allow people to work from home or from other remote locations and to easily interact with colleagues through collaborative working services. The Ethical Superstore helps customers find products that meet their individual environmental and ethical requirements.

Annex 1 lists examples of areas with growth potential and the primary and supporting supply chains required to deliver them to the market. These three lists combine to create a three dimensional matrix of hundreds if not thousands of business opportunities.

Commercial Considerations

To exploit business opportunities in this space requires top level entrepreneurial skills to identify opportunities and exploit them. Too many green entrepreneurs have had the vision but not the business skills to bring a successful product to market. Roy Stanley of the Tanfield Group says:

> *The rules of green business are just the same as any other business – you need a scalable business model in an expanding market. You either have to be able to do it quicker, smarter or better than everyone else or own some intellectual property.*

Vic Morgan of Ethical Superstore says 'If you are coming at business from a green or ethical orientation, then you had better over compensate on the commercial side'. We look at some commercial issues in detail in the following paragraphs.

Markets and marketing

The average iTunes customer does not think of downloading music as 'green behaviour' but as a very convenient way of pursuing their hobby. This chimes with the words of green marketer, John Grant: 'Green marketing is not about making normal look green, but about making green look normal.'[7]

Explicit green marketing works where there is a comparator product, for example I can buy a recycled polyester umbrella at Marks & Spencer, but not at other high street stores, so I shop at Marks & Spencer. But to market, say, a car club where the competition is car ownership, the 'green' angle will only attract a limited number of potential customers. Instead many car clubs actively target families who are considering whether they 'need' a second car by demonstrating how much cheaper and convenient it would be to join the club rather than take on all the running costs and maintenance costs of an infrequently used item.[8] This introduces the service to the mainstream market using 'what's in it for me' marketing rather than aiming for the green niche.

So, even more than for the green products we discussed in Chapter 12, selling innovative green business models is about 'selling the sizzle, not the sausage'. The green angle is unlikely to overcome any qualms about the new way of doing business or consuming, therefore it is advisable to:

- Design the product/service to be desirable in the 'what's in it for me' sense;

- Provide a top quality product/service, marketed strongly;
- Make 'green' the second or third benefit you present to the customer, not the first.

Product portfolios

Established companies will need to consider how innovative business models fit into their existing product portfolio. Innovation brings with it risk and, for some organizations, the PR fallout from failure can damage the rest of the company. Some companies spin out a subsidiary company (for example Airworx) or a joint venture vehicle for high risk products and services so they can be trialled without impacting on the rest of the business and mainstreamed later if the venture is successful.

In the digital economy, there are no rules. Apple used to be a moderately successful hardware and software developer, but now sells huge 'quantities' of electronic music, movies and books via its iTunes store thanks to some innovative (some would say aggressive) vertical integration. At the other end of the scale, many entrepreneurs have exploited the low costs of entry and developed green services from scratch, for example eBay.

Part of the problem or part of the solution?

One issue that will have to be accepted is that, if you develop and deliver a very successful product or service that enables other people to go green, then it is very likely that your own emissions will rise while their emissions fall. For example, the public transport sector will find that their emissions rise if there is a modal shift away from private transport. Likewise a shift to information products will increase the demand for servers and other ICT services. Care needs to be taken here with the green hyenas (see Chapter 4). If your company is promoting itself as green but your own carbon footprint is growing, the hyenas could well pounce on the apparent discrepancy. You will need to have your facts straight and get your argument across robustly. There are two approaches to communicating the big picture (using carbon emissions as an example): (1) expressing the carbon savings elsewhere as well as the carbon emissions from the company and showing the net saving; and (2) using the carbon intensity of the company, i.e. carbon emissions per service delivered, for example passenger kilometres travelled.

Conversely you must not get caught in the trap that, because your overall impact is positive, you start to believe you do not need to improve your own environmental performance. While your business is expanding you still need to work on how those products are delivered. The ICT industry is doing this through virtualization and technological improvements and the public transport industry has been trialling aerodynamic vehicles, alternative fuels and technological innovations such as regenerative breaking on trains.

Chapter summary

1   The pinnacle of green business is to develop innovative business models to deliver sustainability;
2   Three key strategies are: replacing products with services, replacing products with data, and developing new products and services to enable others to go green – there may be more;
3   With innovation comes risk – these new models must be designed to be highly desirable to the customer or consumer;
4   'Green' will probably be the second or third benefit pushed in marketing such products and services, if it is mentioned to the end-user at all.

The View from the Front Line: Vic Morgan, Ethical Superstore

The Ethical Superstore is an online retail business based in Gateshead, UK. The company was established in 2003 and started trading in 2005. In 2009 the company merged with The Natural Collection catalogue business. It also does some wholesaling for independent shops and manages third party online stores for companies such as the Guardian Online. It now has 50 staff and a £6 million turnover. Vic Morgan is the co-founder of the business and has the job title of Chief Innovation Officer, responsible for developing new business and raising capital. He describes the business as 'somewhere between an ethical Amazon and an ethical Costco'.

Why and how did you get involved in this agenda?

I did an MBA at Harvard Business School. During the course I undertook a career profile assessment that identified the three most important values in my life as being altruism, money and independence. This is the classic profile of a philanthropist but I realized I would have to earn money before I gave it away. I worked as a management consultant for a while, which paid off my student loans but my heart wasn't in it. I was always interested in the intersection between business and social issues so a friend and I started an online FairTrade business during the first dotcom boom. Personal reasons brought me to the UK where I started developing e-commerce services for Traidcraft before setting up Ethical Superstore.

What are the business drivers for Ethical Superstore to engage in this agenda?

The Ethical Superstore is a limited, for-profit company, but we really do see ourselves as a business with a double bottom line – the financial and the ethical. Other businesses will have part of their business as ethical such as Cadbury with their FairTrade Dairy Milk bars, but the question is what about the rest of the business? That is not a challenge for us, but it gives us even more responsibility, and some risk, to be true to the ethical side of what we do. We are a very ambitious company and are after very fast growth, which requires a lot of investment. We've raised a little over £2 million of venture capital in the last three years.

The ethical market is worth £30 billion and still growing at 10 per cent per annum. We have three main markets: FairTrade products, organic food and energy efficiency products. The organic market has suffered in the recession, but also due to the sterling/euro exchange rate. This has been more than offset by the boom in FairTrade and energy efficiency markets.

What successes have you had?

We have been growing very fast, 50 per cent a year for four years in a row. While we get customer loyalty due to the warm, fuzzy feeling of shopping ethically, we find that consumers are still price conscious. They see us as an ethical Tesco, where they get competitive prices as well as the ethical standpoint. Natural Collection has won the Observer Ethical Retailer of the Year Award three years in a row.

Online shopping is much less carbon intensive than traditional retailing. We get a good deal from courier firms for deliveries as they don't want to drive an empty van back to, say, London. This backloading makes further carbon savings.

We are very proud to have made the Ethical Superstore what it is today and we're still ambitious for the future. We'd like to see it as a £100 million plus business and would like to then float it as a public company. Currently 5 per cent of our orders are from overseas and we'd like to expand internationally.

What are the big challenges for your organization?

Managing the speed of growth is always a challenge and we would like to grow it to a £100 million business and expand overseas. We have moved premises four times in four years. Running a retail business is expensive – it costs a lot of money to buy and store these products. As a relatively small retailer we cannot afford loss leaders like bigger supermarkets.

Making sure the products we stock are sufficiently ethical is a challenge – stocking the wrong product could really backfire on us. While the checks might appear to be an extra burden, it is more than compensated by avoiding the defensive public relations exercises that mainstream retailers have to undertake to refute allegations about their activities, for example sourcing clothes from sweatshops. We always try to be as transparent as possible and we don't see that as a cost, but rather as a service we provide for our customers.

What's your advice for others in your position?

You have to start breaking all the old rules of business. For example it is traditional not to reveal who your suppliers are, but we do.

If you are coming at business from a green or ethical orientation, then you had better overcompensate on the commercial side. In my first business we recruited people who were passionate about the ethical agenda but were less interested in commerce. Now we do it the other way around – we recruit people who are strong commercially and then school them in our company culture.

Part IV
Making It Happen

Making It Happen

To recap, in Part I we looked at why businesses should go green. In Part II we looked at the big picture in terms of global challenges and solutions, and developed some scenarios for a sustainable economy. In Part III we looked at implementing practical actions to transform a business to form part of that economy, and the strategic commercial context within which those actions would have to take place.

Implementing the higher level practical techniques in Part III will require substantial change to your organization and its business processes. If you successfully reformulate your product or service, or your whole business model, and your supply chain and your internal processes, you will have integrated sustainability into the DNA of the organization. However, this is easier said than done and in Part IV we look at the skills, techniques and systems required to deliver this vision:

- Chapter 14 Overview: derives the requirements for embedding sustainability into your organization, taking a steer from the total quality management (TQM) revolution;
- Chapter 15 Leadership: explores why leadership is essential to green business success and considers some of the key qualities and behaviours required of a green business leader;
- Chapter 16 Strategy: how to break 'the environment' down into themes, set headline targets and adopt strategic principles. It also looks at how to translate strategy into action plans;
- Chapter 17 Stakeholders: considers how to engage and mobilize stakeholders;
- Chapter 18 Management Systems: looks at how to align management systems to facilitate the implementation of the sustainability strategy.

The topics in these five chapters overlap considerably, for example staff issues are covered in leadership (delegation, company culture), stakeholders (staff engagement) and management systems (job descriptions, recruitment, structures). This 'messiness' reflects the holistic nature of sustainability.

14

Embedding Sustainability

Sustainability Maturity Model

Figure 14.1 shows my model of the maturity of sustainability practices in organizations. The ultimate aim is the full integration of sustainability into every part of the business – many of the interviewees in this book refer to sustainability being 'in the DNA of the organization'. The stages don't have to be followed sequentially, on the contrary it is often better to aim for the full integration level from wherever you are at present, avoiding the baggage of the less effective approaches.

As well as providing a conceptual framework, the model has proven to be an excellent way to engage high level staff. I often put it in front of a group of senior executives and get them to discuss where they are on it. There is an interesting psychological effect of doing this – people usually quickly come to the conclusion that they must progress to the full integration level and don't need further persuasion.

The following paragraphs describe each stage in more detail. In practice, most people conclude that in some parts of the business they are at one stage and in others they are doing better or worse. So the stages shouldn't be seen as rigid, but more of a rule of thumb.

Compliance

The first stage is 'compliance' – the traditional business approach to environmental drivers. Companies at this stage will typically only act if a piece of legislation compels them to do so and many will try to dodge the tougher implications of compliance if they can find a loophole. There is no proactive attempt to address sustainability; the attitude is completely reactive.

Some other models of green business have a pre-compliance level, but I take compliance as a given. If you are not compliant with legislation, I strongly suggest you put down this book and go and get compliant.

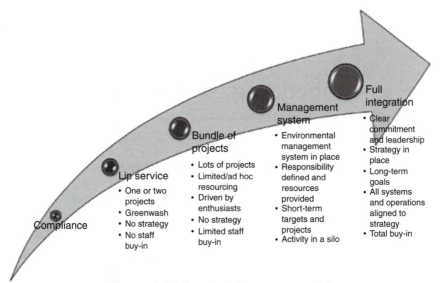

Figure 14.1 *Sustainability maturity model*

All organizations at this level will be at severe risk from the business pressures outlined in Chapter 1, even the smallest. Contrary to popular belief, compliance is an expensive attitude as you will constantly be trying to stay ahead of the hundreds of pieces of legislation that are coming into law while all the time suffering financially from increasing levels of green taxation. As costs rise and clients and customers are picking greener alternatives, reactive companies will be left further behind. Aiming for mere compliance also raises the risk of falling short – more proactive approaches will give you a margin of error against non-compliance, by, for example, eradicating stocks of toxic material.

Lip service

Moving one small step forward, many businesses and organizations simply play lip service to the environment. Typically they have a couple of pet projects that they roll out whenever challenged, or for the annual report. This is effectively a form of greenwash as those projects are an attempt to cover a lack of substantial progress. I find that many people at this stage are fooling themselves into believing they have done their bit.

Companies at the lip service stage are at almost as much risk, if not more so, as those who are merely compliant. Green claims will start to look thin compared to competitors, compliance costs will rise, and employees will become cynical, particularly if they initiated the few projects involved. The worse thing that a company at this stage can do is to try and present their miniscule progress as a selling point – the green hyenas we discussed in Chapter 4 will pounce.

Bundle of projects

The next level I call the 'bundle of projects'. Typically a group of enthusiasts will have formed a committee and put together a substantial number of projects, but there is no strategic buy-in and resources are hard to come by. Staff associated with the committee will have bought into the concept, but most of the workforce will not be aware of its existence.

There is nothing fundamentally wrong with this stage in the short term, in fact it is the typical starting point for generating 'bottom-up' momentum that can result in a breakthrough to leadership. If you are at one of the earlier stages on the model, this is a good place to start properly as it is very action oriented and requires little or no preparation or bureaucracy. You can involve staff with a natural inclination and start to build momentum while simultaneously laying the more strategic plans required for full integration.

Lawyers Muckle LLP started their process in this way, developing a bundle of projects through their Let's Think Green Team, then Julie Parr made a compelling case for more integration during a long car journey with the managing partner. She used the enthusiasm and momentum of the Team, plus the increasing demand from public sector clients as a lever to move towards full integration.

By contrast, I have seen many cases of businesses at this level where the lack of buy-in from senior executives stymies progress on the ground, leading eventually to despair and resentment. If you have a bundle of projects type approach, you must nurture it and let the sapling flourish into a tree.

In the longer term, while the bundle of projects approach can work for smaller companies, companies with a large environmental footprint and a significant investment in capital will find that the bundle of projects will only deliver incremental improvements. Another risk is that they may still find themselves facing rising compliance costs as, without a strategic approach, the projects in the bundle may not cover key issues – for example product issues are rarely addressed at this level.

Management systems

Many businesses, particularly those in the manufacturing sector, will have put together an environmental management system (EMS). Most of these will be accredited to a recognized EMS standard such as ISO 14001.

A management system provides a framework for measuring a baseline, setting targets, actions plans and monitoring results. The formal process of developing a baseline will give a much better understanding of what the company's environmental liabilities are. Resources and responsibilities will be allocated to the action plans and those plans, in general, will get implemented. Emergency procedures and spill kits etc. will be put in place to cover accidents.

The main drawback of the management system level is that, in most cases, 'environment' is usually still seen as operating in a silo. Most staff will see it as someone else's – the environment manager's – job and the business's products, services and processes will rarely change significantly. For example a few years ago I carried out a series of waste minimization visits at manufacturing companies. There was always a point where the environmental manager, who had typically invited me in, realized that the questions I was asking were about cutting waste at source, which was a production issue. There was always an awkward moment when I was introduced to the production manager, who usually took the attitude of 'what are you doing on my patch?' and couldn't wait to get me out of their office as I was 'environmental'. And this was just at the housekeeping level; if we had been trying to implement greener processes or products we would have got nowhere.

Some other risks associated with this stage are:

- It is easy to get stuck here if people start thinking 'we've got the accreditation, what more do you want?' – similar to the self-delusion at the lip service stage;
- Environmental managers often have very little authority compared to their level of responsibility, even within the environmental silo;
- Bringing the formality of a system into play, with all its documentation, processes and meetings, can smother the enthusiasm and drive of the informal bundle of projects teams under a deluge of paperwork.

It is imperative that any EMS is designed and seen as a tool to support green business rather than an end in itself. We look at the use of management systems from a strategic point of view in Chapter 18.

Full integration

The highest level of maturity is where the top management in the organization realizes that, to do 'green' properly, it needs to be integrated into the core functions and processes in the business with total (or near total) buy-in from all staff and other key stakeholders. We're not talking about perfection here, but rather the area beyond the tipping point in the journey where green becomes the norm rather than the exception.

All the executives who have been interviewed for this book are from organizations that are moving towards full integration. Marks & Spencer's Plan A is a great example: championed by Chairman and (then) CEO Sir Stuart Rose, Plan A permeates every part of the business from product design through logistics to advertising. It is pumping through the arteries and veins of the company like adrenaline. Chris Tuppen of BT says he knows that the values of sustainability are embedded into the fabric of the business as spontaneous sustainability projects emerge without the direct influence of his team. Nigel Stansfield of InterfaceFLOR relishes killing off product lines that will hold the company back from their goal of a zero footprint by 2020. Speaking to these executives, you can feel the commitment and the determination to deliver sustainability.

Looking back at the opportunities, threats and risks in Part I, it is clear that to maximize benefits and reduce drawbacks, only the full integration level will ultimately deliver. But it is not an end in itself, merely a platform for continual improvement through implementing the kind of practical actions we saw in Part III.

Lessons from TQM

The Total Quality Management (TQM) movement that flourished in Japan in the 1950s triggered a transformation in the way businesses operate. It certainly transformed the Japanese economy from being associated with cheap low quality products to some of the highest quality manufacturing in the world.

What TQM did was to drag quality out of the quality manager's office and embed it into the fabric of the whole organization. It became everybody's responsibility and a core value of the company rather than a subsidiary issue. There is a clear parallel here with moving from the management systems level of the maturity model to full integration. If we emulate the TQM revolution, we take environment and sustainability out of the environmental manager's office and embed it throughout the organization.

There are two types of change in TQM, known by their Japanese names: kaikaku – big radical changes that align the whole system to deliver quality products, and kaizen – continual, incremental improvements within a system to squeeze the best performance out of it. Kaikaku can be considered as 'doing the right thing' and kaizen as 'doing things right'. By definition, kaikaku has to be planned whereas kaizen can be a mixture of planned and spontaneous change.

So if we apply TQM thinking to sustainability we need to make a series of changes that realign systems to sustainability and create a culture of continuous improvement. It would be virtually impossible and foolhardy to try to make all the necessary kaikaku changes in an existing organization of any size overnight, so it is more realistic to plan a series of step changes over time.

The result is the slightly dangerous looking 'sloping staircase' model (see Figure 14.2). Periodic step changes (kaikaku) align the business to sustainability, for example new cleaner processes, changes to the supply chain, new product development or new business models. Some steps will be to change organizational structures, strategies or investment decision processes to enable further physical changes. Between the step changes are continuous incremental improvements (kaizen) such as good housekeeping, as we saw in Chapter 9, or the minor improvements in purchasing decisions from Chapter 11. Figure 14.2 shows the benefits of this model over simply making incremental improvements that end in diminishing returns.

It is essential that each move upwards must be to a 'flexible platform', i.e. one that allows further progress. 'Cul-de-sacs' are initiatives that, while giving a short-term advantage, eventually lead to a dead end. This particularly applies to capital investments that can lock a business into a particular path for years to come. For example, if a company has invested in a new heating system that was, say, 10 per cent more efficient than its old system, it would very unlikely to

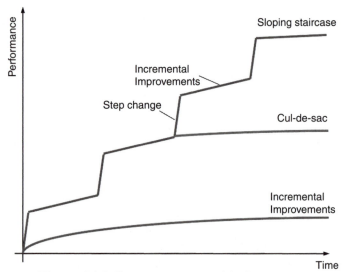

Figure 14.2 *Sloping staircase model of innovation*

rip it out if joining an even more efficient district heating system became an opportunity six months later.

For new ventures, obviously the kaikaku-style alignment of the system to sustainability can be designed in from the beginning. But to keep pace with the cutting edge, future kaikaku and kaizen changes will be required.

How Do We Do This?

So if we want to deliver these radical step changes, develop a culture of continuous improvements and truly embed green into the DNA of the organization, what is required from the company leadership? From the maturity model, the important elements are:

- Leadership and commitment;
- Strategy;
- Stakeholder buy-in;
- Management processes to deliver the strategy effectively.

The following chapters cover each of these elements in detail.

Chapter summary

1 To exploit the opportunities of green business, sustainability must be embedded into the DNA of the organization;
2 Full integration of sustainability into the business means that all processes (physical and managerial) are aligned to sustainability goals;
3 For businesses starting from little/no action, the 'bundle of projects' level of the sustainability maturity model is a good place to start to 'learn by doing';
4 There is a clear parallel between the embedding of 'green' into businesses and the TQM revolution;
5 TQM requires two types of change: big radical realignments of systems to quality (kaikaku) and continual incremental improvement (kaizen). A truly green company will require both these types of change.

The View from the Front Line: Nick Coad, National Express Group

The National Express Group is an international public transport business operating in the US, Spain and the UK. Everyday a million American school kids travel to school on the Group's yellow buses. In the UK the group provides 500 million passenger journeys a year in buses, coaches and trains. The group as a whole employs 40,000 people and has a turnover of £2.75 billion.

Nick Coad is the Group Environment Director. He heads up environmental and corporate responsibility reporting across the Group's devolved management structure.

Why and how did you get involved in this agenda?

I trained as an environmental scientist but never thought I would be able to make a career doing environmental work – the kind of work I'm doing now didn't exist ten years ago. I did voluntary work doing ecology fieldwork in Africa – I joke that I'm basically a failed elephant tracker. I started off as a management trainee where I started doing an MBA but left before completing and did an MSc in Environmental Science instead. I then worked for a couple of environmental consultancies – latterly being at ERMA, working with blue chip companies delivering environmental management systems, environmental impact assessments and air quality assessments. And then I joined National Express.

What are the business drivers for National Express to engage in this agenda?

Initially we focused on three issues – managing risk and liability, improving efficiency and strategic branding and reputation. We needed to get our heads around the environmental agenda. In terms of CSR reporting we weren't doing enough and there was an expectation from our ethical investors to do so. Since climate change has topped the political agenda, we have realized that our core business, public transport, is part of the solution, so it is a huge opportunity for us. So we shifted our focus from internal risk and liability function akin to health and safety, to working with people in sales, marketing and branding.

What successes have you had?

We have had a lot of success in implementing systems for risk and liability and some good performance improvements in terms of efficiency. In the last three years, we've reduced our bus garage energy use by 40 per cent and that of our train maintenance facilities by 25 per cent. Our Anglia trains won a green award in 2007 for reducing fleet energy use by 6 per cent. We have also introduced regenerative braking into our c2c train franchise – a stop/start commuter service – which reduces train energy consumption by 20 per cent.

Externally, we have found our voice. We've punched above our weight in the sustainability debate, getting involved with policy makers, big businesses and customers. Our 'More is Less' position paper was seen as visionary by the trade press and has moved the debate on from the efficiency of transport systems to modal shift.

We have also got involved in the Together campaign run by the Climate Group and the We Will If You Will campaign encouraging sustainable living. We're getting our staff engaged by arranging some home insulation deals.

But there's much more than we can do.

What are the big challenges for your organization?

We are a simple business – we use fossil fuels to move people around. Unfortunately government policy until recently only covered the efficiency of vehicles, not modal shift. Of course a modal shift to public transport will increase the carbon emissions of companies like National Express, but it will cut emissions overall – the gist of our 'More is Less' paper.

We find we are restricted by technology. There is no such thing as a low carbon coach yet – in fact we're finding newer vehicles have a higher fuel consumption than older models. We experimented with hybrid vehicles but they didn't deliver what we needed. We pulled out of trials of biodiesel due to wider sustainability concerns. This was a brave move at the time and made the front pages of the press, but it has been completely vindicated by studies since.

We see the low carbon future as a really exciting, positive future. We would like to reclaim cities from the car using public transport. And we would like to flip the business model for electric cars by combining them with coach services. If you have an electric car, which is limited in range, there is no point running it up a motorway when there are coaches doing that journey. If there were high occupancy lanes on motorways, then we could do that part of the journey faster. You would drive your electric vehicle to a motorway service station, pick up the coach to another service station where an electric hire car would be waiting. As business models change, there are lots of opportunities for us.

What's your advice for others in your position?

You've really got to understand the importance of sustainability to your business. Most CSR efforts will only deliver incremental change, but the low carbon economy requires step changes. You need to work out what those step changes mean for you in terms of opportunities. Then you must take it to the top for buy-in and get it into the strategic planning process. That's the key trick – if it is not in your strategic planning process then it will never be at the centre of your business.

15

Leadership

Leadership is the key factor in attaining the 'full integration' level of the sustainability maturity model. In my experience, most organizations are stuck at the stage of trying to *manage* their way towards sustainability rather than *leading* the way forward. Given the scale of the changes required to deliver a sustainable business, without leadership, strategies will ultimately fail.

Effectively this book is about leadership. Most of it is about how to apply leadership to the organization, but this chapter looks at the personal aspects of green leadership – the qualities, skills and attitudes you need as a green executive to deliver this vast agenda.

Some of the leaders of the businesses featured in this book are high profile, swashbuckling, lead-from-the-front types like Sir Stuart Rose of Marks & Spencer or Ray Anderson of InterfaceFLOR. But many others have proved effective through quiet influence and change with very little fuss. The actual style is down to the organization and the individual, but some key characteristics are essential.

What Is Leadership?

It is worth taking a step back here to consider what leadership means in a corporate environment. Leadership guru Warren Bennis makes the following distinction between management and leadership:[1] management involves power by position; leadership involves power by influence. Bennis goes on to make 12 other comparisons between management and leadership, as shown in Table 15.1.

When you look at the leadership side of each row – innovation, originality, long-term perspective, developing trust, focusing on people – these are key

Table 15.1 *Managers vs. leaders according to Bennis*

Managers	Leaders
Managers administer	Leaders innovate
Managers ask how and when	Leaders ask what and why
Managers focus on systems	Leaders focus on people
Managers do things right	Leaders do the right things
Managers maintain	Leaders develop
Managers rely on control	Leaders inspire trust
Managers have short-term perspective	Leaders have long-term perspective
Managers accept the status quo	Leaders challenge the status quo
Managers have an eye on the bottom line	Leaders have an eye on the horizon
Managers imitate	Leaders originate
Managers emulate the classic good soldier	Leaders are their own person
Managers copy	Leaders show originality

competences required to embed sustainability into an organization, taking it from the management systems level up to full integration. That's not to say that good management isn't required to deliver the end product – it is still an essential part of the mix. We look at the alignment of management functions to sustainability in Chapter 18.

What Makes a Green Leader?

Bennis developed four rules of leadership, as shown in Table 15.2.

Table 15.2 *Bennis' rules of leadership[2]*

In Service of Constituent Needs for	Leaders Provide	To Help Create
Meaning and direction	Sense of purpose	Goals and objectives
Trust	Authentic relationships	Reliability and consistency
Hope and optimism	'Hardiness' (I prefer 'Resilience')	Energy and commitment
Results	Bias toward action, risk, curiosity, and courage	Confidence and creativity

The following sections consider each of these factors from a green leadership perspective.

Sense of purpose

The best organizations have made a true commitment to sustainability. Given the green hyenas we discussed in Chapter 4, the old cliché of actions speaking louder than words applies here as much as in any other field. In Marks & Spencer, Sir Stuart Rose committed £200 million to Plan A before he had any idea what they were actually going to do. The tagline to Plan A 'there is no plan B' makes it clear to stakeholders that there is no going back. Ray Anderson, CEO of InterfaceFLOR, declared his business would have a zero footprint by 2020, and demonstrates commitment by killing off products seen as environmental liabilities. When Apple and Nike walked out on the US Chamber of Commerce in 2009 over its stance on climate change legislation, they made a clear statement: 'The environment is so important it's a showstopper.'

Such commitment is not just for larger businesses. EAE Ltd makes it clear to their staff that a commitment to the environment will help them progress in the company, whereas a lack of commitment could lead to the door. Gentoo have demonstrated commitment by building social housing whose environmental performance way exceeds the requirements of government or the demands of their customers. The Sage Gateshead made a very public commitment to the 10:10 campaign (to cut carbon emissions by 10 per cent by 2010). All of these acts show a sense of purpose.

Trust and authentic relationships

Trust and authenticity are key to your commitment being taken seriously. Andrew Witty, CEO of GlaxoSmithKline, has gone so far as making 'Building Trust' one of the business's five strategic goals. Bennis lists five factors for trust: competence, constancy, caring, candour and congruity (or authenticity).

Regarding authenticity, it is noticeable that almost all the executives interviewed for this book have a personal passion for the environment and sustainability. Sally Hancox of Gentoo says, 'Give responsibility for sustainability to someone with a real passion for it, otherwise it will just disappear into a spreadsheet'; Paula Widdowson of Northern Foods says, 'I believe I've got the best job you could ever have'; Julie Parr of Muckle says, 'It just fits well with me as a person'. Vic Morgan of Ethical Superstore was rated as the classic philanthropist when doing personality tests at business school. This is where the moral imperative we discussed in Chapter 3 comes in – truly believing in sustainability provides the authenticity required.

Conversely, I have heard many tales of chief executives declaring a new green dawn for the company one day and then turning up in a new large gas guzzling company car the next. This destroys the optimism and trust of staff members and partners who are keen on sustainability and feeds the cynicism of those who are unconvinced. If you don't feel it, is this job really for you?

We look at how to engender trust with stakeholders, including staff members, in more detail in Chapter 17.

Hardiness/resilience

EAE boss Glen Bennett had to work with 22 different organizations over two years just to get a modest wind turbine installed on his site. One planning conflict was fought virtually to the death – well, until the planner in question was sacked from the local authority. Bennett then had to fight a media campaign to reverse a business rate rise as the turbine was judged to have raised the value of his site. When he says that a green executive needs to 'be stubborn and bloody-minded', it is an understatement. As we saw above, if you are going to innovate and break new ground then failure is inevitable, so resilience is essential. Others concur: 'stick with it – stickability is the key', says Nigel Stansfield of InterfaceFLOR, 'Don't take no for an answer and don't ever give up', says Martin Blake of Royal Mail, 'The single most important quality for anyone in this game is perseverance', says Roy Stanley of the Tanfield Group.

As we have seen, Marks & Spencer have even made a play of their resilience by advertising the fact they've maintained their green performance through a recession while their competitors (they imply) haven't.

Bias to action

Many organizations have a tendency to suffer from 'paralysis by analysis'. By refusing to act before gathering exhaustive data on the subject (and using that data to write lengthy and hugely detailed positional papers), they get caught up in process and deliver nothing in the way of tangible output. Despite the risks we covered in Chapter 4, a bias to action sets the sustainability leaders ahead of the competition.

Sir Stuart Rose, CEO of Marks & Spencer, committed £200m to Plan A before the programme of activity had been costed – the message was 'we're going to do this, get on with it'. Toon Bossuyt of BOSS Paints advises 'learn by doing'. Glen Bennett of EAE Ltd says 'you shouldn't be afraid to make mistakes'. The bias to action must extend to the whole organization. Paula

Widdowson of Northern Foods says 'We give people permission to act, give them confidence to move forward and allow them to fail until they get it right.'

What You Need to Do

To become a great green executive, you need to:

- Understand the business case as it applies to your business;
- Make and maintain a clear commitment in terms of words, money and action;
- Develop and implement a game changing strategy;
- Align management structures and systems to that strategy;
- Engage stakeholders and create a culture of positive change.

We cover the 'how to' aspects of these points in Chapters 16–18, but first we look at them from a leader's perspective.

Understand the business case

It is vital that you get a good grasp of the business case as it applies to your business. Part I of this book gave a wide range of opportunities and threats that can apply to different business, but you must understand which of these are most relevant to your particular circumstances. Ask:

- What are the key drivers?
- What are the risks of inaction (Chapter 1)?
- What are the opportunities (Chapter 2)?
- What are the risks of action (Chapter 4)?
- What elements of your business are up for change and what must be retained at all costs?

We consider the finessing of the business case for individual organizations in more detail when we cover strategy in Chapter 16.

Make a commitment

Moving from management to full integration requires demonstrable commitment – the sense of purpose we described above. Not just from a single leader either. Given the fact that your company must align all of its systems and processes to sustainability, the commitment ideally comes from everyone who sits around the boardroom table (more on what to do if it isn't there later).

This commitment will manifest itself as follows:

- Public declaration(s); via websites, branding, reports;
- Development and implementation of strategy to meet that declaration (Chapter 16);
- Financial and resource allocations (see Chapter 18) as no budget = no commitment;
- Personal behaviour: you have to be seen to 'walk the talk'.

Public declarations are usually in the form of a written policy (see Chapter 18), most of which are extremely dull and undistinguished – anybody can say they are committed to X, Y or Z. It is more effective to use what management gurus James Collins and Jerry Porras would call a BHAG or 'big hairy audacious goal'[3] such as InterfaceFLOR's commitment to a zero ecological footprint by 2020. Another approach is to integrate goals into everything the company does. Marks & Spencer have used their Plan A goals as branding throughout their stores, making a very public and everyday commitment.

Personal behaviour is a success factor for most leadership issues, but probably even more critical for sustainability. Little things matter and cynics like our green hyenas will leap on small failings such as leaving lights or IT switched on. More proactively, a green business leader should be seen to take part in all sustainability programmes, voluntary projects and engagement programmes. They should also consider demonstrating their authenticity by making a highly visible personal commitment such as cycling to work or installing solar panels at home.

Organizational culture and delegation

Ray Anderson, CEO of InterfaceFLOR, tells a story of how a visitor to one of his factories stopped a forklift driver to ask what the man did. The driver answered 'Ma'am, I come to work every day to help save the Earth.'[4]

A strong buy-in from all staff will help with the implementation of kaikaku style step changes and will lead to organic kaizen improvements. BT's Chris Tuppen says that he knows he has been successful in creating the right culture as sustainability projects spring up in the business spontaneously without his section's input. Richard Gillies of Marks & Spencer says 'devolve responsibility, get everyone involved'. Northern Foods didn't want 'green' to exist solely in a silo, so they deliberately didn't create a green function to ensure it was everybody's responsibility. These examples show the kind of culture change for sustainability that occurred for quality under TQM.

It is important that authority goes with responsibility. I once met with a director of a company that worked across multiple retail sites. At each site responsibility for meeting energy efficiency targets had been given to 'energy champions' who were all junior members of staff. The director wondered why the targets weren't being met. I told them they needed to shift responsibility to the site manager who had the authority to make things happen.

Unfortunately this isn't an isolated experience. Again and again I meet environmental managers who are responsible for reducing waste and energy costs but who have no authority to spend their budget on, say, waste minimization or energy efficiency projects. This is insane. If you want someone to take responsibility, you must give them authority to act.

Conversely, delegation must not dilute commitment from the top. Another frequent problem I find is low or middle ranking managers who have been delegated the job of writing a 'sustainability strategy' and then get no further input or commitment to the results from their superiors. This is not delegation but derogation of responsibility.

Overcoming Internal Resistance

We have seen that going green is not easy and there are many challenges to overcome. We looked at external challenges in Chapter 4, but one of the key obstacles you will face personally as a green executive is resistance from people within the organization. I often say the biggest barrier to sustainability is just 6 inches wide – the space between our ears. This barrier occurs for a number of reasons:

- Anti-green sentiments: to many people the idea of natural limits is anathema to their worldview and, at worst, some pernicious form of communism in disguise;
- Narrow economic focus: 'sustainability is not a business issue and should be left to politicians';
- 'Too busy/not my problem': this is a genuine issue, particularly in middle management where there are many requirements to juggle and adding a new one is often not welcome;

- Limited horizons: 'OK, we've got a recycling system, what more do you want?';
- Fear for the future: while some resistance to change is simply fear of an uncertain future, some of it will be more personal, for example 'old timers' fearing that their skills will be redundant in the new way of working;
- Staff/management friction: staff members and/or unions may feel that sustainability programmes will benefit the upper echelons but not people at the front line.

One very obvious option is simply to get rid of people who do not fit in with the company culture you are trying to create. This is the ultimate sanction, and shouldn't be ruled out, but I recommend more subtle tactics, which I call 'green jujitsu'.

The martial art of jujitsu is founded on the principle of using your opponent's strength against them. You should avoid toe-to-toe confrontation at all costs as you can just get stuck in a stalemate. We look here at four ways of using your 'opponent's' strength against them.

Speak their language

Whether people are anti-green, too narrow in their focus or too busy, a key green jujitsu tactic is to speak their language, not yours. Take care in using words such as 'carbon', 'environment' or 'green' unless they are part of a piece of legislation or taxation. Words like 'energy', 'waste' and 'risk' are more powerful to the ears of the unconverted.

These skills are important even between people who have bought in to 'green'. Richard Gillies of M&S talks about the language barrier between the 'CSR junkies' and the 'economic animals' – while their aims are aligned, it can be difficult to get them on the same wavelength.

Table 15.3 has some suggestions of 'green language' that you might want to avoid for certain audiences and some 'jujitsu' alternatives that might help.

Use questions, not statements

Bold statements of fact to a cynic or sceptic can be like a red rag to a bull. In contrast, asking questions (maybe with a fact embedded in the middle) tends to give you momentum, as questions are less threatening and your opponent has to respond thoughtfully.[5] Make the question directly relevant to your organization, for example:

Table 15.3 *Green and jujitsu language*

Green Language	Jujitsu Language
Green	Waste
The environment	Energy efficiency
The planet	Resource efficiency
Sustainable development	Lean manufacturing
Sustainability	Productivity
Climate change	Return on investment
Global warming	Legislation
Carbon emissions	Pollution
Carbon footprint	Liabilities
Corporate social responsibility	Risk
Community	Energy security
	Savings
	Product differentiation
	Market opportunity
	Hazardous
	Health and safety

- 'Our biggest customer has declared they want to slash the carbon footprint of their supply chain – how do we respond?';
- 'How robust is the business to rising oil prices?';
- 'Do you know that we are wasting £2 million on energy every year?';
- 'How are we going to respond to the EU's latest product stewardship legislation?'.

Asking for help

Asking your opponent to use their wisdom, expertise and knowledge to help develop solutions is a powerful way of obtaining their buy-in. People love to be asked for help and once they start getting their teeth into an issue, they will often start to take more of an interest in the surrounding problem.

If the person is of a financial bent, ask them to help cost the impact of a piece of legislation, or the potential return on investment on energy efficient equipment. If they have an engineering or technical role, find a technical problem for them to help you with, for example reusing waste heat within your site. If they are from the commercial side, ask their advice on how to compete against a rival product or service that is playing the green card in its promotion.

Choose your problem carefully. If it is too simple, they will see through it. If it is insoluble, or the ultimate answer is genuinely 'it's not worth it', you may turn them further from green issues. It has to be something reasonably challenging with a very good chance that the 'correct' answer will make the organization greener.

Guerrilla tactics

If your opponent is powerful, then you may have to work around them. Military history shows myriad examples of where small, determined and resourceful bands of fighters have kept much more powerful armies at bay. Again, the jujitsu principle applies – guerrillas who confront their opponents on a conventional battlefield will lose very quickly.

Building momentum from the bottom up can create a movement that is too powerful to resist higher up. Julie Parr of Muckle LLP set up their Let's Think Green Team in response to staff interest, but when prospective clients in the public sector started asking for more and more environmental information in tenders, she was able to use the momentum created to persuade the managing partner to make it a corporate priority. She did this on a long car journey where she could get and keep his attention. Martin Blake of Royal Mail says 'sometimes you need to be a fifth columnist and get in there and shake it up a bit'.

The usual approach to starting guerrilla activity is:

- Get together a team of interested people – as per the 'bundle of projects' stage on the sustainability maturity model;
- Start developing projects to deliver quick wins in economic savings, engaging staff and winning new business;
- Start making small requests or suggestions to management;
- Repeat and keep building.

Chapter summary

1   Leadership is the key success factor in moving to the full integration level of sustainability;
2   Leadership is the difference between the best in class and the rest, who are generally 'managing' environmental affairs;
3   The key leadership qualities of a sense of purpose, trust, hardiness and a bias to action, are all required to deliver sustainability;
4   The green leader needs to understand the business case, make a commitment, set a strategy, create the right culture for change and walk the talk;
5   Overcoming internal resistance is a key skill for delivering sustainability. Green jujitsu techniques can go a long way to bringing people on board.

The View from the Front Line: Glen Bennett, EAE Ltd

EAE is Scotland's largest leaflet marketing company. It distributes 'what's on' type leaflets and publications to thousands of information racks across Scotland. The company has a permanent staff of 45 and takes on a further 15 temporary staff every summer. CEO Glen Bennett founded the company in 1987 and its main base is situated in Loanhead on the outskirts of Edinburgh.

Why and how did you get involved in this agenda?

It fits with my personal values. My parents grew up in the post-war era of frugality and hated waste – I remember recycling glass as a child back in 1972. They were also great outdoors fanatics – my father was a scout leader.

When I started my own business I decided I wanted to bring this belief set into the values of the organization.

What are the drivers for EAE to engage in this agenda?

Apart from my own philosophy, the two big drivers are costs and PR. We prioritize the latter as we've always striven to be a market leading, cutting-edge company and we see our environmental performance as proof of this.

We have won major tenders where the deciding issue has been our environmental performance. Having a wind turbine is a much better demonstration of that performance than ticking a box to say we have an environmental policy. So we often take options without a direct economic return as the PR benefits outweigh the costs many times over.

What successes have you had?

We started with a free environmental audit from the Business Environment Partnership (a Scottish business support organization). This gave us a good baseline and a clear action plan to work from. It also uncovered a major water leak under our front drive that we've now fixed.

We installed a 6kW wind turbine inside our front gate. This supplies 50 per cent of our electricity and charges our electric forklift overnight. We are in the process of purchasing an electric van for urban deliveries in Edinburgh. This will also be charged overnight by the wind so it will be truly zero emissions. Currently our excess electricity spills for free into the grid – under current regulations it would cost too much to sell it!

To try and cut fuel consumption, we now have trackers on all our vehicles to cut out unauthorized use and use software to design efficient rounds. Our drivers have gone through eco-driving training.

We recycle about 95–97 per cent of our waste and have shifted to duplex printing which has cut our paper use by 30 per cent. We have a strict 'switch it off' policy and altered our IT back-up system to work at the end of the day rather than the middle of the night, which allows a full power down of personal computers.

We have put the grassed area of our site over to a wildlife garden. This includes a compost heap for recycling all our kitchen and garden waste.

We were awarded the Business Environment Award by Midlothian and East Lothian Chamber of Commerce in 2008 and a Gold Green Tourism Business Award in 2009. This was a great endorsement as we didn't apply for it, we were nominated by someone else which shows how respected our efforts are.

What are the big challenges for your organization?

The number 1 challenge has been bureaucracy. It took us two and a half years to get our wind turbine installed and we had to work with 22 different organizations to do it. Many were not up to the job – one planner asked what 'kWh' stood for, another tried to kill the project at the last minute for noise testing. Then, as soon as it was installed, we were hit with a business rate increase as the turbine counted as a business improvement! That levy has now been removed, but only after we ran a media campaign to point out the stupidity of the situation.

Another problem is that many equipment suppliers are boffins and enthusiasts rather than business people. They don't understand that whatever happens, we need to run our business.

Internally we have had to change attitudes. One of our management team made it very clear he had no interest in all of this – he is no longer with the firm. Some of our drivers are real petrol heads and are resistant to the idea of an electric vehicle. Others objected to our vehicle tracking system, but newer staff members take it as a standard part of the job.

What's your advice for others in your position?

You have to be a bit of a maverick to make things happen. Be stubborn and bloody-minded. It can be daunting when you start but you have to do one thing at a time, do it properly and move on to the next. We found it very useful to get an external set of eyes to come in and do an audit – this gave us an action plan of how to move forward. And of course, you shouldn't be afraid to make mistakes.

16

Strategy

Overview

In Chapter 14 we saw that one of the key requirements of full integration was a long-term sustainability strategy embedded into the company's long-term business strategy. If the two strategies exist side by side then the former will always be the poor cousin of the latter. As Nick Coad of National Express says, 'That's the key trick – if it's not in your strategic planning process then it will never be at the centre of your business.'

Some organizations give their strategy a brand name of its own, for example Plan A from Marks & Spencer or Mission Zero from InterfaceFLOR. Alternatively others incorporate the green agenda into the existing corporate culture brand, for example, The Northern Way at Northern Foods or kyosei at Canon.

Looking back at our sloping staircase model in Chapter 14, the strategy will provide the framework for planning and delivering the step changes, and facilitating and enabling the incremental improvements.

Timescales

So how long is long term? For Marks & Spencer, the timescale for Plan A was seven years. By contrast, InterfaceFLOR has been committed to hitting their zero footprint by 2020 since 1994, so there is quite a range. Choosing a timescale is highly dependent on the type of business you are in and your organizational culture. Some sectors can reinvent themselves in a couple of years if not months (for example smart phones, web 2.0) whereas others take decades to transform due to the capital already invested in existing infrastructure and the fresh capital required to effect the change (for example the energy sector).

When working with clients I usually recommend five to ten years for sustainability strategy development. Looking forward less than, say, three years tends to result in tactics rather than strategy – for example the good housekeeping efforts we saw in Chapter 9 – as the group focuses on current concerns and economic conditions. Innovation in terms of product ranges, building new supply chains or reorganizing distribution networks can be visualized, planned, implemented and completed in the five year plus time frame. However, looking ahead longer than ten years can remove the personal link and feeling of responsibility as many staff will either have retired or will expect to have moved to another organization. Too long a time frame can also lead to too high a reliance on technological advances – 'we'll all be flying solar powered hover cars by then, job done'.

Before You Start

There are three things you need to understand – the current state of your business (i.e. the baseline), the unfolding business, political, social and technological landscape, and the business case for sustainability as it applies to your business.

Developing a baseline

Getting a good understanding of what your business does, how it does it and how it relates to sustainability is an essential first step. A baseline should cover all aspects of your business upstream and downstream of your organization. It should be made up of both quantitative data and qualitative information, such as:

- The company's current mission, values and purpose;
- Environmental baseline (carbon footprint, product lifecycle assessment, other environmental parameters – see Chapter 18);
- Operations: capital equipment (age, performance, value), process flow, risks drawbacks;
- Supply chain: key supplies and suppliers, reputations, risks and liabilities;
- Product/service: lifecycle performance indicators, sacred cows;
- Staff: age profile, diversity, culture, skill sets, engagement;
- Customers and/or clients: preferences, reputation;
- Branding: position in the market(s), public perception of the organization;
- Views of external stakeholders (regulators, non-governmental organizations etc.).

The landscape ahead

The second element is to look at the unfolding future landscape and consider how it might change over the timescale of your strategy. I use the following extended PESTLE analysis (I've added a C for commercial at the end):

- Political: how is the political landscape evolving in the countries and regions where you operate? What strategies have governments and key regional and local authorities got in place?
- Economic: as well as usual suspects like economic growth, interest rates, exchange rates and the inflation rate, you need to consider how the environmental agenda might affect the economic system (for example oil prices rising due to peak oil, insurance premiums rising under climate change);
- Social: what demographic changes are affecting you? What is coming in and out of fashion? What ethical issues are emerging?
- Technological: what emerging technological developments may effect your business or provide opportunities?
- Legal: in what direction is legislation moving? What issues are likely to become more strictly regulated?
- Environmental: what environmental impacts will directly affect your business? For example, resource issues such as supply of fish or wood, or impacts such as more frequent flooding, more severe storms and sea level rises under climate change;
- Commercial: what are your customers demanding now? How is this demand likely to evolve? What new markets are evolving? How are supply chains changing? How are your competitors responding to the challenge?

Exploring the business case

The third step for the strategy team is to take the baseline and the unfolding landscape and explore the business case for your business. Try asking the following questions:

- What are the risks of inaction (Chapter 1)?
- What are the key drivers (Chapter 2) – personal, costs, customer demand, branding, staff demand, risks?
- How do corporate values impact on your business (Chapter 3)?
- What are the strengths of your business that you must maintain?

- What can be sacrificed?
- What are the risks of going green (see Chapter 4)?

It is essential to understand how the generic business case outlined in Part I applies to your business. For example, if you look at many business support organizations' literature, it tends to start and finish with the message 'save energy, cut waste, save money'. This is indeed true, but it is very short-sighted and frankly dangerous as it limits thinking to measures that will provide a direct economic benefit. Most service sector organizations will not save an appreciable amount of cash compared with their turnover or profit margin. The benefit for these companies is in branding and winning new business. Cash savings are a large distraction to these companies. Manufacturing industries and other resource intensive businesses can save significant sums of money and boost their profits. But if they use cost as the sole measure of success, they will miss out on the wider PR and marketing opportunities. For example, BT may have saved £100 million in 2009 through sustainability, but it also helped bring in £1.9 billion of work in the same year.[1] So BT could have made a loss on the direct return on investment and still made money out of sustainability.

Developing a Strategy

A sustainability strategy provides the framework for making the following decisions: what are we going to do in the future and what are we not going to do?

The second of these is often forgotten, but legacies can hold companies back and can be a hostage to fortune on the PR side. For example, in BP's ill-fated 'Beyond Petroleum' rebranding, the backlash came because, while BP may have been investing renewable technology (now divested again), it was not moving away from fossil fuels.

Figure 16.1 shows the elements of a generic sustainability strategy. To integrate a sustainability strategy into your main business strategy you should adapt this to your organization's standard template, unless of course that template requires changing to make room for sustainability. The four elements are:

- The mission giving the overall goal;
- Strategic principles: these produce the overall shape of the strategy;
- Strategic themes: these are the elements that will be addressed;
- Headline goals for each theme.

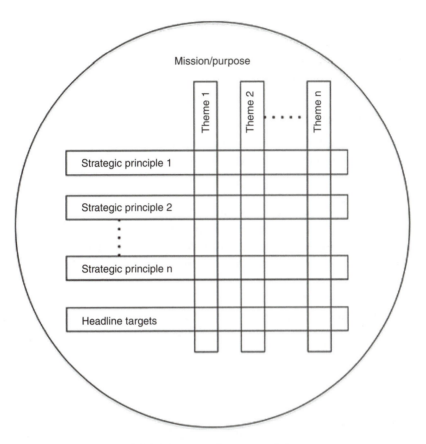

Figure 16.1 *Elements of a sustainability strategy*

We consider each of these in turn.

The mission

The mission, or purpose, should succinctly define what the strategy is trying to achieve. A compelling mission is required to enthuse others about the task ahead – and will give you a yardstick against which to compare any difficult decision. InterfaceFLOR's Mission Zero is clear and ambitious, a zero ecological footprint by 2020. Marks & Spencer's Plan A tagline forms a compelling mission: 'There is no Plan B'.

The sustainability mission must align with the mission, values and principles of the company as a whole. Conversely those elements may change to incorporate sustainability. Procter & Gamble changed their statement of purpose to incorporate sustainability by appending six words to the end: 'We provide branded products and services of superior quality and value that improve the lives of the world's consumers, *now and for generations to come.*'

Strategic principles

The strategic principles define the framework within which action will take place. Here are some candidate strategic principles that you can consider for your organization:

- Tackle the big issues first: this may seem obvious, but it can be more complex than it first appears. For many companies, the lifecycle impacts of their products are either upstream or downstream of 'the factory fence' – are they going to prioritize internal improvements or lifecycle improvements?
- No trade-offs: having struggled to sell a 'green product range' in the 1990s, Procter & Gamble now has a strict 'no trade-offs' rule – a product has to perform on performance, value and sustainability;
- Problems are opportunities: InterfaceFLOR turned a potential economic loss from installing solar panels at a factory into a new product 'Solar-Made carpet', which landed a contract worth 20 times the cost of the panels. This is where understanding the business case really comes into its own;
- Creative destruction: InterfaceFLOR deliberately kills off product lines (over 30 to date) that stand in the way of their Mission Zero goal, whether they are profitable or not;
- Innovation: whether it is new processes, new products or new business models, how much is the business prepared to innovate to develop solutions? Or should the focus be on greening what is already there?
- Be part of the solution: some businesses may be, or could be, part of the solution as much as they're part of the problem, i.e. if they provide enabling solutions to others (see Chapter 13). This requires a different strategic mindset to a company that simply wants to be 'less bad';
- Revolution vs. evolution: some businesses dive in at the deep end (revolution) for example InterfaceFLOR and Marks & Spencer, while others are building up their sustainability programme organically (evolution) for example Procter & Gamble and Royal Mail. Pick whichever suits your company culture;

- Learn by doing: BOSS Paints, Northern Foods and EAE Ltd have taken an action-based approach to their strategies – they're not afraid to make mistakes.

It is important to choose some of these or develop similar principles in order to give action plans and decision makers strategic direction. Principles should be allowed to evolve with time as experience feeds back into the strategic process.

Strategic themes

As well as adopting strategic principles, you will need to break the sustainability agenda down into broad strategic themes to give the problem some focus. These should be chosen to address the key issues emerging from the baseline and horizon scanning activities. As a guide, the strategic themes of three major companies are listed in Table 16.1.

The themes in Marks & Spencer's Plan A are defined by sustainability topic for example climate change, waste and health. Procter & Gamble has taken a different approach to their themes, focusing on company activities such as developing green products and engaging employees. InterfaceFLOR uses a

Table 16.1 *Example strategic themes*[2]

Marks & Spencer	Procter & Gamble	InterfaceFLOR
1 Climate change performance	1 Delight the consumer with sustainable innovations that improve the environmental profile of our products	1 Zero waste
2 Waste performance		2 Eliminating emissions and effluent
3 Sustainable raw material performance	2 Improve the environmental profile of our own operations	3 Renewable energy
4 Fair partner performance	3 Improve lives through our social responsibility programmes	4 Closing the loop: recycled or renewable materials
5 Health performance	4 Engage and equip all employees to build sustainability thinking and practices into their everyday work	5 Making transport resource efficient
	5 Shape the future by working transparently with stakeholders to enable continued freedom to innovate in a sustainable way	6 Sensitizing stakeholders
		7 Redesigning commerce

mixture of sustainability topics (for example waste, energy) and activities (redefining commerce, sensitizing stakeholders).

Whichever approach you take, it is important that these themes do not become silos as many of the best solutions straddle themes. To take Diageo's bioenergy project as an example, the company took one problem – liquid effluent with a high organic content – and turned it into a source of renewable energy using anaerobic digestion. If they had strictly segregated wastewater treatment and energy into different silos, the solution may never have been identified.

Headline goals

Headline goals make the aspirations above concrete and tangible. Many organizations set incremental goals, for example a 2 per cent improvement in energy efficiency year on year. However, more and more are finding that these promote a focus on incremental improvements rather than the step changes we discussed in Parts II and III. So more and more companies are setting stretch goals, for example Diageo switched in 2007 from a year on year target to a stretch target of cutting carbon emissions by 50 per cent by 2015. This manifested itself in a change in focus away from incremental improvements to developing its large-scale bioenergy projects to convert waste effluent to energy. These projects will hit the stretch goals but their lead times mean that they would have missed the old incremental goals in the interim.

The most impressive of the stretch goals is InterfaceFLOR's goal to have a zero ecological footprint by 2020, but such a goal can sometimes frighten people into passive inaction. A solution is to have an extremely ambitious stretch target to set the endpoint and an intermediate goal or goals to provide a stepping stone to get there.

Setting the Wider Agenda

So far, our strategy has only considered the direct sphere of influence of your business. Often you will find that your strategic ambitions are limited by the wider political, economic and commercial circumstances within which you operate. While some of these restraints can be overcome by clever innovation and marketing, you may find that you need to change those factors. This can be undertaken as a lone crusade or in collaboration with other organizations.

Opportunities to change the wider agenda include: calling for stricter legislation; campaigning to remove perverse incentives; and reframing the argument.

Calling for stricter legislation

The traditional approach of industry to new legislation is to complain about its financial impacts. So it is always surprising (and newsworthy) when a commercial company calls for stricter environmental legislation. In 2009, airlines such as British Airways, Air France-KLM, Cathay Pacific and Virgin Atlantic called for a global cap and trade scheme to force the industry to take greener technologies.[3] This kind of intervention gives governments room to act and can shame reactive companies into silence.

This tactic has two main benefits for the business: (1) it positions the company as proactive and willing to change in the eyes of external stakeholders; and (2) if the legislation is implemented, it will reward greener companies and punish less green rivals, creating further competitive advantage for the former.

Campaigning against perverse incentives

There are structural obstacles in many economies to sustainability. For example there is no tax on airline fuel, making it relatively cheap compared to less polluting forms of transport such as rail. Often the regulators will either not understand that regulation can be an obstacle to progress or the problem legislation is outside their particular silo.

Such campaigns are not restricted to larger organizations. EAE Ltd successfully got their local authority to remove a business rates hike imposed on their site as their wind turbine was deemed a site improvement. UK renewables company Solar Century has been campaigning for years to remove unfair advantages they perceive as helping their larger fossil fuel-based energy competitors, for example government energy strategies that assume oil will remain cheap compared to renewables.[4]

Reframing the argument

National Express produced its 'More is Less' position paper to reframe the argument over how to reduce transport emissions in the UK. Up to that point the government had focused on reducing the carbon footprint of each type of transport, rather than encouraging a modal shift from high carbon transport (air, private car) to low carbon modes (train, coach). The company has won recognition from the government that such a modal shift is essential to deliver the UK's carbon reduction targets, but that it will necessitate an increase in emissions in the public transport sector to deliver the wider cut.

This is a great example of how a company can change the whole landscape within which it operates. The downside risk here is that these moves could be seen externally as self-serving and/or a form of greenwash. Care must be taken that the argument is genuine and backed up with hard data.

From Strategy to Action Planning

So we've looked at how we can develop a strategy that will both direct internal programmes and influence external factors. Now we're going to look at how to convert that strategy into action plans. Broadly speaking, there are two main techniques: planning forwards (forecasting) and developing a vision of the future, then working backwards (backcasting).

Forecasting

The forecasting approach is the one most people take in planning – working out which way the trends are going and trying to 'bend the trend' to hit the target (see Figure 16.2).

A typical forecasting approach would be:

- Carry out a baseline analysis of the strategic themes (this may be more detailed than the strategic baseline);
- Develop a set of targets and/or objectives;
- Develop a list of potential interventions;
- Assess the cost/benefit of each intervention to determine a priority list;
- Add more interventions if the list does not add up to the target;
- Analyse actual progress during implementation and revise the plan where necessary.

Marks and Spencer's Plan A is a good example of this approach. The sustainability team sat down with a range of other stakeholders to develop a list of 100 commitments that they felt would cover all angles from their strategic themes from in-store energy use to animal welfare. As the project moved into

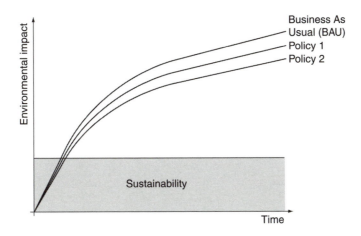

Figure 16.2 *Incremental policies resulting from forecasting*

the implementation phase, a further 24 commitments were added to the original list.

The advantages of forecasting are that it is simple, quick, flexible and responsive to 'learning by doing'. The disadvantage is that the focus on the present means that step changes we require under the sloping staircase model are less likely to come under consideration and driving up a cul-de-sac is more likely.

Backcasting: Starting at the end

To escape 'the tyranny of the present' and avoid cul-de-sacs, you need a vision of where you want the business to be in the future. Then you can work backwards to today, working out which steps you need to take when. Barriers and current trends will then only influence the pace and initial scale of the transition, not its direction. This approach is known as backcasting.[5]

Backcasting sets up desirable future scenarios and then attempts to map policy paths back to the current situation (see Figure 16.3). The benefits of backcasting are that it is:

- Strategic: policies are developed with a long-term view;
- Holistic: policies are developed in compatible packages rather than as individual initiatives;
- Proactive: the focus is on a desirable outcome rather than trying to buck trends;

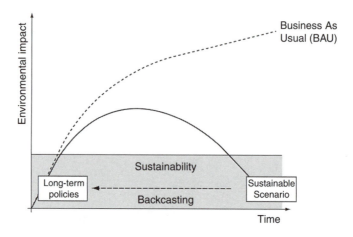

Figure 16.3 *Setting sustainable future norms with backcasting*[6]

- Participative: backcasting is highly suitable for engaging a range of staff and possibly other stakeholders in the strategy process;
- Radical: along with the use of stretch targets, backcasting promotes innovation and creative thinking.

The disadvantages are that it could possibly lock the company into a path that is inflexible to unforeseen events, and of course it takes more work before the strategy can be implemented. However, there is nothing wrong with a twin track approach – forecasting in the short term to achieve quick wins while the backcasting process develops a medium-/long-term action plan.

The following steps are involved in backcasting:

- Develop a set of idealized scenarios outlining different approaches to meeting the headline goals;
- Develop the detailed baseline for each theme;
- Determine the steps required to meet each scenario, i.e. define the steps required on the staircase model, avoiding cul-de-sacs;
- Identify policies, projects and action plans to start the company along the strategic path from the current position;
- Assess each scenario's solution against cost, risk, business opportunity and/or any other assessment criteria and choose the best options.

The backcasting approach lends itself to a collaborative, brainstorming approach. The development of scenarios, strategic paths and projects is best performed in multidisciplinary workshops. This has other advantages, in particular it brings more key staff and stakeholders into the process, improving their understanding and securing their buy-in.

Chapter summary

1 To deliver sustainability you need a long-term environmental strategy integrated with your core business strategy;

2 The strategy is the framework within which your organization develops action plans, makes decisions and assigns resources;

3 Before you start, you need to carry out a baseline analysis, develop a feel for the unfolding landscape and get a good understanding of the business case as it applies to your business;

4 A strategy should consist of a mission, strategic principles, strategic themes and headline goals;

5 Stretch goals stimulate innovation much more than incremental goals;

6 You may have to influence the wider sustainability agenda, including changing government policy, in order to get the most out of your strategy;

7 There are two main methods for developing action plans from the strategy: forecasting and backcasting. The former is fast and flexible, the latter radical and stretching.

The View from the Front Line:
Surrie Everett-Pascoe, Canon Europe Ltd

Surrie Everett-Pascoe is the CSR, Environmental and Product Safety Director for the European strategic headquarters of Canon, the global imaging and optical products giant. Surrie's responsibilities cover strategic and operational environmental issues including compliance with Canon's global ISO 14001 EMS.

How and why did you personally get involved in this role?

I've had three different careers within Canon. I qualified as a company secretary and became the Group Secretary and Head of Legal, before moving into project and change management. Then I was asked to move into a new position as UK environmental manager. No one had done this role before so I saw it as a great challenge to get it up and running. My next thought was, 'I'm a business person in an environmental role' so I went out and got an IEMA [Institute for Environmental Management and Auditing] accreditation so I would know what I was talking about.

   In less than five years I was promoted into the European Director's role and that's been another new challenge. While environmental issues are not new to Canon, it was a relatively new organizational set up and I have had to create a new team.

What are the drivers for Canon to engage in this agenda?

Canon has a global philosophy of 'kyosei', which translates as 'living and working together for the common good'. This has been Canon's policy for a very long time so the environmental angle has always been there – it is not just jumping on the green bandwagon, it's actually embedded into the corporate philosophy. We have a very strong global brand and we want to demonstrate strong corporate citizenship. We're doing these things because they're right for the environment and right for our business – a win–win.

What are the big challenges for your organization?

We have a global ISO 14001 environmental management system, so one site could cause us a problem. This is a high risk strategy and I think it's a real measure of the commitment that Canon Inc has made.

   In the current (mid-2009) economic climate it can be difficult to find the budget for environmental projects. When the economy is buoyant and we're making lots of profit, it is easier to divert some of that profit into longer term projects.

A big challenge is to motivate middle management. The top level management can be committed, the general staff can be committed, but middle management have sales targets, costs targets, an organization to run and we're saying, 'in addition to all that we want you to do these things as well'. There are ways around this: incentives, making it part of their job role, part of their objectives and finding keen green champions to take the agenda forward.

What successes have you had?

I would like to see Canon as market leaders in green initiatives. We have done a lot of work in many areas – our products are very advanced, in some cases using less than 80 per cent energy in use than previous versions; consumer products such as cameras are smaller and use less material; and we've launched a green calculator made from recycled material from photocopiers. At every stage of the product lifecycle we're improving all the time.

Operationally we've got the global ISO 14001 standard and our European company car policy will reduce vehicle emissions by switching to efficient models.

In Japan, Canon Inc has installed co-generation plants at our factories, changed the whole production line to efficient cell manufacturing and we've changed the logistics systems to save carbon emissions.

What's your advice for others in your position?

Focus on what is good for the business – identify what are the minimum things you must do and then what are the things that will have biggest benefits for the organization.

Mobilizing Stakeholders

Stakeholders

On our maturity model of sustainability, the full integration model requires total (or, more realistically, near total) buy-in from stakeholders. It is often said that stakeholders own the reputation of the business – certainly no amount of spend on PR can overcome a bad repute. Having good stakeholder relationships has many benefits:

- Protecting the brand and hence market share;
- Going further, it can enhance the brand and improve market share;
- Developing a broader and deeper understanding of key sustainability issues that the company needs to tackle; these may not be apparent from within;
- Encouraging and stimulating innovation through collaborative working and sharing of ideas;
- Building goodwill that can buffer the company's reputation from long-term damage if things do go wrong.

Trying to develop and implement a sustainability strategy without, at the very least, taking into consideration the views of stakeholders is foolhardy. In this chapter we look at how to engage stakeholders effectively.

Types of stakeholder

A stakeholder is any person or group of persons with an interest in your business. In environmental terms, stakeholders include:

- Staff;
- Shareholders;
- Customers;
- Suppliers;

- Supplier's employees;
- Collaborators, associates and partners;
- Regulators and government;
- Non-governmental organizations and pressure groups;
- Local communities;
- Communities local to suppliers;
- Sectoral organizations.

Stakeholder attitudes and conflict

Attitudes towards the environment and concepts such as sustainable development vary across a wide spectrum. As in any relationship, it is important to understand the other party's point of view or 'where they are coming from' to build mutual respect. Conversely, completely different attitudes to the same problem or issue often cause conflict and rancour. So it is worth considering different attitudes to sustainability.

Some social scientists use the model in Figure 17.1 to categorize beliefs about society and nature, each belief being defined by the degree of equality and individualism. The model uses a small ball on a surface to represent the state of the environment. If the ball is moved a small amount (an environmental impact), then it will either stay where it is (another stable state), return to its original position (i.e. it is resilient to change), or drop off the model (ecological disaster).

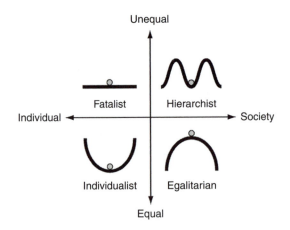

Figure 17.1 *Attitudes to the environment and sustainability*[1]

The four attitudes are:

- Individualist: individualists believe the environment is benign, robust and there to be exploited. They have an abundance mentality, believing that resources are effectively infinite and you can use as much of them as you want. They believe in jam today rather than jam tomorrow. They believe that environmental risks are generally overstated and will ignore data that contradicts their view. This is the typical belief of free marketeers and so-called 'climate change deniers'.
- Hierarchist: hierarchists believe the environment is there to be exploited but has to be protected to remain within limits. It is the typical approach of governments and public sector bodies. A hierarchist believes that analysis is key – everything (impacts, risks etc.) can be measured and that the results of an assessment are the right results.
- Egalitarian: egalitarians believe that the environment is fragile and requires protection. Environmental damage must be minimized at all costs. They believe that risks are understated and will ignore any evidence to the contrary. This is the typical approach of environmental pressure groups.
- Fatalist: fatalists believe that the environment shifts from one state to another, but no state is any better or worse than any other. Fatalists feel they have no power over their lives. The environmental debate passes them by.

Conflicts are usually caused by different perspectives on a problem and nowhere can this be seen more clearly than when it comes to the interaction between corporations and environmental pressure groups. Arne Naess, the late Norwegian philosopher and founder of the deep ecology movement, gives a great theoretical example.[2] A developer and a protest group are in conflict over a proposed new road that will cut through a forest. The protest group (egalitarian) see the forest as a unified entity and when they talk about 'the heart of the forest' they are not talking about its geometric centre, rather its soul. The developer (individualist) sees trees of certain economic and ecological value and has calculated that the width of the road will have a negligible impact on the overall number. As a concession to the protest group they offer to avoid the centre of the forest if that is what is important to them (a hierarchist offer). The protest group snorts in derision.

This illustrates the mismatch between the values of each group and the misunderstanding of the deeper meaning of the language they are using. This is both a risk of working with outside bodies and a potential benefit. If you can work to truly understand the perspective and values of the other organization it will give you a richer understanding of the problem you are jointly trying to solve.

When to engage stakeholders

There are different types of stakeholder engagement, for example:

- General relationship maintenance;
- Specific problem solving;
- New project/venture consultation.

Some formal processes such as environmental impact assessments (EIAs) require stakeholder engagement at set points. Otherwise the general rule is that engagement should take place as early in a process as possible so the results of the engagement can have a meaningful influence on decision making.

Effective Stakeholder Engagement

Trust

Trust is key to good stakeholder engagement or any relationship for that matter, yet trust is often taken for granted. Many of us will have volunteered for some form of consultation in the past where the residual feeling was that we had been used simply to tick a box somewhere and the key decisions had already been made. This kind of breach of trust can turn stakeholder engagement from a potential opportunity into a disaster.

Going back to Bennis,[3] the factors affecting trust were:

- Competence: the technical and managerial competence to engage properly and deliver on promises;
- Constancy: that the company can be relied upon to do what it says it will do, even when the going gets tough;
- Caring: stakeholders have to feel that the engagement is meaningful and their welfare is of genuine concern to the business;
- Candour: openness, transparency and honesty, which we discuss further below;
- Congruity (or authenticity), which we covered in Chapter 15.

One trap that many fall into when working with stakeholders is to raise expectations too high. If stakeholders start to believe that they have ultimate say, they will get very angry if and when they are told they can't have what they want. Tell them clearly: 'We are listening to you, but at the end of the day we have to make the decisions, and sometimes we will disagree.'

Transparency

Transparency is fast becoming a crucial sustainability issue. Secrecy undermines trust and, if something is shrouded in secrecy, the natural inclination is to assume things are even worse than they really are. Legislative requirements such as the US Toxic Release Inventory are driving ever greater exposure of information. Many companies including big names like Nike, Gap and Hewlett-Packard are deliberately releasing previously confidential information into the public domain so people can see what the truth is.[4]

Traditional industrial secrecy can actually be a practical restriction on improving environmental performance. For example, if you would like to take part in collaborations to identify and develop industrial symbiosis opportunities (see Chapters 7 and 11), an insistence on non-disclosure agreements from other parties has been known to kill projects completely.

Transparency is a driver to change in itself. If you have a skeleton in your cupboard, don't wallpaper over the door, chuck it out. The Ethical Superstore makes a great play of making their suppliers public, against normal practice in traditional retailers. This drives them to make sure their supply chain is as ethical and green as it can be, and which, in turn, forms a major plank of their market differentiation.

Different levels of engagement

I base my model for stakeholder engagement (see Figure 17.2) on Arnstein's ladder of public participation.[5] Arnstein's ladder is a model of citizen engagement in political and social issues and it is easily adapted for business purposes.

The ladder has the following levels:

- Information provision: objective information is provided to stakeholders so they can see the 'true' picture;
- Consultation: stakeholders are asked for their views on a proposed solution. These views are considered during the decision making process;
- Participation: stakeholders are given an opportunity to take part in solving problems and the proposed solutions are considered as options during decision making;
- Partnership: more formal relationships are formed with stakeholders and they become part of the formal decision making process, finding mutually acceptable solutions through negotiation;
- Delegated power: stakeholders are given decision making powers over a number of issues.

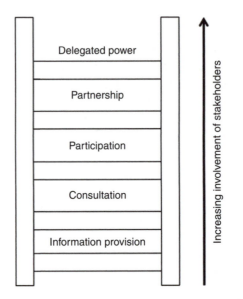

Figure 17.2 *Levels of stakeholder engagement (adapted from Arnstein)*

The appropriate level of engagement can be chosen for each stakeholder depending on the circumstances. The basic principle is that the further up the ladder you go, the richer the engagement for both parties. Some examples include:

- Many companies provide sustainability information in an annual report and through their websites;
- Focus groups may be set up to consult stakeholders' opinions on key priorities for sustainability programmes;
- Staff engagement workshops are used to actively develop solutions to sustainability problems through participation;
- Partnerships may be formed with suppliers to develop new products (see Chapter 11) or with pressure groups to provide a 'critical friend'. For example Coca-Cola and the World Wildlife Fund have formed a partnership to develop sustainable water management for the company's operations in India;[6]
- A conservation group may be given delegated power to manage an area on site for wildlife.

Storytelling

Facts and figures, while important, are intrinsically dull and less than compelling. Many organizations are finding that storytelling is a powerful tool for communicating their vision and engaging stakeholders. For example, rather than saying 'In 2020, we will have reduced our carbon footprint by 35 per cent', it is more inspirational to say:

> *Jane Jones wakes up on 25 May 2020 and, after breakfast with her family and walking her kids to school, she switches on her computer, her daily commute to work a relic of the past. She logs into GreenCorp's highly efficient solar-powered server and starts a web conference with colleagues in the US and Senegal on the new biopolymer the company is developing for the post-oil economy. Afterwards she takes her coffee and laptop into the garden and peruses the latest draft of GreenCorp's five year procurement strategy for eradicating fossil fuels completely from the company's supply chain, tweaking the text on line.*

When I work with clients to create a vision of the future, I often get brainstorming participants to draft the chief executive's introduction to the company report for the year 2020.

Journalistic principles can help communicate with stakeholders. Of particular use are the human interest story – one person's journey to sustainability – and the 'and, finally . . .' quirky news story. When Muckle started sending shredded confidential paper waste to be used as horse bedding, their newsletter headline was 'Reuse of resources and happy horses'.[7]

Feedback

An important way of demonstrating respect for stakeholders is to close the informational loop and provide feedback on how their contribution has influenced decision making or future plans. There are many options, including using annual reports, company newsletters, email bulletins, letters of thanks and special award ceremonies.

Staff Engagement

A particularly important element of stakeholder engagement is to engage staff in the sustainability process. We examine more formal human resource issues in Chapter 18, but this section is about creating the right culture in the business.

Proper engagement is key to the success of sustainability programmes as no matter what new technologies, systems or processes the company introduces, they will be useless unless employees play ball. For example, many companies have invested in teleconferencing facilities, but these are often underused as staff have not made a habit of working in this way. Habit is an important word here; not only do you need to make some kind of intervention to change staff behaviour, you need to reinforce that change until it becomes the norm (see Figure 17.3). Paula Widdowson of Northern Foods works with staff on a change for six weeks as this is as long as she believes it takes to turn new ways of working into a habit.

However, the problems can be very deep-seated. Martin Blake of Royal Mail initially struggled to convince the postal unions to get on board – in fact his first attempt to engage with them ended in a very short and colloquial answer.[8] The union leadership were suspicious that this was simply another job to be given to the workers to make more profits for the management. Blake used some of the green jujitsu techniques described in Chapter 15, but it still took time, patience and charm to persuade them that sustainability was in the interest of front line workers as well as the top executives. Now the unions are proactively involved in the sustainability programme and have become one of its cheerleaders.

Typically, staff engagement programmes have involved activities such as:

- Appointing sustainability champions who will provide information and 'fly the flag' for the sustainability programme;
- Running competitions to set site vs. site or team vs. team to see who can cut energy use the most;

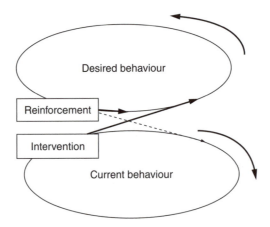

Figure 17.3 *Staff engagement and behavioural change*

- Running awareness programmes such as 'switch it off' campaigns with stickers on light switches and posters.

While these are all effective up to a point, the more effective engagement comes further up the participation model. Engaging staff in developing solutions means that:

- They get enthused about sustainability in general;
- Buy-in for the change is automatic. As staff own the solution, much less effort is required to reinforce new behaviour;
- The process engages the intellectual capital in the organization, leading to better solutions and happier employees.

As with external stakeholders, trust is a key issue for success. It is important that the hard work and contribution to sustainability by employees is met with redoubled commitment from corporate leaders. It is also essential, as we saw in Chapter 15, that the behaviour of the leaders reinforces and doesn't undermine the change being sought.

Chapter summary

1 Engaging stakeholders is a key part of any sustainability strategy;
2 Trust is the key issue in successful engagement;
3 The active involvement of stakeholders in developing solutions will lead to deeper trust, better mutual understanding and stronger relationships;
4 Different people have different perspectives and may need to be engaged differently;
5 The message should be inspiring. Storytelling is one method of making this relevant to all;
6 Staff engagement is critical to the success of sustainability strategies.

The View from the Front Line: Toon Bossuyt, BOSS Paints

BOSS Paints is a family business currently in its third generation of ownership and currently has 19 shareholders from the Bossuyt family. The company manufacturers, distributes and sells paints, providing a complete service with telephone advisors to ensure that customers choose the right colour, buy the right type of paint for the job and use it properly. The company's factory is located near Kortrijk in Belgium and the paints are distributed to professional painters, independent stores and a chain of 36 franchise shops. It employs 230 people and has a turnover of more than €40 million per annum. Toon Bossuyt is Managing Director and one of the 19 shareholders.

Why and how did you personally get involved in this agenda?

I believe that if you run a company you should try to do it in a way that doesn't affect the environment. But we have to be honest that this is not possible yet, but we have to do what we can while still running a profitable company.

What are the drivers for BOSS Paints to engage in this agenda?

Our shareholders want to be proud of the company they own and it is hard to be proud of a company that is very polluting. Shareholders always drive the business and this is the main driver for us to engage.

We have three parts to our mission: producing a quality product, being environmentally friendly and looking after our people. This is what drives us; we believe that if we do all three properly then profit will follow.

What are the big challenges for your organization?

We do get conflicts between our values. For example, our people want big company cars – everyone wants a company car and most people want a big one! We have a policy of modest company cars and policies to reward those who take a more efficient model, but it is not always easy and sometimes we must make a choice between values.

Bringing staff along is a big challenge. I get asked by managers why should we employ an environmental coach when they can't employ an extra person in their department. We have a consensus style of management at BOSS and try to decide things together, so we often have to make compromises.

There can also be a conflict between product quality and environmental aspects. Many customers (paint shops and painters) think solvent-based paint is better quality than water-based paint. We can't just tell them they are wrong and we will only sell water-based paints. But we try to push customers towards the water-based paints and reduce the solvents in the rest. We believe that the end-users of the paints want their paints to be as green as possible, so we think this will change.

Our current policy is to optimize paints for quality. We have had discussions within the family over whether to produce environmentally optimized paints but the market for these is currently too small. What we would like to produce is paints optimized for both quality and the environment.

What successes have you had?

We have significantly reduced our consumption of electricity and water per litre of paint produced. We have a large number of small projects underway to reduce consumption further throughout the factory, looking at lighting, air conditioning and the operation of equipment.

We have 1477 solar panels on the roof, which provide 25 per cent of our power. This was an easy decision to make as we get a return of 10 per cent, which is more than we would get on the stock market. The government subsidizes the investment, which is why there is so much solar energy appearing in Belgium. When we started with solar, we had only 64 panels and it was nearly the biggest array in the country. Now our array is over 20 times as big and we're not close to being the biggest anymore. We are also considering wind power, but there are a large number of issues we need to investigate first.

For projects that do not have an economic return we have a 'People and Planet' programme that is funded from a sliding proportion of profits (the higher the profits the higher percentage goes to the fund). Example projects include the original solar panels, free fruit for staff, staff tyre pressure checks and free cycle maintenance for those cycling to work.

We provide advice to our users and we try to advise them to take the greenest option where possible. We find that motivating people on health grounds is easier than motivating them on green issues. So it is easy to sell water-based paints as being low odour and healthier than on wider environmental issues.

What's your advice for others in your position?

Learn by doing. Get passionate people in, get started and gain competence as you go along.

Aligning Management Functions

Overview

If leadership is making sure you are doing the right thing, then management is making sure things are done right. While this book is focused on leadership rather than management, part of the leadership challenge is to ensure that the correct management elements are in place to deliver strategies effectively and to encourage and benefit from spontaneous change.

We cover four elements here: environmental management systems; measuring and reporting progress; budgeting and investment; and human resources management.

Environmental Management Systems

An environmental management system (EMS) is a framework for measuring environmental impacts, setting objectives, developing and implementing action plans, and monitoring the result. There are a number of formal EMS standards, most notably ISO 14001. The resulting certificate is a powerful statement to your stakeholders both inside and outside the organization. Even if you don't intend to pursue certification in the first instance, it makes sense to follow a recognized approach in case you change your mind later, for example, if major customers start favouring suppliers with the standard.

An EMS is a process and not an end in itself. A cynic once said 'an EMS allows you to destroy the environment in a well documented manner'. There is some truth in this – while EMS standards require continual improvement, none require compliance with any absolute requirement stricter than the law of the land and none expects you to make major changes to your product, process or facilities.

ISO 14001

The ISO 14001 standard has three overarching requirements:[1]

- Compliance with legislation;
- Pollution prevention;
- Continuous improvement.

It is the last of these that catches companies out. Auditors will expect to see evidence of how performance has improved. This is where many companies falter as it becomes more difficult year on year to show an incremental improvement. Eventually you may be forced into taking a step change in order to keep moving forward.

ISO 14001 has six main clauses:

- General requirements: where the scope of the system is set;
- Policy: this forms the bedrock of the system (see below);
- Planning: identify legal requirements and significant environmental impacts, set objectives and targets;
- Implementation and operation: covers resources, roles, responsibility and authority, competence, training and awareness, communication, documentation system, document control, operational control, emergency preparedness and response;
- Checking and corrective action: covers monitoring and measurement, evaluation of compliance, non-conformity, corrective and preventive action, control of records and internal audit;
- Management review: reviews the effectiveness of the EMS in the face of changing internal and external factors. Identifies changes required to maintain that effectiveness.

These clauses are followed in a loop. The continual improvement requirement means that performance must improve at each iteration (normally taken to be yearly). The standard is based on the same cycle as the ISO 9001 Quality Management System, ISO 16001 Energy Management System and OHAS 18001 Health and Safety Management standards, so the four can be combined if required.

Environmental policy

An environmental policy is a written statement outlining an organization's mission in relation to managing the environmental impacts of its operations. Policies are often seen in the foyers of head offices and on websites and most are extremely dull and uninspiring.

A policy is your public declaration of your commitment to improving your environmental performance, so it must be drafted carefully. There is no standard format for writing an environmental policy, but the style should reflect your organization's culture. Here are a few basic tips to follow to ensure the policy is clearly written and concise:

- Keep the statement short – if it's longer than a sheet of A4, then it's probably too long;
- Make sure it is easy to read and understand;
- Be as specific as possible, making the policy relevant to your organization's activities and practices rather than the standard, interchangeable policies adopted by many organizations;
- ISO 14001 requires the policy to commit the organization to compliance with legislation, pollution prevention and continuous improvement;
- Demonstrate your commitment to making the policy work and get the statement signed, dated and endorsed by the managing director or chief executive;
- It should be regularly reviewed – for ISO 14001 purposes this needs to be done on an annual basis.

Measuring and Reporting Performance

The old managerial maxim, 'If you can't measure it, you can't manage it' must be one of the most often repeated. While it is not the most glamorous of green business aspects, it is important to get hold of the data for the following reasons:

- Reporting and making green claims;
- Prioritizing resources;
- Backing up arguments;
- Identifying problems and opportunities.

As we have discussed before, gathering information and data should not be at the expense of action.

Key performance indicators

KPIs must be chosen to both to reflect your strategy and EMS. It makes sense to divide them in two: (1) headline indicators that measure progress towards the stretch targets adopted in the strategy (Chapter 16); and (2) secondary indicators that cover a wider range of lesser issues including those identified in the EMS.

The Global Reporting Initiative's sustainability guidelines provide a framework for choosing indicators.[2] The key criterion is 'materiality', a function of the significance of the impact of a particular indicator and the degree of influence over that indicator that the organization has. Indicators with a low materiality can be ignored; those with a high materiality must be included. While this framework was produced for choosing indicators to report, it is also useful for choosing indicators for internal management processes.

As well as which indicators to choose, another strategic decision is in what resolution you collect data in terms of processes and time. Most organizations can produce aggregated figures for, say electricity consumption, but being able to meter individual processes is essential for effective management and prioritization. Time-based monitoring for certain indicators, for example electricity consumption and water consumption, can also be highly useful as comparing data from downtime and operating times can identify underlying problems such as faulty equipment or water leaks. An early investment decision for green businesses is whether to improve monitoring and data collection systems.

Carbon footprinting

Carbon footprinting has become ubiquitous for environmental management, and many people will be interested in what a green business is doing to reduce its carbon footprint, so it is worth discussing in a little more detail. A carbon footprint is a measurement of the total amount of greenhouse gases associated with a person, an organization or a product. It is expressed in terms of equivalent amounts of CO_2, for which an individual, organization, product or event is responsible.

When it comes to carbon footprints, the 'Greenhouse Gas Protocol' lays down the standard method.[3] The six greenhouse gases as specified in the protocol are: CO_2, methane (CH_4), nitrous oxide (N_2O), hydrofluorocarbons (HFCs), perfluorocarbons (PFCs) and sulphur hexafluoride (SF_6). There are other greenhouse gases, for example nitrogen fluoride NF_3, which was omitted from the protocol because at that time its use was highly limited. However, NF_3 use is now fast increasing with the popularity of thin film transistor (TFT) televisions[4] so it should be included if appropriate. CO_2 is the baseline greenhouse gas and carbon footprints are expressed in terms of CO_2 equivalent, for example 1 tonne of methane has a global warming potential of 21 tonnes CO_2 equivalent.

As shown in Figure 18.1, there are four different 'scopes' of emissions that make up a footprint:

- Scope 1 Direct emissions: usually emissions from burning fossil fuels, powering vehicles or other equipment. Other emissions may come from chemical reactions, fugitive emissions (leaks) or the decomposition of organic materials (for example in composting);
- Scope 2 Indirect emissions from the use of electricity: the amount of CO_2 emitted in the power stations to produce mains (or other) electricity;
- Scope 3 Indirect emissions from your supply chain, i.e. scope 1 and 2 emissions from your suppliers, and their suppliers and so on;
- Scope 4 Emissions from the distribution, use and disposal of the products and services you provide.[5]

The Greenhouse Gas Protocol states that scope 1 and 2 are mandatory, but scope 3 is optional, but in practice scope 3 is normally included as it tends to dominate the footprint for many organizations as we saw in Chapter 11. This turns measuring a carbon footprint into a significant task as even the smallest organization will have a large network of suppliers between them and the primary industries extracting raw materials and energy. In practice this can be

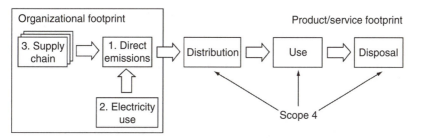

Figure 18.1 *Different scopes of carbon footprints*

managed by 80:20 thinking to cut out insignificant elements and using generic data where real data is unavailable. Taking a carbon footprint of a product (scope 1–4), is effectively a lifecycle assessment expressed in carbon terms (see Chapter 12).

Reporting

The standard annual sustainability report produced by businesses is still the bedrock of sustainability and CSR reporting. Most now look inviting and interesting and mix up technical detail with more accessible translations of the information for less technically minded readers. As mentioned above, the Global Reporting Initiative has developed guidelines for sustainability reporting in organizations.[6] The guidelines cover strategy and governance, management approach and performance indicators across the whole range of sustainability issues: environmental, social and economic. They not only cover which issues to report but how they should be reported.

As well as formal reporting, there are many other opportunities to report to stakeholders in a more proactive way, for example advertising, product information, conference sessions, the mainstream media, blogs, viral marketing methods, and even transactional collateral such as receipts.

The biggest pitfall to avoid in reporting is greenwash. As we saw back in Chapter 4, overstating your case is a cardinal sin and will be punished by the authorities, pressure groups and the public. As a result, some reports now include a review by a respected and independent third body – for example Marks & Spencer's report contains an assessment by well known environmentalist Jonathan Porritt.[7] People such as Porritt can be trusted to tell it how it is and will not risk their reputation by putting their name to something that is overstated.

Staff feedback

It is important not to forget internal communications as feedback will support the staff engagement efforts described in Chapter 17. There is a wide range of opportunities, for example public display screens, company intranets, in-house journals or, more simply, graphs of monthly performance in places were people tend to linger, for example by coffee machines, water coolers, staff rooms or the mail room. As with other forms of communication, it is important to mix the delivery method and style to match the interests of the user. Financial people will tend to be interested in cost savings, engineers in clever technical solutions and marketeers in the development of new green markets. Again, storytelling can help bring the agenda down to the personal, human interest level, so stories on say, how a particular engineer solved a particular problem can be used to liven up messages on overall achievements.

Finance and Budgeting

Financial commitment

My killer question for current or potential clients is, 'What's your budget?'. The answer usually comes in the form of a red face and some muttering. This is a tough test and most of them fail. Organizations routinely declare they are 'committed' to minimizing their impact on the environment yet that commitment does not even extend to setting a budget. Instead the environmental manager must go cap in hand to higher authorities to fund each project on a case-by-case basis. The impacts of this approach are:

- Environmental projects will always be seen as a discretionary spend and will have to fight it out with other, short-term pressures;
- It is impossible to put together a long-term strategy if the funds to deliver each stage are uncertain, leading to a piecemeal approach;
- The commitment will appear paper thin to internal and external stakeholders.

Let's face it, no budget = no commitment. As Chris Jofeh of Arup says 'Don't make funding the last thing you think about, make it the first thing you think about.' The following sections explore the types of investment that a green business will need to make and how budgeting can be adjusted to improve the decision making process.

Different ways of counting

Two financial costing techniques can help make investment decisions 'greener': (1) through life costing: operating costs are given equal weight to the capital cost of any option. This encourages the purchase of more efficient equipment and plant; and (2) activity-based costing: where all 'overheads' (including energy, water and waste costs) are apportioned directly to each activity. This means that an energy intensive process will show up in the accounts as much more expensive than a low energy process.

Both approaches attempt to capture the true financial cost into investment decisions. This makes it more likely that, say, either an energy intensive process option will be seen to be unprofitable and rejected, or that an investment will be made to improve the energy efficiency of existing, inefficient plant.

Types of investment

While some simple environmental actions will save you money very quickly at little or no cost, others will require investment, particularly changes to your process, product or business model. Marks & Spencer's Plan A may have saved the company money overall, but they started off with a £200 million budget to get the programme going. From a generic point of view, most industrial projects fall into one of three categories:

1   Compliance: the things you really have to do to stay out of court whether environmental compliance, health and safety or financial auditing;
2   Investment for a direct benefit: projects that give an immediate return on investment (ROI), for example factory automation or installing energy efficient motors;
3   Investment for an indirect benefit: projects where the economic benefit cannot be accurately predicted, for example a PR exercise or staff training.

The problem with low carbon/environmental projects is that they often straddle two, if not all three, of these bases. This causes confusion in budgeting as, if there is a direct ROI, this is often used as the sole measure of success. In the industrial sector, the cash saved from waste minimization and energy efficiency can often be substantial, for example Northern Foods is already saving £2–4 million per year. Such investments can easily stand up to simple assessments, but, as we have seen, for many organizations the indirect benefits are much larger, for example by building a trusted, progressive brand. These benefits cannot easily be factored into a simplistic ROI calculation. For example, EAE Ltd is not expecting to make a direct financial return on their wind turbine, but they believe it has helped them to win at least one major contract – 'one wind turbine is worth 100 environmental policies', says boss Glen Bennett. InterfaceFLOR turned the perceived cost of a large array of solar panels at a factory into a new product brand – SolarMade™ carpet – whose increased sales covered the cost of the array 20 times over.[8] So we need a budgeting strategy that can handle this complexity.

Ring-fenced budget

As mentioned above, Sir Stuart Rose of Marks & Spencer committed £200 million to the company's Plan A programme. This kind of ring-fenced budget makes a very clear statement of intent and commitment. It allows proper planning of sustainability issues, unlike the ad hoc funding approach we see at the bundle of projects stage of sustainability we discussed in Chapter 14.

There are a few disadvantages to this approach:

- By making 'green' a separate issue, it is less likely to be integrated into business planning;
- If times get tough, the budget may be vulnerable to early cuts;
- There may be a tendency to dress up any project as 'green' to try and tap into the ring-fenced budget;
- Similarly, other budget holders may be reluctant to approve any project with a hint of green as 'there's another budget for that'.

Certainly it is the intention of Marks & Spencer to reintegrate the funding for Plan A type activity, but this will put the company back at the stage of having to make very complex investment decisions.

Split budgets

To overcome the direct/indirect benefits confusion, one approach is to separate your budgets into those for: (1) investments that can stand up on a direct benefits ROI (for example energy efficiency investments). These can be considered alongside other projects on the company's standard assessment criteria; and (2) investments that don't make this cut, but which have clear sustainability benefits. These are then evaluated for their indirect benefits against a different budget.

BOSS Paints use this approach. 'Green' projects with a reasonable financial return are assessed alongside all the other company investments. Projects that do not get funded on ROI but that meet certain sustainability criteria may instead be considered for the company's 'People and Planet' programme, alongside other project ideas that may have no direct return on investment. The programme has funded a wide range of projects including the company's first solar panel array, cycle maintenance classes for employees, and a free ironing service. A proportion of each year's profits are fed into the programme budget with the proportion increasing as profits rise. This has the additional benefit of incentivizing the workforce to maximize profits as there is a clear communal benefit when the company does well.

Committing savings

Another approach that has proved successful is to provide a fighting fund that is topped up from a proportion of the financial savings gained from each project. In other words, if the fund invests in a new compressed air system leading to savings, then, say, 50 per cent or more of the savings every year go back into the fund. This encourages the fund manager to start off implementing the projects with the best return on investment in order to build up funds for projects that have a lower ROI but that will deliver benefits to the brand. This is a very efficient way of maximizing the original investment and protecting 'green projects' from other financial pressures. In the UK, Woking Council have been operating such a fund for 13 years and have managed to save over £1 million and cut carbon emissions from council buildings by 77.4 per cent.[9]

Human Resources Management

In Chapter 17 we looked at stakeholder engagement and noted that the key stakeholders when it comes to the success of green projects were the company's employees. In this section we look at what formal human resources (HR) systems and processes are required to ensure the workforce is part of the solution and not part of the problem.

Training and awareness

Along with the specialized staff engagement techniques discussed in Chapter 17, many leading businesses implement formal training programmes for all staff. InterfaceFLOR has a four level training programme – all employees must take Level 1 and the higher levels are for those who need a deeper understanding. Procter & Gamble have developed bespoke training for every function of the business (production, design, sales, marketing) so every employee understands how their role effects the sustainability agenda and vice versa.

When I run training courses I always ensure that each session has a practical outcome by getting the participants to apply the lessons to their own organization or department. This not only makes the training more relevant, builds buy-in (as we saw in Chapter 17), but is also a useful source of solutions and innovative ideas.

Recruitment

We saw in Chapter 2 that job seekers are increasingly favouring businesses with a green/ethical reputation. The question is whether green businesses should seek recruits who have a good understanding of green issues. While this sounds straightforward, Vic Morgan of the Ethical Superstore urges caution. He has found through experience that it is easier to recruit people with a strong commercial instinct and train them in the company values than to take people whose first instinct is green/ethical and train them in their mainstream role.

Where the recruitment process is important is to make sure that new recruits do not have values that directly conflict with sustainability efforts. Value driven organizations will already have processes to test alignment with company values. These guidelines should be adapted to include values relating to sustainability.

Job descriptions and performance assessment

Related to recruitment is the issue of job descriptions and assessment of staff performance against those descriptions. Sustainability efforts will never be integrated into the company unless every staff member understands their role. Management guru Charles Handy talks about the inside out doughnut model – at the centre is the formal job description, but beyond that are a vague ring of informal requirements on any position that we have to meet to make the job happen.[10] Sustainability is usually regarded as being a 'soft' issue in that outer ring, but to integrate it into the business, it must penetrate the formal job descriptions. This should be as specific as possible as opposed to vague requirements to, say, 'promote the values of the company'. For example, site managers can be assigned formal energy performance targets against which they will be assessed, or sales managers could be given a target to increase the proportion of green products in the sales mix. The most important level of the business for such targets is middle management as this is where issues tend to get stuck or lost. We saw in Chapter 15 how staff must be given appropriate authority as well as responsibility to deliver sustainability requirements effectively.

Change agents

To implement change, the organization will require change agents – members of staff whose role is in total or in part to help transform the organization towards the sustainability goals. There are four main options, all but the last can be mixed and matched:

- Formal, dedicated sustainability staff team operating as an internal consultancy;
- Part-time staff committee: volunteer (or volunteered!) members have 'day jobs' but meet periodically to review and monitor progress;
- Part-time 'sustainability champions' or 'energy champions' who are responsible for encouraging sustainability in their immediate working environment;
- No team: either use a facilitator to work with staff across business functions or the 'benign dictatorship' approach of small companies with strong and determined leaders.

The organizations interviewed for this book were split on these options. Gentoo felt that getting the right people in their internal consultancy was paramount, whereas Northern Foods deliberately avoided teams and simply had one senior member of staff, Paula Widdowson, to facilitate change and make sure no one thought that 'green' was someone else's job. Muckle LLP found that an informal committee allowed them to build a critical mass of enthusiastic employees who began to get good results and caught the attention of senior management.

The advantages of the four systems are shown in Table 18.1.

The choice comes down to organizational culture. The formal team approach works best where there are project teams and sustainability team members can be seconded into those teams. The 'no team' approach will only work when the facilitator has enough authority and/or charisma to bring staff with them.

External resources: Dream teams

As well as internal resources, many of the companies interviewed for this book have put together teams of external experts to oversee and advise progress on sustainability. InterfaceFLOR, BT and Marks & Spencer have such individuals advising their senior staff. Some of the individuals on these dream teams are high profile figures in the sustainability world, such as Jonathan Porritt and Amory Lovins.

Table 18.1 *Advantages of different staffing approaches*

Dedicated Team	Part-time Committee	Sustainability Champions	No Team
Breadth of expertise in-house	Cross-section of functions represented	Cross-section of functions represented	Ownership with mainstream employees
Defined responsibility and accountability	Buy-in ensured	Cheaper than formal team – only part-time requirement of staff time	No 'us and them' ghetto-ization of 'green'
More projects can be launched and monitored	Centre of gravity around which activity can coalesce	Local 'experts' can apply their domain knowledge	Agile – no bureaucracy
	Much cheaper than formal team in terms of salaries	Peer-to-peer communications may be better trusted	Cheap – no bureaucracy
	Can be effective in a 'leadership vacuum'		Requires use of existing intellectual capital

The advantages of the dream team approach are:

- You can pick idealists who will really drive you along and hold you to the highest standards;
- An external eye will spot issues and opportunities that the internal eye will miss;
- The right individual will bring a wealth of experience across a wide range of sectors;
- The individuals do not get bogged down in the day to day drudgery of management;
- The individuals do not get tied up in internal politics.

Chapter summary

1   While sustainability requires leadership, management procedures must also be aligned to the sustainability strategy

2   EMSs provide a useful framework for delivering the sustainability strategy, but are not an end in themselves;

3   The correct KPIs must be chosen to cover headline targets and subsidiary issues;

4   Reporting of progress internally and externally is essential to maintain trust in stakeholder relationships;

5   Budgets and investment decision making procedures must be aligned to capture all aspects of sustainability;

6   To integrate sustainability throughout the organization, specific requirements must be put in job descriptions throughout the organization;

7   Recruiting the right people is essential, ensuring new recruits are at least open to sustainability thinking, but not at the expense of their ability to deliver their 'day job';

8   There are a number of options to delivering the sustainability function of a business; the 'right' approach is the one that best matches company culture;

9   Dream teams of external advisors can add a huge amount of value.

The View from the Front Line: Chris Jofeh, Arup

Arup provides engineering and consulting services for all aspects of the built environment. The company has over 10,000 staff based in 92 offices in 37 countries and turned over £750 million in 2008. Famous projects include the Sydney Opera House, 30 St Mary's Axe (aka the 'London Gherkin') and the Beijing National Stadium (aka 'The Bird's Nest'). The firm was founded in 1946 by legendary engineer Ove Nyquist Arup.

Chris Jofeh is a Director of Arup, leading the Existing Buildings Consultancy side of the business. His primary role is to grow a business around improving, upgrading and retrofitting existing buildings.

Why and how did you get involved in this agenda?

By training I'm a structural engineer, but I've always leaned to the environmental side of things. The green movement of the early 1970s hit me at just the right time – I was very taken with it. In fact I wrote a guide for solar and wind energy in the UK for Friends of the Earth in the mid-1970s. At university I heard a marathon talk by the visionary architect and engineer Buckminster Fuller and became a fan of his. He took a very holistic view in his work.

Whereas my career has taken me in and out of the environmental field, it's something I've never abandoned. For example, I've had a long running research project running in the background for many years. It is a means of designing very large structures, such as domes, big enough to go over cities in hot arid climates. Without any moving parts or power consumption, they create a climate inside which is much more pleasant than that outside.

What are the business drivers for Arup to engage in this agenda?

Arup has always tried to deliver what is now called sustainable design. Ove Arup believed that this is what we had to do because it is important, necessary and right. He called it 'Total Architecture' in the early days and if you read how he defined total architecture, it is very close to today's definition of sustainable design – it's all just good design, really. This approach is one of the things that attracted me to Arup before I joined.

Arup has a strong social purpose and it is a core belief of ours that you need to behave responsibly in what you do, not just in your dealings with others but in your impact on the environment.

Sustainability is fast becoming a reputational issue for our clients. In the commercial world, they are coming under pressure from their investors, a lot of them have their own CSR agendas and the majority want to do more than just pay lip service to it. These days it need not cost any more to build a green building, and the right upgrades pay for themselves via reduced running costs, improved productivity and enhanced asset values. The evidence is increasing that these buildings will be more valuable assets, counting for more on your balance sheet, and will probably have a healthier and more productive workforce with lower absenteeism, sickness and turnover of staff. The data is not consistent or conclusive, but the trend is definitely in that direction. The public sector has an increasingly strong sustainability agenda too. It is rare these days to find an organization that says 'No. Not interested.'

What successes have you had?

We've had some great successes. We have a client in the US whose campus of buildings we took a look at. There were seven buildings, four of which were LEED certified. Under our guidance, and a cost of less than $400,000, the client reduced his annual energy bill by over $1 million in the first year.

On the completely opposite end of the scale, we were involved in a college building in London. It's a typical 1960s concrete framed building by a main road so they had to keep the windows closed which meant they had mechanical ventilation and air conditioning systems running 24/7. We put an acoustic glass screen just outside the main elevation of the building which sufficiently attenuated the noise that the occupants could open the windows instead of using the mechanical systems. This was a nice intelligent solution which was popular as people like to be able to open their windows and control their environment.

We've done 19,000 existing building projects – about 15 per cent of all Arup's projects. Looking forward, I would like to get to the stage where substantially more than half our building projects would be on existing buildings. Looking at greenhouse gas emissions, new buildings just slow the rate at which things get worse: they don't actually make it better. Tackling existing buildings makes it better.

I have the sense now that people are seeing the value of the proposition that we're taking to the marketplace and I'm getting lots of feedback that this is an important part of the business that we are growing and that we're going about it in a good way.

What are the big challenges for your organization?

Designing a, say, new BREEAM Excellent building is relatively straightforward. It is much more of a challenge and you can have much more fun seeing what you can do with an existing asset. In terms of carbon you can usually do more good improving the performance of an existing building than knocking it down and building a new one with even lower carbon emissions.

In terms of refurbishing the existing housing stock, this needs to be done at scale. There are 25 million domestic buildings in the UK and at a conservative estimate, probably 24.5 million of them could do with upgrading. The challenge is not so much a technical one as a procurement and funding one. Piecemeal improvements – a house here, a flat there – will be disproportionately expensive. I've done the sums and tested them with various audiences and I think it's affordable for us a society to upgrade all those buildings in 15 years. Getting enough skilled builders to do it is another problem.

There are lots of barriers still, particularly on the carbon agenda. 'Why me first?' is a big one, but it is slowly being overcome.

We need to get away from the idea that sustainability means simply 'green'. Sustainability has three pillars to it – environmental, social and economic – and they're equally important. If you just focus on green without it working socially and, particularly, financially, it just isn't going to happen. So for us, the challenge is to see it as a business opportunity, not as a 'save the planet' opportunity. We've got to reframe the argument, looking for the opportunities that support business as well as drive down pollution, CO_2 emissions and so on.

What's your advice for others in your position?

Forget saving the planet as the primary driver – focus on enhancing the client's business, helping them do what they want to do, but do it better. Use this as the route to delivering green solutions.

This one might sound a bit like advice from a motorway service station management book, but don't be discouraged and always try to turn challenges into opportunities.

Architect Louis Sullivan is credited with the line 'form follows function'. This was rewritten by NASA in the 1960s as 'form follows funding' and then to 'no bucks, no Buck Rogers'. Joking aside, the availability and form of funding will determine what you can do. Don't make funding the last thing you think about, make it the first thing you think about.

Notes

BREEAM is the Building Research Establishment Environmental Assessment Method, the main UK system for rating the environmental performance of non-residential buildings. 'Excellent' is the second highest BREEAM ranking, below 'Outstanding'.

LEED is the Leadership in Energy and Environmental Design, the main US and increasingly international system for rating the environmental performance of buildings.

A Time for Leaders

It is no exaggeration to say that we are at a crossroads in human history. The challenges of climate change, resource depletion and toxic pollution are immense and pressing, but the opportunities are equally huge. Sustainability should not be seen as a move backwards, but an inspiring vision of mankind flourishing within the natural limits of the planet. A sustainable society will enjoy clean air and water, energy security, thriving wildlife, preserved natural habitats, a stable climate, sustainable resources, less poverty, stronger more vibrant communities and the reduced risk of environmental accidents.

Traditionally, sustainability and environmental issues have been regarded as issues to be *managed* through procedures, systems and reports. But addressing such enormous challenges head on requires *leadership*, and it is our leaders in politics, business and civil society who must deliver. This book provides a road map for the new breed of corporate green leaders to transform their business to become part of the solution rather than part of the problem. It attempts to equip them with the knowledge, skills and case studies they need to deliver this vision.

We have covered a lot of ground and packed in a huge number of concepts, techniques and facts and figures. But if you are to take just seven key learning points from it, I would recommend the following:

- Doing nothing is not an option. Companies who think they are standing still on this agenda will find they are actually going backwards;
- 'Go green, save money' is for amateurs. The key opportunities are in recruiting and retaining staff, winning market share and opening up new markets rather than the simplistic cost cutting agenda that many organizations push;
- Don't forget you are still running a business. The business case for sustainability is compelling, but not without risks. You need to find the solutions that are good for the planet and good for business;

- Sustainability needs to be embedded into the DNA of the organization. In most companies, green is stuck in a silo and/or at a managerial level and requires bold and strategic leadership to make the necessary changes happen;
- Acknowledge and relish the challenge. The ultimate aim is to comply with the ecosystem model (solar, cyclic, safe) of environmental sustainability, using large eco-efficiency improvements to make that model feasible. This will require huge changes in processes, supply chains, products and business models;
- You've got to walk the walk. Commitment is more than words on a policy declaration, it must manifest itself in bold decisions, actions, behaviour, resourcing and results. Leadership means not only doing the right thing, but stopping doing the wrong thing.
- You can't do it alone. The transformation will need buy-in from a wide range of stakeholders. Staff, suppliers, customers, pressure groups and regulators all have a role to play in helping develop solutions. But if your existing stakeholders are holding you back, change them.

What this book can't give you is the experience, understanding and gut instinct you get from actually doing it. A bias to action and resilience were two of the key leadership attributes we have identified. The winners in sustainability keep trying, keep learning, but, most of all, keep going.

Resilience and a bias to action are certainly two things that unite the 18 people interviewed for this book; a third is enthusiasm. They love what they are doing with a passion and their optimism helps them find solutions where others see only problems. They are, in their own way, heroes of our time – I hope their stories have inspired you.

So, the challenge is there, and the risks and rewards are immense. Can you step up and lead?

Annex: New and Emerging Green Markets

Market	Supply Chain Segments
Energy generation, storage and distribution	**Direct supply chain**
Large scale renewables	Research and development
Micro-renewables	Commercialization
Heat distribution	Design
Energy storage, e.g. batteries, hydrogen	Supply chain
Control systems, smart grids and home energy	Manufacturing
management systems	Retail, rental and distribution
Buildings	Operation/service provision
Zero carbon building concepts	Maintenance
Insulation and other high performance building materials	Maintenance equipment and spares
Efficient heating and lighting systems	Emergency repair/response
Vehicles and transport	Safety products and services
Alternative fuels: electric, hydrogen and biofuels	Disposal and reverse logistics
Efficient vehicles	**Secondary supply chain**
Food	IT systems
Low carbon food supplies	Consulting
Local production techniques for imported foods	Compliance
Water supply	Training
Sustainable sourcing	Legal services
Efficient use	Sales/marketing
Treatment	Public relations
Waste	Finance
Collection and sorting processes	Enabling technology
Recycling processes	
Consumer goods	
Sustainable biomaterials	
Virgin-quality recycled materials	

Notes

Introduction

1   BBC (2010) 'BP boss Hayward says he was "demonised" over oil spill', bbc.co.uk, 27 July 2010, www.bbc.co.uk/news/business-10782429 accessed 24 September 2010.
2   Edwards, T. (2010) 'Bhopal verdict: A most convenient injustice', guardian.-co.uk, 8 June 2010, www.guardian.co.uk/commentisfree/libertycentral/2010/jun/08/bhopal-verdict accessed 24 September 2010.
3   Telegraph (2010) 'Barack Obama: Gulf of Mexico oil spill an "environmental 9/11"', telegraph.co.uk, 14 June 2010, www.telegraph.co.uk/finance/newsbysector/energy/oilandgas/7827301/Barack-Obama-Gulf-of-Mexico-oil-spill-an-environmental-911.html accessed 24 September 2010.
4   Randerson, J. (2010) 'Cameron: I want coalition to be the "greenest government ever"', guardian.co.uk, 14 May 2010, www.guardian.co.uk/environment/2010/may/14/cameron-wants-greenest-government-ever accessed 24 September 2010.
5   French Embassy website, www.ambafrance-uk.org/President-Sarkozy-s-speech-at,15755.html accessed 24 September 2010.
6   AP (2010) 'Merkel calls for strong deal on climate change', 3 November 2009, www.msnbc.msn.com/id/33603930/ns/politics-capitol_hill/ accessed 24 September 2010.
7   Young, T. (2010) 'Chinese premier threatens to use "iron hand" to meet energy targets', BusinessGreen, 6 May 2010, www.businessgreen.com/business-green/news/2262571/chinese-premier-threatens-iron accessed 24 September 2010.
8   Rogers, S. (2010) 'How China overtook the US in renewable energy', guardian.co.uk, 25 March 2010, www.guardian.co.uk/news/datablog/2010/mar/25/china-renewable-energy-pew-research accessed 24 September 2010.
9   Shankleman, J. (2010) 'Blue chip firms warn against green skills crisis' BusinessGreen, 1 July 2010, www.businessgreen.com/business-green/news/2265777/leadership-skills-gap-threatens accessed 24 September 2010.

Chapter 1: Business as Usual is Not an Option

1   EA (2009) 'SME-nvironment Survey 2009', Environment Agency, www.environment-agency.gov.uk/static/documents/NetRegs/NetRegs_SME_ Environment_2009_UK_summary.pdf accessed 24 September 2010.

2   Frost & Sullivan (2006) 'The impact of REACH on the chemical industry', www.frost.com/prod/servlet/market-insight-top.pag?docid=63485355 accessed 24 September 2010.

3   EPA (2008) 'Massey Energy Company Inc. Clean Water Act Settlement', US Environmental Protection Agency, www.epa.gov/compliance/resources/cases/civil/cwa/massey.html accessed 24 September 2010.

4   Guardian (2008) 'US supreme court kicks Exxon Valdez case back to California court', *The Guardian*, 13 August, www.guardian.co.uk/environment/2008/aug/13/oilspills.usa accessed 24 September 2010.

5   Goldstein, S. (2009) 'Red Bull hit with record £270k packaging waste fine', www.packagingnews.co.uk, 29 July, www.packagingnews.co.uk/news/923655/Red-Bull-hit-record-270k-packaging-waste-fine/ accessed 24 September 2010.

6   GEMI (2004) 'Forging new links – enhancing supply chain value through environmental excellence', Global Environmental Management Initiative,   www.gemi.org/supplychain/resources/ForgingNewLinks.pdf accessed 24 September 2010.

7   Wachman, R. (2010) 'BP "to divest all North Sea assets" in dramatic attempt to reduce its costs', *The Observer*, 20 June, www.guardian.co.uk/business/2010/jun/20/bp-north-sea-assets-sale accessed 24 September 2010.

8   Macalister, T. (2010) 'BP's Deepwater Horizon oil spill likely to cost more than Exxon Valdez', guardian.co.uk, 30 April, www.guardian.co.uk/environment/2010/apr/30/bp-cost-deepwater-horizon-spill accessed 24 September 2010.

9   www.greenpeace.org/apple accessed 24 September 2010.

10   Fried, I. (2005) 'Jobs defends Apple's record on environment', CNET News, 21 April, http://news.cnet.com/Jobs-defends-Apples-record-on-environment/2100-1041_3-5680152.html accessed 24 September 2010.

11   Stockman, L., Rowell, A. and Kretzmann, S. (2009) 'Irresponsible energy, Shell: The world's most carbon intensive oil company', Oil Change International, PLATFORM, Friends of the Earth International, Greenpeace UK, http://priceofoil.org/wp-content/uploads/2009/05/shelliefinal.pdf accessed 25 September 2010.

12   Royal Society (2006) 'Royal Society and ExxonMobil', http://royalsociety.org/Report_WF.aspx?pageid=8256&terms = exxon accessed 24 September 2010.

13   Adam, D. (2008), 'Exxon to cut funding to climate change denial groups', guardian.co.uk, 28 May, www.guardian.co.uk/environment/2008/may/28/climatechange.fossilfuels accessed 24 September 2010.

14   BBC (2006) 'State sues car firms on climate', www.bbc.co.uk, 20 September, http://news.bbc.co.uk/1/hi/sci/tech/5365728.stm accessed 24 September 2010.

15   BBC (2008) 'Oil hits new high on Iran fears', bbc.co.uk, 11 July, http://newsvote.bbc.co.uk/1/hi/business/7501939.stm   last   accessed 24 September 2010.

16   Hess, J. B. (2009) 'Oil and the future', Oil and Money Conference, London, 20 October, http://phx.corporate-ir.net/External.File?item=UGFyZW50SUQ9 MzU1MTY2fENoaWxkSUQ9MzQ3ODM5fFR5cGU9MQ = = &t = 1 accessed 24 September 2010.

17   Letsrecycle.com (2008) 'Budget confirms £32 per tonne Landfill Tax from April', www.letsrecycle.com, 12 March, www.letsrecycle.com/do/ecco.py/view_item? listid=37&listcatid = 217&listitemid = 9782 accessed 24 September 2010.

18   BBC (2004) 'Rallies held over Bhopal disaster', bbc.co.uk, 3 December, http://news.bbc.co.uk/1/hi/world/south_asia/4064527.stm accessed 24 September 2010.

19   Eccleston, P. (2007) 'Big supermarkets "are all getting greener"', *The Daily Telegraph*, 15 October, www.telegraph.co.uk/earth/earthnews/3310497/ Big-supermarkets-are-all-getting-greener.html accessed 24 September 2010.

20   BBC (2009) 'GM enters bankruptcy protection', bbc.co.uk, 1 June, http://news.bbc.co.uk/1/hi/business/8077255.stm accessed 24 September 2010.

21   Wood, C. (2009) 'General Motors going green: Even the logo?', www. autoguide.com, 9 July, www.autoguide.com/auto-news/2009/07/general-motors-going-green-even-the-logo.html accessed 24 September 2010.

Chapter 2: Green Business Opportunities

1   Business In the Community (2008) 'The value of corporate governance: The positive return of responsible business', www.bitc.org.uk/document.rm? id=8354 accessed 24 September 2010.

2   AT Kearny (2009) 'Companies with a commitment to sustainability tend to outperform their peers during the financial crisis', www.atkearney.com/index. php/News-media/companies-with-a-commitment-to-sustainability-tend-to-outperform-their-peers-during-the-financial-crisis.html accessed 24 September 2010.

3   CIPD (2009) 'Corporate social responsibility', Chartered Institute of Personnel and Development, www.cipd.co.uk/subjects/corpstrtgy/corpsocres/ csrfact.htm accessed 24 September 2010.

4   Murray, J. (2007) 'Green initiatives deliver employee retention benefits', www. computing.co.uk/business-green/news/2201847/green-initiatives-deliver accessed 24 September 2010.

5   Press Association (2003) 'Job seekers choose morals over money', *The Guardian*, 12 September, www.guardian.co.uk/money/2003/sep/12/ethicalmoney.workandcareers accessed 24 September 2010.

6   Personal communication, Liz Lipton-McCombie, WH Smith, 10 June 2010.

7   BERR (2009) 'Low carbon and environmental goods and services', Department for Business, Enterprise and Regulatory Reform, www.berr.gov. uk/files/file50253.pdf accessed 24 September 2010.

8   IGD (2007) 'Ethical consumerism', IGD, www.igd.com/index.asp?id=1& fid = 1&sid = 5&tid = 48&cid = 166 last accessed 25 September 2010.

9   DEFRA (2006) 'Evaluation of the energy efficiency commitment 2002–05', Department for the Environment, Food and Rural Affairs, www.defra.gov.uk/ environment/climatechange/uk/household/supplier/pdf/eec-evaluation.pdf accessed 24 September 2010.

10 The Co-operative Bank (2008) 'The Ethical Consumerism Report 2008', www.ethicalconsumer.org/Portals/0/Downloads/ETHICAL%20CON-SUMER%20REPORT.pdf accessed 24 September 2010.

11 The Soil Association (2009) 'Organic Market Report 2009', www. soilassociation.org/LinkClick.aspx?fileticket=GPynfoJoPh0 = &tabid = 116 last accessed 24 September 2010.

12 The Co-operative Bank (2008) 'The Ethical Consumerism Report 2008', www.ethicalconsumer.org/Portals/0/Downloads/ETHICAL%20CON-SUMER%20REPORT.pdf accessed 24 September 2010.

13 Macalister, T. (2009) '"Green energy overtakes fossil fuel investment", says UN', *The Guardian*, 3 June, www.guardian.co.uk/environment/2009/jun/03/ renewables-energy accessed 25 September 2010.

14 Bernard, S., Asokan, S., Warrell, H. and Lemer, J. (2009) 'The greenest bail-out?', *Financial Times*, 2 March, www.ft.com/cms/s/0/cc207678-0738-11de-9294-000077b07658.html?nclick_check=1 accessed 24 September 2010.

15 UNEP (2009) 'REN21 Renewables Global Status Report 2009 Update', United Nations Environment Programme, www.unep.fr/shared/docs/ publications/RE_GSR_2009_Update.pdf accessed 24 September 2010.

16 www.betterplace.com/ accessed 24 September 2010.

Chapter 3: The Moral Imperative

1   WHO (2005) 'Climate change', World Health Organization, www.who.int/heli/ risks/climate/climatechange/en/index.html accessed 30 September 2010.

2   Thomas, C. D., Cameron, A., Green, R. E., Bakkenes, M. J., Beaumont, L. J., Collingham, Y. C., Erasmus, B. F. N., Ferreira de Siqueira, M., Grainger, A. and Hannah, L. (2004) 'Extinction risk from climate change', *Nature*, no 427, pp145–148.

3   Stern, N. (2009) *A Blueprint for a Safer Planet: How to Manage Climate and Create a New Era of Progress and Prosperity*, The Bodley Head, London.

4   World Resources Institute (2007) 'How much of the world's resource consumption occurs in rich countries?', *Earth Trends*, http://earthtrends.wri. org/updates/node/236 accessed 25 September 2010.

5   Wilson, A. N. (2010) 'How the Cadbury family of the Victorian age would put today's fat cats to shame', *Daily Mail*, 25 January.

6   Dougan, D. (1970) *The Great Gun-Maker*, Sandhill Press Ltd, Newcastle.

7   Sheumaker, H. and Wajda, S. T. (2007) 'Material culture in America: Understanding everyday life', ABC-CLIO, Santa Barbara, CA.

8   Carson, R. (2000) *Silent Spring*, Penguin Classics, London.

9   www.google.org/about.html accessed 24 September 2010.

10   Collins, J. C. and Porras, J. I (1997) *Built to Last: Successful Habits of Visionary Companies*, HarperCollins, New York, NY.

11   Entine, J. (2010) '*The Body Shop file: Beyond "Shattered Image"*', www. jonentine.com/the-body-shop.html accessed 24 September 2010.

12   Roddick, A. (2005) *Business as Unusual: My Entrepreneurial Journey: Profits with Principles*, Anita Roddick Books, Arundel.

13   BBC (2010) 'Google stops censoring search results in China', bbc.co.uk, 23 March, http://news.bbc.co.uk/1/hi/business/8581393.stm accessed 24 September 2010.

14   Prahalad, C. K. (2004) *The Fortune at the Bottom of the Pyramid: Eradicating Poverty through Profits*, Wharton School Publishing, Upper Saddle River, NJ.

15   Maren, M. (1997) *The Road to Hell: The Ravaging Effects of Foreign Aid and International Charity*, Simon & Schuster, New York, NY.

16   Allen, N. (2009) 'Al Gore "profiting" from climate change agenda', *The Daily Telegraph*, 3 November, www.telegraph.co.uk/earth/environment/climatechange/6496196/Al-Gore-profiting-from-climate-change-agenda.html accessed 25 September 2010.

Chapter 4: Green Business Risks

1   White, P. (2009) 'Building a sustainability strategy into the business', *Corporate Governance*, vol 9, no 4, pp386–394.

2   Ottman, J. (2003) 'Lessons from the green graveyard', www.greenmarketing. com, March/April, www.greenmarketing.com/articles/complete/lessons-from-the-green-graveyard/ accessed 25 September 2010.

3   Reason, P., Coleman, G., Ballard, D., Williams, M., Gearty, M., Bond, C., Seeley, C. and Maughan McLachlan, E. (2008) *Insider Voices: Human Dimensions of Low Carbon Technology*, www.bath.ac.uk/management/news_events/pdf/lowcarbon_insider_voices.pdf accessed 25 September 2010.

4   NHS (2010) 'NHS England carbon footprint: GHG emissions,1990–2020 baseline emissions update', National Health Service Sustainable Development Unit, 26 January, www.sdu.nhs.uk/page.php?page_id=160 accessed 28 September 2010.

5   Grant, J. (2007) *The Green Marketing Manifesto*, Wiley, Chichester, UK.

6   ASA (2008) 'ASA adjudication on Lexus (GB) Ltd', Advertising Standards Agency, 8 October, www.asa.org.uk/asa/adjudications/Public/TF_ADJ_45114. htm accessed 12 September 2009.

7   Personal communication, John Hinton, Ethical Superstore, 29 June 2010.

8   Murphy, C. (2002) 'Is BP Beyond Petroleum? Hardly', *Fortune*, 30 September, http://money.cnn.com/magazines/fortune/fortune_archive/2002/09/30/ 329277/index.htm accessed 25 September 2010.

9   Pearce, F. (2009) 'Shell's promise of a bright future turns out to be yet another false dawn', guardian.co.uk, 17 December, www.guardian.co.uk/environment/ 2009/dec/17/shell-copenhagen-climate-summit accessed 25 September 2010.

10 Greenpeace (2006) 'Illegal rainforest timber used in parliament refurbishment', www.greenpeace.org.uk, 29 September, www.greenpeace. org.uk/media/press-releases/illegal-rainforest-timber-used-in-parliament-re-furbishment accessed 25 September 2010.

Chapter 5: Global Problems

1   I have not included 'biodiversity' in my Big Three as biodiversity loss is the end result of the environmental impacts in this chapter rather than a standalone problem.

2   The facts in this section have been extracted from Stern, N. (2009) *A Blueprint for a Safer Planet: How to Manage Climate and Create a New Era of Progress and Prosperity*, The Bodley Head, London.

3   Hubbert, M. K. (1956) 'Nuclear energy and the fossil fuels', Spring Meeting of the Southern District, American Petroleum Institute, San Antonio, Texas, 7–9 March.

4   Macalister, T. and Monbiot, G. (2008) 'Global oil supply will peak in 2020, says energy agency', *The Guardian*, www.guardian.co.uk/business/2008/dec/ 15/global-oil-supply-peak-2020-prediction accessed 25 September 2010.

5   Macalister, T. (2009) 'Oil: Future world shortages are being drastically underplayed, say experts', guardian.co.uk, 12 November, www.guardian.co. uk/business/2009/nov/12/oil-shortage-uppsala-aleklett accessed 25 September 2010.

6   Jackson, P. M., (2006) 'Why the peak oil theory falls down: Myths, legends, and the future of oil resources', Cambridge Energy Research Associates (CERA),

www.cera.com/aspx/cda/public1/news/pressReleases/press Release Details. aspx?CID=8444 accessed 26 September 2010.

7   IEA (2005) 'World Energy Outlook 2005: Middle East and North Africa Insights', International Energy Agency, pp125–126, www.iea.org/textbase/ nppdf/free/2005/weo2005.pdf accessed 25 September 2010.

8   World Coal Institute, www.worldcoal.org/coal/uses-of-coal/coal-to-liquids/ accessed 26 September 2010

9   Ditmarr, M. (2009) 'The future of nuclear energy: Facts and fiction', Institute of Particle Physics, Zurich, Switzerland, www.technologyreview.com/blog/ arxiv/24414/ accessed 25 September 2010.

10   UNEP (2007) 'Global Environmental Outlook 4', United Nations Environment Programme, www.unep.org/geo/geo4/media/ accessed 25 September 2010.

11   IUCN (2010) 'World's most endangered primates revealed', www.iucn.org, 18 February, www.iucn.org/?4753/Worlds-most-endangered-primates-revealed accessed 25 September 2010.

12   National Geographic 'Deforestation', *National Geographic*, http://environ-ment.nationalgeographic.com/environment/global-warming/deforestation-overview.html accessed 25 September 2010.

13   World Resources Institute (2007) 'How much of the world's resource consumption occurs in rich countries?', *Earth Trends*, http://earthtrends.wri. org/updates/node/236 accessed 25 September 2010.

14   Carson, R. (2000) *Silent Spring*, Penguin Classics, London.

15   Ritter, L., Solomon, K. R., Forget, J., Stemeroff, M. and O'Leary, C. (1996) 'Persistent organic pollutants', United Nations Environment Programme, www.chem.unep.ch/pops/ritter/en/ritteren.pdf accessed 25 September 2010.

16   Lee, D. H., Lee, I. K., Song, K., Steffes, M., Toscano, W., Baker, B. A. and Jacobs Jr, D. R. (2006) 'A strong dose-response relation between serum concentrations of persistent organic pollutants and diabetes', *Diabetes Care*, vol 29, pp1638–1644.

17   WWF (2004) 'Contamination: The next generation. Results of the family chemical contamination survey', www.wwf.org.uk/filelibrary/pdf/ family_biomonitoring.pdf accessed 26 September 2010.

18   Hawken, P., Lovins, A. B. and Lovins, L. H. (1999) *Natural Capitalism*, Earthscan, London.

19   Details on the Stockholm Convention on Persistent Organic Pollutants can be seen at http://chm.pops.int.

20   IPCC/TEAP (2005) *Safeguarding the Ozone Layer and the Global Climate System: Issues Related to Hydrofluorocarbons and Perfluorocarbons – Summary for Policy Makers*, Cambridge University Press, UK, www.ipcc.ch/pdf/special-reports/sroc/sroc_spm.pdf accessed 26 September 2010.

21   Cooley, S. R. and Doney, S. C. (2009) 'Anticipating ocean acidification's economic consequences for commercial fisheries', *Environmental Research Letters*, vol 4.

22   Ezzati, M., Lopez, A. D., Rodgers, A., Vander Hoorn, S. and Murray, C. J. L. (2002) 'Comparative Risk Assessment Collaborating Group, 2002. Selected major risk factors and global and regional burden of disease', *Lancet*, vol 360, pp1347–1360.

23   Bell, M. L., Davis, D. L. and Fletcher, T. (2004) 'A retrospective assessment of mortality from the London smog episode of 1952: The role of influenza and pollution', *Environ Health Perspectives*, vol 112, no 1, pp6–8.

Chapter 6: Global Solutions

1   Porritt, J. (2006) *Capitalism as if the World Matters*, Earthscan, London.

2   WCED (1987) *Our Common Future*, World Commission on Environment and Development, Oxford Paperbacks, Oxford (aka The Brundtland Report).

3   Schmidheiny, S. (1992) *Changing Course: A Global Business Perspective on Development and the Environment*, MIT Press, Cambridge, MA.

4   von Weizsäcker, E., Lovins, A. B. and Lovins, L. H, (1997) *Factor Four: Doubling Wealth, Halving Resource Use*, Earthscan, London.

5   Schmidt-Bleek, F. (1997) 'Statement to government and business leaders', Factor 10 Institute, Carnoules.

6   Ookubo, S. (2006) 'Nichia unveils white LED with 150 lm/W luminous efficiency', TechOn, 21 December, http://techon.nikkeibp.co.jp/english/-NEWS_ EN/20061221/125713/ accessed 26 September 2010.

7   PassivHaus Institute (2007) 'Information on Passive Houses', www.passivhaustagung.de/Passive_House_E/passivehouse.html accessed 26 September 2010.

8   Cappuccio, D. J. (2008) 'Energy savings via virtualization: Green IT on a budget', Report, November 12, www.gartner.com.

9   BusinessCar (2009) 'New Toyota Prius mpg and CO_2 revealed', 26 February, www.businesscar.co.uk/story.asp?storycode=4211&sectioncode = 1 accessed 26 September 2010.

10   Boeing website, www.boeing.com/commercial/787family/787-3prod.html accessed 26 September 2010.

11   'Fossil record of cyanobacteria', University of California Museum of Paleontology, Berkley University, www.ucmp.berkeley.edu/bacteria/cyanofr.html accessed 26 September 2010.

12   Bey, C. (2001) 'Quo vadis industrial ecology? Realigning the discipline with its roots', *Greener Management International*, no 34, pp35–42.

13   Datchefski, E. (2001) *The Total Beauty of Sustainable Products*, Rotovision, Hove, England.

14   McDonough, W. and Braungart, M. (2003) *Cradle to Cradle: Remaking the Way We Make Things*, Rodale Press, New York, NY.

15   Pearce, F. (2005) 'Forests paying the price for biofuels', *New Scientist*, no 2526, 22 November, pp19.

16   The source of this quote is obscure, but it has been attributed to Drucker in dozens of quotation databases such as: www.qfinance.com/quotes/efficiency.

17   Bowater, D. (2010) 'Family holiday abroad could cost £300 in tax', *Daily Express*, 4 June.

18   Maher, S. (2010) 'ETS backlash sees home turf turn on Rudd', *The Australian*, 22 June, www.theaustralian.com.au/politics/ets-backlash-sees-home-turf-turn-on-rudd/story-e6frgczf-1225882960269 accessed 26 September 2010.

19   Jackson, T. (2009) *Prosperity without Growth: Economics for a Finite Planet*, Earthscan, London.

20   Sustainable Development Commission (2009) 'Prosperity without growth?', Sustainable Development Commission, www.sd-commission.org.uk/pages/redefining-prosperity.html accessed 26 September 2010.

21   HM Treasury (2006) *Stern Review: The Economics of Climate Change*, HM Treasury, London.

22   Nordhaus, W. (2007) 'The Stern Review on the economics of climate change', Yale University, http://nordhaus.econ.yale.edu/stern_050307.pdf accessed 26 September 2010.

Chapter 7: Visions of a Sustainable Economy

1   Kay, A. (1971) 'Reported from an early meeting in 1971 of PARC', Palo Alto Research Center, Palo Alto, CA.

2   Jackson, T. (1996) *Material Concerns: Pollution, Profit and Quality of Life*, Routledge, Abingdon, UK.

3   Hawken, P., Lovins, A. B. and Lovins, L. H. (1999) *Natural Capitalism*, Earthscan, London.

4   Hawken, P., Lovins, A. B. and Lovins, L. H. (1999) *Natural Capitalism*, Earthscan, London.

5   Hawken, P., Lovins, A. B. and Lovins, L. H. (1999) *Natural Capitalism*, Earthscan, London.

6   If every stage in the improved supply chain uses 80 per cent of the resources as normal, the total resources across ten links would be 0.810 or 10.7 per cent.

7   Sweney, M. (2010) 'Government to continue climate change ads despite criticism from watchdog', *The Guardian*, 17 March.

8   ScienceDaily (2007) 'Over 50s have the highest carbon footprint in the UK', 2 March, www.sciencedaily.com/releases/2007/02/070218135655.htm accessed 26 September 2010.

9   Kane, G. (2004) 'Product design and the rebound effect', Design History Society Annual Conference, University of Ulster, Belfast, 9–11 September.

10 Davies, E. (2005) 'Consumers enjoy falling prices', bbc.co.uk, http://news.bbc.co.uk/1/hi/business/4174587.stm accessed 26 September 2010.

11 Frosch, R. A. and Gallopoulos, N. E. (1989) 'Strategies for manufacturing', *Scientific American*, vol 261, no 3, pp144–152.

12 Based on information from the Kalundborg Symbiosis Institution, www.symbiosis.dk/ accessed 26 September 2010.

13 McDonough, W. and Braungart, M. (2003) *Cradle to Cradle: Remaking the Way We Make Things*, Rodale Press, New York, NY.

14 physorg.com (2009) 'New hull coatings for Navy ships cut fuel use, protect environment', 4 June, www.physorg.com/news163361728.html accessed 26 September 2010.

Chapter 8: Outreach

1   Personal communication, Ben Wielgus, KPMG, 2 April 2009.

2   Google.org, www.google.org/rec.html accessed 27 September 2010.

3   World Business Council for Sustainable Development website, www.wbcsd.org/templates/TemplateWBCSD5/layout.asp?type=p&Menuid = NjA& doOpen = 1&ClickMenu = LeftMenu accessed 27 October 2009.

4   WRAP website, www.wrap.org.uk/retail/courtauld_commitment/phase_1/ accessed 27 September 2010.

5   Responsible Care website, www.responsiblecare.org/ accessed 27 September 2010.

6   Revkin, A. C. (2009) 'Industry ignored its scientists on climate', *New York Times*, 23 April, www.nytimes.com/2009/04/24/science/earth/24deny.html?_r=1 accessed 27 October 2009.

7   Schwartz, A. (2009) 'Why did Apple quit the US Chamber of Commerce?', Fast Company, 6 October, www.fastcompany.com/blog/ariel-schwartz/sustainability/why-did-apple-quit-us-chamber-commerce?partner=ethonomics_newsletter accessed 9 October 2009.

8   Monbiot, G. (2006) 'Selling indulgences', Monbiot.com, 19 October, www.monbiot.com/archives/2006/10/19/selling-indulgences/ accessed 27 September 2010.

9   *New Internationalist* (2006) Issue 391, www.newint.org/issues/2006/07/01/ accessed 27 September 2010.

10   CheatNeutral.com website, www.cheatneutral.com/ accessed 27 September 2010.

11   Dhillon, A. and Harnden, T. (2006) 'How Coldplay's green hopes died in the arid soil of India', *The Daily Telegraph*, 30 April, www.telegraph.co.uk/ news/worldnews/asia/india/1517031/How-Coldplays-green-hopes-died-in-the-arid-soil-of-India.html accessed 27 September 2010.

Chapter 9: Good Housekeeping

1   AP (2009) 'Worst industrial disaster still haunts India', 12 February, www. msnbc.msn.com/id/34247132/ns/world_news-south_and_central_asia accessed 27 September 2010.

2   Jardine, C. N., Boardman, B., Osman, A., Vowles, J. and Palmer, J. (2006) *Methane UK*, Environmental Change Institute, University of Oxford, www.eci. ox.ac.uk/research/energy/downloads/methaneuk/methaneukreport.pdf accessed 27 September 2010.

3   Turner, R. (2007) 'Underground Welsh dump of ten million tyres smouldered for 15 years', walesonline.co.uk, 28 May, www.walesonline.co.uk/news/ wales-news/tm_headline=underground-welsh-dump-of-ten-million-tyres-smouldered-for-15-years&method = full&objectid = 19208352&siteid = 50082-name_page.html accessed 27 September 2010.

4   Waste Online (2005) 'Metals – aluminium and steel recycling', www. wasteonline.org.uk/resources/InformationSheets/metals.htm accessed 27 September 2010.

5   Goodall, C. (2007) 'Carbon emissions and the service sector', www. lowcarbonlife.net/downloads/Emissions%20data%20from%20companies.pdf accessed 27 September 2010.

6   WRI (2007) 'World GHG emissions flow chart', http://cait.wri.org/ figures.php?page=/World-FlowChart accessed 27 September 2010.

7   Main source of data is: www.transportdirect.info/Web2/JourneyPlanning/ JourneyEmissionsCompare.aspx. accessed 27 September 2010. Air transport has been factored up by 1.9 as a conservative estimation of the additional radiative forcing of emissions higher in the atmosphere (IPCC (2001) 'Aviation and the global atmosphere', International Panel on Climate Change, www.grida. no/publications/other/ipcc%5Fsr/?src=/climate/ipcc/aviation/064.htm accessed 27 September 2010). The carbon emissions from food production have not been factored into walking/cycling.

8   Webb, M. (ed) (2008) 'SMART 2020: Enabling the low carbon economy in the information age', A report by The Climate Group on behalf of the Global Sustainability Initiative (GeSI), www.smart2020.org/_assets/files/03_Smart2020Report_lo_res.pdf accessed 27 September 2010.

9   BBC (2009) 'Eco-employee wins bid to appeal', bbc.co.uk, 3 November, http://news.bbc.co.uk/1/hi/england/oxfordshire/8339652.stm   accessed 27 September 2010.

10 Webb, M. (ed) (2008) 'SMART 2020: Enabling the low carbon economy in the information age', A report by The Climate Group on behalf of the Global Sustainability Initiative (GeSI), www.smart2020.org/_assets/files/03_Smart2020Report_lo_res.pdf accessed 27 September 2010.

11 Enomoto, K. (2010) 'The ECO Assist System in insight', SAE 2010 Hybrid Vehicle Technologies Symposium, February, San Diego.

12 Newnet (2008) 'Diageo gets approval for £65m Scottish biomass power facility', newnet.com, 5 November, www.newenergyworldnetwork.com/renewable-energy-news/by_technology/biofuel_biomass/diageo-gets-approval-for-65m-scottish-biomass-power-facility.html accessed 27 September 2010.

Chapter 10: Greener Operations

1   Bulleid, R. (2009) 'Energy cravings of the data explosion', *ENDS Report*, no 415, pp28–31.

2   Webb, M. (ed) (2008) 'SMART 2020: Enabling the low carbon economy in the information age', A report by The Climate Group on behalf of the Global Sustainability Initiative (GeSI), www.smart2020.org/_assets/files/03_Smart2020Report_lo_res.pdf accessed 27 September 2010.

3   von Weizsäcker, E., Hargroves, C., Smith, M. H., Desha, C. and Stasinopoulos, P. (2009) *Factor Five: Transforming the Global Economy Through 80% Improvements in Resource Productivity*, Earthscan, London.

4   Envirowise (2006) 'Cut waste and build profit', www.envirowise.gov.uk/uk/Press-Office/Press-Releases/Scotland/Cut-waste-and-build-profit.html accessed 27 September 2010.

5   WRI (2007) 'World GHG emissions flow chart', http://cait.wri.org/figures.php?page=/World-FlowChart accessed 27 September 2010.

6   For more information, see the Process Intensification Network, www.pinetwork.org/ last accessed 27 September 2010.

7   von Weizsäcker, E., Hargroves, C., Smith, M. H., Desha, C. and Stasinopoulos, P. (2009) *Factor Five: Transforming the Global Economy Through 80% Improvements in Resource Productivity*, Earthscan, London.

8   von Weizsäcker, E., Hargroves, C., Smith, M. H., Desha, C. and Stasinopoulos, P. (2009) *Factor Five: Transforming the Global Economy Through 80% Improvements in Resource Productivity*, Earthscan, London.

9   Marks & Spencer (2009) 'How We Do Business Report 2009', http://corporate.marksandspencer.com/file.axd?pointerid=f3ccae91d1d348 ff8f523ab8afe9d8a8&versionid = fbb46819901a428ca70ecf5a44aa8ddc accessed 27 September 2010.

10   Poulter, S. (2009) 'Put doors on freezers to bring food prices down, supermarkets are told', *Daily Mail*, 9 November, www.dailymail.co.uk/news/article-1226168/Asda-supermarkets-told-doors-freezers.html accessed 27 September 2010.

11   Monbiot, G. (2006) *Heat, How to Stop the Planet Burning*, Penguin Press, London.

12   Brignall, M. (2008) 'B&Q to end sale of patio heaters', guardian.co.uk, 22 January, www.guardian.co.uk/environment/2008/jan/22/carbonemissions.climatechange accessed 27 September 2010.

13   Webb, M. (ed) (2008) 'SMART 2020: Enabling the low carbon economy in the information age', A report by The Climate Group on behalf of the Global Sustainability Initiative (GeSI), www.smart2020.org/_assets/files/03_Smart2020Report_lo_res.pdf accessed 27 September 2010.

Chapter 11: Greening the Supply Chain

1   Canon (2009) 'Canon Sustainability Report 2009', www.canon.com/environment/report/pdf/report2009e.pdf accessed 27 September 2009.

2   NHS (2010) 'NHS England carbon footprint: GHG emissions, 1990–2020 baseline emissions update', National Health Service Sustainable Development Unit, 26 January, www.sdu.nhs.uk/page.php?page_id=160 accessed 28 September 2010.

3   Volvo Global Group 'Always the life cycle', www.volvogroup.com/group/global/en-gb/responsibility/envdev/env_work/prod_development/pages/product_development.aspx accessed 28 September 2010.

4   IKEA (2008) 'IKEA Sustainability Report 2008', www.ikea.com/ms/en_US/about_ikea/pdf/Sustainability_report_2008.pdf accessed 28 September 2010.

5   Sharp green procurement guide at http://sharp-world.com/corporate/eco/customer/pdf/gguide3e.pdf accessed 28 September 2008.

6   CCC Newsdesk (2007) 'The climate change dividend – cutting carbon and saving money', Climate Change Corp, 13 March, www.climatechangecorp.com/content.asp?ContentID=4801 accessed 28 September 2010.

7 A Better Place (2008) 'Renault-Nissan and Project Better Place prepare for first mass produced electric vehicles', 21 January, www.betterplace.com/the-company-pressroom-pressreleases-detail/index/id/renault-nissan-and-project-better-place-prepare-for-first-mass-produced-ele accessed 28 September 2010.

8 Anderson, R. (2010) *Confessions of a Radical Industrialist: How Interface Proved That You Can Build a Successful Business Without Destroying the Planet*, Random House Business, London.

Chapter 12: Greening the Product Portfolio

1 EC (2009) 'Ecodesign your future: How Ecodesign can help the environment by making products smarter', European Commission, http://ec.europa.eu/enterprise/policies/sustainable-business/ecodesign/files/brochure_ecodesign_en.pdf accessed 28 September 2010.

2 Computer data taken from www.apple.com/environment/ accessed 1 July 2010; Toyota car data taken from http://findarticles.com/p/articles/mi_m3012/is_2_185/ai_n12937459/ accessed 1 July 2010; washing powder data taken from www.pg.com/en_US/sustainability/products_packaging/our_approach.shtml accessed 1 July 2010; food data compiled from Goodall, C. (2007) *How to Live a Low-carbon Life: The Individual's Guide to Stopping Climate Change*, Earthscan, London.

3 ENDS (1993) 'Critical review of LCA practice', *ENDS Report*, no 219, 1 April.

4 Designtex.com, www.designtex.com/climatex_Environments.aspx?f=36310 accessed 28 September 2010.

5 PassivHaus Institiute 'Information on passive houses', www.passivhaustagung.de/Passive_House_E/passivehouse.html accessed 26 September 2010.

6 Ookubo, S. (2006) 'Nichia unveils white LED with 150 lm/W luminous efficiency', TechOn, 21 December, http://techon.nikkeibp.co.jp/english/NEWS_EN/20061221/125713/ accessed 26 September 2010.

7 White, M. (2008) 'Consumer society is made to break', Adbusters, 20 October, www.adbusters.org/category/tags/obsolescence accessed 28 September 2010.

8 McDonough, W. and Braungart, M. (2003) *Cradle to Cradle: Remaking the Way We Make Things*, Rodale Press, New York, NY.

9 CorpWatch (2000) 'CorpWatch names winners of Earth Day 2000 Greenwash Sweepstakes', 20 April, www.corpwatch.org/article.php?id=944 accessed 28 September 2010.

10 Chon, G. (2006) 'Big three struggle as Toyota beats Ford in US sales', *Wall Street Journal*, 2 August, http://online.wsj.com/article/SB115435195999822145.html accessed 28 September 2010.

11   This rule of thumb has been taken from sources such as DEFRA (2008) 'A framework for pro-environmental behaviours', www.defra.gov.uk/evidence/ social/behaviour/documents/behaviours-jan08-report.pdf accessed 28 September 2010.

Chapter 13: Green Business Models

1   Galbraith, K. (2009) 'The carbon case for downloading music', *New York Times*, 17 August, http://green.blogs.nytimes.com/2009/08/17/the-carbon-case-for-downloading-music/ accessed 28 September 2010.
2   Webb, M. (ed) (2008) 'SMART 2020: Enabling the low carbon economy in the information age', A report by The Climate Group on behalf of the Global Sustainability Initiative (GeSI), www.smart2020.org/_assets/files/03_Smart20 20Report_lo_res.pdf accessed 27 September 2010.
3   7th Annual Chemical Management Services Workshop: The Growing Trend of CMS, GM Pontiac Campus, Pontiac, Michigan, 23 October 2003, www. chemicalstrategies.org/pdf/workshop_events/Workshop_Summary_10_23_03. pdf accessed 28 September 2010.
4   Xerox (2009) 'Environmental solutions that work', www.xerox.com/down loads/usa/en/e/Environmental_Overview.pdf accessed 28 September 2010.
5   Allen, K. (200) 'Amazon e-book sales overtake print for first time', guardian.co.uk, 28 December, www.guardian.co.uk/business/2009/dec/28/ama zon-ebook-kindle-sales-surge accessed 28 September 2010.
6   Personal communication Rasha Sami and Penelope Crossley, Linklaters, 16 March 2010.
7   Grant, J. (2007) *The Green Marketing Manifesto*, Wiley, Chichester, UK.
8   Personal communication, Andy Haddon, Option C, 8 April 2009.

Chapter 15: Leadership

1   Bennis, W. (1989) *On Becoming a Leader*, Addison Wesley, New York, NY
2   Bennis, W. (1999) 'The leadership advantage', *Leader To Leader*, no 12, Spring, www.leadertoleader.org/knowledgecenter/journal.aspx?ArticleID= 53 accessed 28 September 2010.
3   Collins J. C. and Porras J. I (1997) *Built to Last: Successful Habits of Visionary Companies*, HarperCollins, New York, NY.
4   Anderson, R. (2010) *Confessions of a Radical Industrialist: How Interface Proved That You Can Build a Successful Business Without Destroying the Planet*, Random House Business, London.

5   For more on this, see Senge, P. M., Smith, B., Schley, S., Laur, J. and
    Kruschwitz, N. (2008) *The Necessary Revolution: How Individuals and
    Organizations Are Working Together to Create a Sustainable World*, Nicholas
    Brearley Publishing, London.

Chapter 16: Strategy

1   BT (2009) 'Changing world: Sustained values: Our 2009 sustainability review',
    www.btplc.com/Responsiblebusiness/Ourstory/Sustainabilityreport/pdf/2009/
    BTSustainabilityReview2009.pdf accessed 28 September 2010.
2   The themes were extracted from Marks & Spencer (2009) 'How We Do
    Business Report 2009', http://corporate.marksandspencer.com/file.axd?
    pointerid=f3ccae91d1d348ff8f523ab8afe9d8a8&versionid=
    fbb46819901a428ca70ecf5a44aa8ddc accessed 27 September 2010; White, P.
    (2009) 'Building a sustainability strategy into the business', *Corporate
    Governance*, vol 9, no 4, pp386–394; and Anderson, R. (2010) *Confessions of
    a Radical Industrialist: How Interface Proved That You Can Build a Successful
    Business Without Destroying the Planet*, Random House Business, London.
3   Brahic, C. (2009) 'Airlines want governments to be stricter on emissions', *New
    Scientist*, 6 April, www.newscientist.com/article/dn16909-airlines-want-
    governments-to-be-stricter-on-emissions.html accessed 28 September 2010.
4   Leggett, J. (2008) 'A low carbon diet', guardian.co.uk, 10 July, www.guardian.
    co.uk/commentisfree/2008/jul/10/renewableenergy.oil accessed 28 September
    2008.
5   Robinson R. B. (1982) 'Energy backcasting: A proposed method of policy
    analysis', *Energy Policy*, vol 10, no 4, pp337–344.
6   Adapted from Bannister, D. and Hickman, R. (2005) 'Looking over the horizon:
    Visioning and backcasting for UK transport policy', Department of Transport,
    London.

Chapter 17: Mobilizing Stakeholders

1   Thompson, M., Ellis, R. and Widavsky, A. (1990) *Cultural Theory*, Westview,
    Boulder, CO.
2   Naess, A. and Rothenberg, D. (1990) *Ecology, Community and Lifestyle: Outline
    of an Ecosophy*, Cambridge University Press, Cambridge.
3   Bennis, W. (1999) 'The leadership advantage', *Leader To Leader*, no 12, Spring,
    www.leadertoleader.org/knowledgecenter/journal.aspx?ArticleID= 53 accessed
    28 September 2010.

4   Segran, G. (2008) 'New CSR marketing trends: Transparency and dialogue', INSEAD, http://knowledge.insead.edu/CSRMarketingTrends080902.cfm accessed 28 September 2010.

5   Arnstein, S. R. (1969) 'A ladder of citizen participation', *JAIP*, vol 35, no 4, pp216–224.

6   See www.worldwildlife.org/sites/videos/wwf-coke-water.html accessed 28 September 2010.

7   'It's all going on', Muckle LLP's internal newsletter, supplied to author 24 June 2010.

8   Blake, M. (2010) quoted at Low Carbon Best Practice Exchange, London, 10 June 2010.

Chapter 18: Aligning Management Functions

1   ISO (2004) BS EN ISO 14001 Environmental management systems, International Organization for Standardization.

2   GRI (2006) 'Sustainability reporting guidelines', Global Reporting Initiative, www.globalreporting.org/NR/rdonlyres/ED9E9B36-AB54-4DE1-BFF2-5F735235CA44/0/G3_GuidelinesENU.pdf accessed 28 September 2010.

3   The GHG Protocol Initiative (2004) 'The Greenhouse Gas Protocol: A Corporate Accounting and Reporting Standard', www.ghgprotocol.org/files/ghg-protocol-revised.pdf accessed 28 September 2010.

4   ENDS (2008) 'Scientists call for control on new greenhouse gas', *ENDS Report*, no 402, p27.

5   Note, the GHG Protocol only covers scopes 1–3, but many practitioners add scope 4 to allow compatibility between organizational and product footprints.

6   See www.globalreporting.org/NR/rdonlyres/ED9E9B36-AB54-4DE1- BFF2-5F735235CA44/0/G3_GuidelinesENU.pdf accessed 27 September 2010.

7   Marks & Spencer (2009) 'How We Do Business Report 2009', http://corporate.marksandspencer.com/file.axd?pointerid=f3ccae91d1d34 8ff8f523ab8afe9d8a8&versionid = fbb46819901a428ca70ecf5a44aa8ddc accessed 27 September 2010.

8   Anderson, R. (2010) *Confessions of a Radical Industrialist: How Interface Proved That You Can Build a Successful Business Without Destroying the Planet*, Random House Business, London.

9   Woking Borough Council 'Carbon neutral development: A good practice guide', www.woking.gov.uk/council/planning/publications/climateneutral2/energy.pdf accessed 28 September 2010.

10   Handy, C. B. (1995) *The Empty Raincoat: Making Sense of the Future*, Random House Business Books, London.

Index